If you want a fresh and insightful overview of the Scriptures, Dr. Larry Richards' newest contribution to biblical scholarship, *How to Read (and Understand) the Bible*, is for you. This refreshing approach to understanding the Scriptures is insightful, stimulating, trustworthy, and creatively instructive. With authentic biblical scholarship, combined with practical applications, you will travel through the entire Bible, gaining new appreciation for God's great gift to us on every page. Bible students and lay readers alike will gain an enriched perspective and understanding of God's Word.

DR. GILBERT A. PETERSON
Former president and chancellor of Lancaster Bible College

Perhaps Larry Richards' enduring legacy—as expressed through the titanic number of books he has published over forty years—will be the immeasurable assistance lent to thousands in understanding not only the basic message of Scripture, but also how to interpret and teach it in a way that propels believers into becoming followers in the mission of God. *How to Read (and Understand) the Bible* is a life-changing book that does just that. Here is an accessible, thoughtful, conceptual, and practical book that every church should use to equip its leaders, small groups, and ministries.

MARK A. LAMPORT
Professor of practical theology of nine theological schools in the US and Europe and coeditor of *Encyclopedia of Christian Education* and *Encyclopedia of Christianity in the United States*

Larry Richards has devoted his life to the serious study of God's Word. Although the content of *How to Read (and Understand) the Bible* reflects the good scholarship behind it, it is not a dry, academic tome. This book is an enjoyable read, just as reading Scripture itself can be. Larry's engaging, almost conversational style of writing makes you feel as if you and he were sitting together for a stimulating conversation about God's story. As the book takes you through the major themes of the Bible, you'll come away with a big-picture perspective that will make your Bible reading more meaningful and more practical for daily Christian living—as it was meant to be.

KLAUS ISSLER

Professor of Christian education and theology at Talbot School of Theology, Biola University, and author of *Living into the Life of Jesus and understand*

How to Read the Bible

HOW TO READ (and understand) THE BIBLE

Meeting God in the book you love but never fully understood

LARRY RICHARDS

TYNDALE®
MOMENTUM

An Imprint of
Tyndale House Publishers, Inc.

Visit Tyndale online at www.tyndale.com.

Visit Tyndale Momentum online at www.tyndalemomentum.com.

TYNDALE, *Tyndale Momentum*, and the Tyndale Momentum logo are registered trademarks of Tyndale House Publishers, Inc. Tyndale Momentum is an imprint of Tyndale House Publishers, Inc.

How to Read (and Understand) the Bible: Meeting God in the Book You Love but Never Fully Understood

Designed by Mark Anthony Lane II

Published in association with the literary agency of Mark Sweeney and Associates, 28540 Altessa Way, Suite 201, Bonita Springs, FL 34135.

Library of Congress Cataloging-in-Publication Data

Richards, Larry, date, author.
  How to read (and understand) the Bible : meeting God in the book you love but never fully understood / Larry Richards.
    pages cm
  Includes bibliographical references.
  ISBN 978-1-4143-9182-3 (sc)
1. Bible—Reading. I. Title.
  BS617.R52 2015
  220.6′1—dc23   2014043869

Printed in the United States of America

21	20	19	18	17	16	15
7	6	5	4	3	2	1

This book is dedicated to Sue, my wife and partner, who for more than thirty years has enriched all I've written, generously sharing her insights, her suggestions, and her encouragement. I am especially indebted to her for this book, which she insisted I write while she earned her master's in counseling psychology at the Seattle School of Theology and Psychology.

Table of Contents

Preface

EVER SINCE I consciously committed my life to Jesus Christ in 1951 while serving in the US Navy, I have loved God's Word. Knowing little about it at the outset, I started a noontime Bible study on my base and was led deeper and deeper into the wisdom of Scripture. I had been familiar with Jesus from my childhood, but as the study group explored the Gospels and Romans, I was gripped by an awareness of Christ's ability to transform our lives and give them meaning. In particular, I saw that transformation in the life of a shy, young civilian worker on our base, a woman named Lee. For six months, Lee came to the Bible study every day, but she never said a word. A few years later, when I visited the base after leaving the navy, I was invited to Lee's home, where eighteen men and women who had come to know Christ through her witness were gathered. God had used the fruit of a little Bible study I had started to transform and mature the lives of almost twenty people. I now understood the true power of God's Word to change our hearts.

Following my time in the navy, I attended Dallas Theological Seminary, taught for a time at Wheaton College, and then launched a writing career that to date has produced some 250 books, every one deeply rooted in Scripture.

It may seem strange that after sixty years of study, I would write a book about "meeting God in the book you love but never fully understood." But I encounter so many people today who see the Bible as a rule book, or a book packed with stories that teach morals. They believe in Jesus, but don't fully grasp the magnitude of what God is doing—in history and in their own lives. So I began to reread the Bible as *story*—the story of God's purpose in the universe he created, and how we believers fit into God's story to make his story *our* story too.

In reading the Bible as story, I discovered for the first time just how intent God is on fashioning an eternal community of love, and that along history's way, he wants us to experience as much of that community of love as we are willing to accept.

In many ways, my understanding of God changed. I was stunned to see the importance of the little, daily choices you and I make. I came to see how, in his sovereign flexibility, God walks through life with us, responding to our prayers and guiding the outcome of the choices we freely make. I came to wonder at the greatness of a God who responds so generously to us, yet never wavers from the grand future embedded in his covenant promises and overall plan.

I was also gripped by the role of God's antagonist, Satan, as he struggles to spoil God's story for you and me. But most of all, I met God afresh in the book I loved but had never fully understood. I not only came to know him better, but also to love him more deeply and respond to him more joyfully.

Each chapter in the book you're about to read begins with a description of a pivotal event, which introduces an important theme for understanding the Bible and understanding God. We'll then explore these themes, providing keys to help you read and understand Scripture. It's my prayer and my confident expectation that as you follow God's story through his Word, you too will come to know and love him better.

Larry Richards
Raleigh, North Carolina

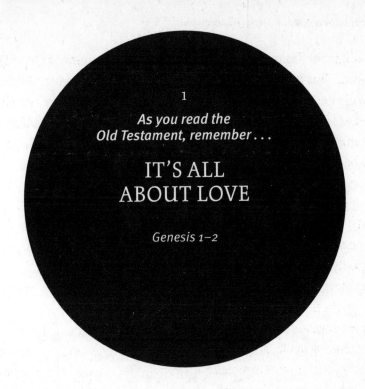

As you read the
Old Testament, remember . . .

IT'S ALL
ABOUT LOVE

Genesis 1–2

The Pivotal Event

The first man opened his eyes and looked around.

What a beautiful place this is. But what is it? Where am I?

He raised himself on one elbow, puzzled now. He heard bees buzzing and smelled the fragrance of ripening fruit. Flowers in riotous colors bloomed all around him. The sky above sparkled an azure blue, illuminating currents that seemed to flow across the heavens.

And who am I?

Slowly Adam stood up, unaware that he was naked.

Digging Deeper into Genesis 1–2

I'm impressed with Sir Arthur Conan Doyle's detective, Sherlock Holmes. He's so aware of the little things. Brown stains on a thumb and forefinger; the way the cuff of a left pant leg shows more wear than the right. Nothing at all like his companion, Dr. Watson, who might notice someone waving his arms and shouting, but who always misses the subtler clues, the things that speak volumes to Holmes.

If Holmes and Watson were called in to investigate the Bible's creation account, I suspect that Watson would immediately see what most of us do. But Holmes would find meanings that others miss.

Our first impressions of Genesis are much like recognizing the type of broad, sweeping gestures that even Dr. Watson couldn't miss. Visualizing the act of creation, we're overwhelmed at the awesome power of a God who can call worlds into existence with a word. Yet there are other clues in the first chapters of Genesis that are more understated and suggestive—the types of clues that Sherlock Holmes would detect, clues that tell us much about the central figure of the Bible's story and set up the story itself. If we focus primarily on the grand gestures, we may miss the more elusive clues embedded in the Creator's words and actions. Still, we mustn't discount the significance conveyed in the overarching grandeur of God's creative act.

The Major Message of Creation

In the opening words of Genesis, God steps boldly onstage: "In the beginning God created the heavens and the earth." Because of the magnificence of creation, the apostle Paul will later write, some knowledge of God is the common heritage of all humankind: "Since the creation of the world God's invisible qualities—his eternal power and divine nature—have been clearly seen, being understood from what has been made."[1]

What Paul means is that the universe is so obviously supernatural, so clearly a God thing, that no one can miss its significance. The universe need not *contend* for God; its very existence bears witness to God's existence and to his awesome, overwhelming, complete, and eternal power. The message of creation is a proclamation, not an argument.

For no argument is necessary. The very shape of creation—its vastness, order, and symmetry—says all that needs to be said. "God has made it plain,"[2] Paul insists. It's as if the universe were a transmitter, constantly broadcasting a single message, and human beings were fashioned with a built-in receiver tuned to its single frequency. A person may turn down the volume to a whisper. But it is impossible to silence creation's voice entirely.

The "great power and mighty strength"[3] of the God revealed in creation might hold terror for those who don't know him. But those of us who see ourselves as part of God's story find that his overwhelming power offers comfort and assurance.

Jesus put it this way to his disciples: "My sheep listen to my voice; I know them, and they follow me. . . . My Father, who has given them to me, is greater than all; no one can snatch them out of my Father's hand."[4] The God we meet in the Genesis creation account is, simply put, *greater than all*. And we have the assurance, as followers of Jesus Christ, that we are held, secure, in God's mighty hand.

The grand proclamation of creation—of God's existence and mighty power—is something we must keep in mind as we read the Bible. There will be times when things don't go the way we think they should. There will be moments when it seems as if God's purposes have failed, when we might think that God himself must be distressed at the way history unfolds. At such moments, we must remember the message of creation—namely, that God, the Creator of all things from one end of the universe to the other, has unlimited power and unequaled strength. He doesn't stumble through history as we do, peering anxiously ahead and haplessly fumbling away opportunity after opportunity. No, the God introduced in Genesis 1 is far greater than his creation, far superior to any created being. Whatever happens along the way, Scripture's unwavering message is that God's purposes will prevail. His power and his mighty strength *guarantee* it.

When we read the Bible, most of us understand the broad gestures, such as the Bible's sweeping claim that in the beginning God created the heavens and the earth. We understand this to mean that God is distinct from and greater than the material universe; that the lifeless sprang from the heart and mind of a living person. But to simply affirm that God exists and that he made all things does not mean we are living within Scripture's narrative.

Dr. Dan Allender, a well-known Christian counselor, tells of a time when he visited New Zealand. One morning as he was hiking, he came to a point of land. Spread out before him was a spectacular range of snow-capped mountains, towering into a vivid blue sky. Overwhelmed by the majesty of the spectacle, Dan found himself filled with praise and thanking God.

Another hiker came out on the point, and his face, too, showed awe and wonder. "It's unbelievable, isn't it?" the newcomer whispered.

Dan nodded and then asked, "So who do you thank?"

The newcomer looked puzzled. "*Thank?* What do you mean?"

Telling the story later, Allender commented, "I felt so sad for him."

Dan Allender lives within the narrative of Scripture, allowing his perspective of life and his experiences to be shaped by Scripture's revelation. When he encounters the beauty of creation, it turns his thoughts to the Creator and fills his heart with praise and thanksgiving. The other hiker he met that morning lived within a different narrative. The beauty of creation overwhelmed him with awe, but he had no one to thank.

The apostle Paul, in his letter to the Romans, concludes that humans are without excuse because God has revealed himself in his creation—and "although they knew God, they neither glorified him as God nor gave thanks to him."[5] The test of a vital relationship with God isn't found in the creeds we recite or in the truths we claim to believe. It's found in our response to God's revelation of himself—not only in creation but also in Scripture and in the person of his Son, Jesus.

Misreading the Narrative

During the past few hundred years, we've been conditioned to look into the Bible and ask certain kinds of questions: *How did (or could) this happen? When did it happen? How can we explain this rationally and scientifically? What evidence is there that our explanation is correct?*

This mind-set, characteristic of what philosophers call *modernism*, has dramatically affected the way most people read Genesis 1 and 2. The modernist mind-set has led us into conflict with non-Christians and into heated debates with our fellow believers. The questions we've asked—and disagreed on the answers to—include such things as, How old is the earth? Do the "days" recorded in Genesis 1 refer to consecutive twenty-four-hour periods? Can a "day" represent a geologic age? Did God create life forms in a *day*, and then permit them to evolve through an *age* extending for millions of years?

Because such questions can't be settled by simply referring to the text of Scripture, we've often tried to answer them by attempting to harmonize Scripture with the shifting views of the scientific community. But science is ultimately nothing more than a different narrative, whose constantly changing paradigms about the nature of reality make it an unreliable tool for understanding God's Word. Perhaps we should wonder why we even ask the kinds of questions that recent generations have found so fascinating.

Some would argue that we raise the questions and use the tools of science to demonstrate that our belief in the God of the Bible is logically defensible. But Scripture reminds us that "faith comes from hearing the message, and the message is heard through the word about Christ."[6] When Paul, while he was with the Corinthians, "resolved to know nothing . . . except Jesus Christ and him crucified,"[7] he consciously rejected reliance on "the wisdom of this age."[8] Paul was convinced that the gospel is self-authenticating. He did not have to argue against or according to first-century philosophy; he simply had to present God's message clearly and trust the Holy Spirit to convict and convince.

In our day, we have no need to argue against or according to contemporary scientific theories or perspectives. Like Paul, we simply need to relate the story of God's Word and trust the Holy Spirit to draw people to faith.

Looking at the Clues

If we look beyond the big-picture aspects of Creation, the first two chapters of Genesis provide fascinating clues to the nature of God's story.

We notice immediately, for instance, that a particular word, *good*, appears seven times in the first chapter and five times in the second. As God fashioned our world, he paused again and again to look at what he had done. The narrative repeatedly tells us, "God saw that it was good."[9] As God evaluates his work, we sense his delight and satisfaction in what he has accomplished. And God's evaluation provides vital insights into his character and his story.

The word *good* first appears in the description of an event that takes place on the first day of creation. "And God said, 'Let there be light,' and there was light. God saw that the light was good, and he separated the light from the darkness. God called the light 'day,' and the darkness he called 'night.' And there was evening, and there was morning—the first day."[10]

We notice immediately that God considers light *good*. He also distinguishes between light and darkness. Clearly, God does not see darkness as good. Without knowing any more than this, we understand that it's important to *see* and to *be seen*. Anything less falls short of being *good*.

As each new day unfolds in the story, God makes other distinctions as well. He divides the earth's surface into land and sea. He creates vegetation and animal forms that reproduce after their kind. Scholars have studied the use of the word *kind* in Scripture, in an effort to find a fit with classifications used by botanists and zoologists. But *kind* simply does not fit the usual categories of phylum, genus, family, and species. Yet each "kind" in Scripture is distinguished from every other kind, and one kind cannot reproduce with another. God calls this distinction *good*.

The text also indicates that the *consistency* in creation's design is part of what makes it so good in God's sight. The reliable rotation of the earth allows day to follow night in an unbroken cycle so regularly that we are able to mark the passage of weeks and months and years. Season consistently follows season. The stars sail majestically in the night skies, their courses so stable that men will one day use them to chart their journeys and find their way. All this, God calls good.

On the sixth day, God created a human being, a life form "in his own image"[11]—yet, like the animals, created male and female. God blessed the human pair and told them to "fill the earth and subdue it"[12]—a phrase that suggests we are to *care* for the earth, not exploit it. On this sixth day, God looked at what he had made and deemed it *very good*. Again we sense his satisfaction and delight.

In evaluating his own work in the opening pages of the Bible's story, God opens himself to our scrutiny. By declaring what he sees as *good*, he opens a window into his character and personality, providing us with deep insights into the person whose story is told throughout the Bible. As we learn what he values—what seems *good* and *right* to him—we find ourselves in agreement with God.

It is good to make distinctions, to evaluate, select out, and choose.

It is good to have light, to be able to see where we are and where we're going. It is good to see and know others, and to be seen and known by them.

It is good to live in a stable universe rather than amid random chaos.

We feel more comfortable in a world marked by regularity and consistency. Uncertainty creates anxiety; instability makes us fearful. In order to feel secure, we need the kind of universe that God created.

Seeing all the *good* in the early chapters of Genesis as a revelation of God's character and nature helps us feel more comfortable with him. We realize that he and we have much in common. As we agree with our Creator about what is good in the world he fashioned, we underscore the truth that we are made in God's image. And as we learn more of God's story in the Bible, we'll find that its narrative fits us better and better. God's story provides a framework within which we feel comfortable, a narrative that rings true.

The events described in Genesis 2 amplify what we've seen in Genesis 1. When I hear some scholars speak of two creation accounts, one in Genesis 1 and another in Genesis 2, I suspect they haven't watched much television. If they had, they might be more familiar with a common strategy that helps viewers follow the action. First, the director will set up an *establishing shot*, a wide-angle view that defines the context in which the action takes place. Then he or she will zoom in to focus on what's most significant within that scene.

This is how the Bible handles the creation story. Genesis 1 is an establishing shot, defining the setting (the creation of the universe) in which the rest of the story will unfold. In this way, the writer tells us that the most significant event in the creation story is the fashioning of human beings. What we have in Genesis 1 and 2 are not two (conflicting) creation stories but one story shot with two cameras, if you will. In Genesis 2, the author simply returns to the sixth day and provides a close-up, detailing God's creation of humanity.

As we carefully read the Genesis 2 account, we realize that it's a close-up shot of the scene established in Genesis 1:27: "God created man in his own image, in the image of God he created them, male and female he created them."

As we zoom in on the action, we see that these beings created in God's image are special. Whereas the rest of the created universe sprang into existence at a word, here God stoops to personally fashion Adam's body from the dust of the earth—and then he breathes his own life into Adam.

Next, the text portrays Adam's early years in Eden, a garden shaped especially for him. In the account of Adam's life in Eden, the likeness between the man and his Creator is further emphasized. There in the Garden, Adam does far more than explore his environment. He explores his own nature—and God's nature as well. In the emotions that Adam experiences in response to the natural world,[13] he discovers his—and God's—capacity to take pleasure in beauty. In working and caring for the Garden,[14] Adam discovers that he—like God—derives deep satisfaction from performing meaningful work. In his freedom to eat from any tree in the Garden,[15] Adam learns that he—like God—can draw distinctions and choose between options. In responding to God's command not to eat from the tree of the knowledge of good and evil,[16] Adam learns that he—like God—can make moral choices. When God permits Adam to name the animals, Adam learns that he—like God— has intellectual abilities that allow him to share in the act of creation. In Scripture, names express something of the essence of the thing named; thus, to give something, or someone, a name is to mold reality.

The sheer act of creation tells us that God is great and powerful, awesome beyond measure. The description of his fashioning of Adam points to how special Adam is. And Adam's experience in Eden, like the use of the word *good*, helps us feel comfortable with the Creator. He made us in his image and likeness, and we have much in common.

But there's another, more subtle indicator in early Genesis that we don't want to miss. God states, "Let *us* make mankind in *our* image."[17] In view of subsequent revelation that the Creator is one God in three persons, it's best to understand the plural as an early expression of God's trinitarian nature.

The Bible tells us that "God is love."[18] It portrays the relationship between the persons of the Trinity as a perfect harmony, as a continual giving and receiving of love. The stunning truth revealed here is that God himself exists in community.

In Genesis 2:20, we're told that when Adam finished naming the animals, "no suitable helper was found" for him. Adam had no one to love and no one of his kind to love him. Yet God's stated purpose was to create human beings in his image and likeness. It was not enough for Adam to appreciate beauty, to find satisfaction in work, or to make moral choices. Adam also had to love and be loved. For Adam to truly reflect the image of God, he too must have someone distinct from but of the same essence as himself, so he could love and be loved in return. No wonder God said, "It is not good for the man to be alone."[19]

If we wonder why God created Adam first and Eve at a later time, perhaps it's because Adam needed time to discover that he was alone, time to sense his need for others of his kind. When Adam's ache of loneliness had grown intolerable, God acted to make a "suitable helper" for him,[20] someone who differed from Adam and yet shared his essence. In Adam's words, Eve was someone who was "bone of my bones and flesh of my flesh";[21] someone with whom he could "be fruitful and multiply," and expand the community within which humans are called to live.

Together, the trinitarian "let us" of Genesis 1:26 and the "not good for the man to be alone" of Genesis 2:18 lead us to a conclusion that helps shape our understanding of God's story and of our own stories as well. God's story is about *relationships*. God's story is about *love*.

God, who is love and who knows perfect love within the Trinity, created humans in his own image so that we too might love and be loved. But he did not create us to love and be loved only by each other. God created human beings for himself to love as well, and so that we might love him in return.

Already we can see that God's intention seems to be to fill the universe with everything that is good for the creatures formed in his image—creatures he has chosen to love. God seems intent on creating a loving community within which humanity can fully experience what it means to be fashioned in God's image and likeness.

Here again we find ourselves in agreement with God. Just as the things God calls good seem good to us, so too the vision of a universe filled with love resonates in the deepest part of our being. The story told so far by the Bible fits perfectly with who we are as human beings—not necessarily with the way things *are*, but definitely with the way we yearn for things to be. In the first two chapters of Genesis, we're given a vision—not so much of the present, but of a day long past and of a new day the Bible claims is on the way.

As we move on in the story, we'll discover why that day has taken such a long time coming.

Discussion Questions

1. How have you experienced God's creation? How do you respond to creation's voice?

2. What seems to you to be especially good about creation? What does this tell you about yourself? What does it suggest about God?

3. The first pages of Genesis reveal that God's story is about relationships, about love. What are the implications for humanity if God's story truly is a love story?

*As you read the
Old Testament, remember . . .*

ADAM CHOSE INDEPENDENCE

Genesis 3

The Pivotal Event

The serpent motioned toward the tree with his head. "Beautiful, isn't it?"

Eve nodded.

"Did God really say you mustn't eat from any tree in the garden?"

Eve shook her head. "No, we may eat fruit from the garden's trees. But we're not to even touch the fruit of this tree, or we'll die."

The serpent smothered a laugh. "You certainly won't die," he said authoritatively. "God knows that when you eat, your eyes will be opened, and you'll be like him. You'll know good and evil."

Digging Deeper into Genesis 3

Love stories are always so suspenseful. Will "Sleepless in Seattle" ever connect with his soul mate in New York? Will Emma realize that she loves her good friend Mr. Knightley? And how will the two strangers who meet briefly in *Serendipity* find each other again before they marry the wrong people?

It isn't only movies that keep us in doubt. Countless novels and short stories give dimension to Shakespeare's observation that "the course of true love never did run smooth."[1]

I suspect these authors and filmmakers realize they must create suspense in order to hold our attention through hundreds of pages or an hour and a half in the theater. Usually these enthralling stories have happy endings, but occasionally an author pulls a nasty trick on us. Take *Titanic*, for example. Jack and Rose fall in love. The future looks bright. But instead of a happy ending, Jack dies in the icy waters of the North Atlantic after urging Rose to live a full and happy life without him. Many decades later, Rose, elderly and alone, stands on the deck of a ship near the spot where Jack died and tosses a fabulous jewel over the side.

Given that the first two chapters of Genesis introduce a love story, perhaps we shouldn't be surprised if the course of God's story doesn't run smoothly. Not that we can fault the Creator. After all, there's something unique about love. True love is something that wells up from the heart. True love is freely given, and an authentic love relationship is one in which both parties spontaneously and voluntarily respond in love to the other.

For God to end up with a universe filled with good, to be enjoyed by those who love him as he loves them, the Creator had to grant Adam and Eve the freedom to love. They had to be able to choose, freely and voluntarily, to love God. But that meant they would also be able to choose *not* to respond to God's love.

God wouldn't settle for puppets. Yes, God could have created individuals who simply *had* to love him. But he wanted beings shaped in his own image, persons who would *choose* to love him.

Or not.

A Test of Love

God planted a tree in Eden. He told Adam, "You are free to eat from any tree in the garden; but you must not eat from the tree of the knowledge of good and evil, for when you eat from it you will certainly die."[2]

It's important to view this verse in the context of *love*. We're much too quick to categorize it as *law*. The problem is that human laws are, always and ultimately, coercive. When the Bible describes how humans should behave, it's only natural, given our familiarity with human law, to jump to the conclusion that God is defining a law of his own that we must obey. We assume that when God said, "You must not eat from the tree of the knowledge of good and evil," he was establishing a *rule*, and that when Adam and Eve chose to break the rule, God used his coercive power to punish them.

But that's not at all what happened!

God didn't issue a command backed by a threat. He simply warned Adam of a danger and of the consequences of that danger. God spoke out of his love for Adam. And if Adam had heeded God's warning, his choice would not have been coerced obedience. It would have been an expression of Adam's confidence in God, with whom he enjoyed a loving relationship.

It follows, therefore, that when Adam chose not to heed God's warning, his decision was not as much an act of disobedience as it was a rejection of the love relationship he enjoyed with the Creator.

Here's how Jesus explained this same concept to his disciples: "Anyone who loves me will obey my teaching. . . . Anyone who does not love me will not obey my teaching."[3] Only the power of love can move us to truly respond to Jesus' teaching. To receive God's word as law may create outward conformity to what the Bible teaches, but only love enables us to respond with glad and willing hearts.

In the same way, Adam and Eve's response to God's instruction— his teaching—on the forbidden fruit was all about love, not law. When

Adam and Eve ate the fruit, they spurned God's love and exchanged the relationship they had with him for something else. They exchanged love for the prospect of independence and freedom.

What's so fascinating is that even though Adam and Eve had enjoyed such an intimate relationship with the Creator and had experienced so many wonderful blessings, they were so easily drawn away when the stranger arrived.

Love Undermined

In a later chapter, we'll look more closely at the stranger who appears in Eden—who he is and what his motives are. He's obviously the villain of the story, intent on destroying the relationship between God and humanity. What's significant for us here is his *strategy*: to undermine the confidence that Adam and Eve have in God—the God who loves them.

"Did God really say, 'You must not eat from any tree in the garden'?"[4]

Eve's answer shows that she is uncertain of what God actually said. "We may eat fruit from the trees in the garden, but God did say, 'You must not eat fruit from the tree that is in the middle of the garden, and you must not touch it, or you will die.'"[5]

Adam, listening nearby, says nothing to correct her.

Then the stranger directly contradicts God's word—"You will not certainly die"—and introduces doubt concerning God's motives: "God knows that when you eat from it your eyes will be opened, and you will be like God, knowing good and evil."[6]

At this point, Eve's confidence in God's love has been thoroughly undermined, and she turns to herself, relying on her senses ("the fruit of the tree was good for food and pleasing to the eye") and interpreting what she thinks the outcome of eating the fruit will be ("gaining wisdom").[7] That was all it took. Eve stretched out her hand, took the fruit, and bit into it. Then she gave the fruit to Adam, who took it from her and ate it.

When the apostle Paul looks back on this moment, he tells us, "Adam was not the one deceived; it was the woman who was deceived and became a sinner."[8] The word translated "sinner" here is not a common term. It is the Greek word *parabasis*, which means "to break" or "to violate." Eve was deceived into violating the love relationship she and Adam had with the Creator, which up to that time had governed their responses to him. Far worse is that "Adam was not . . . deceived." Adam, who was with Eve during the entire conversation with the stranger, and who understood the issues, took the fruit Eve handed him and consciously, purposely, ate.

No wonder Scripture places the greatest responsibility on Adam. Everything that followed, Paul tells us in Romans 5:16, was the result of "one man's sin." Adam's act was a conscious rejection of God's love, a knowing repudiation of the relationship he and Eve shared with the Creator. Adam opted for independence from God.

The Blame Game

Once the decision had been made and the damage done, God stepped into Eden in search of Adam and Eve. What he found was two people at odds with themselves and with each other. In declaring their independence from God, they had unexpectedly reverted to the state of being *alone*, which was the one thing in Eden that God had said was *not good* for mankind.[9] From now on, every person on earth would choose to act as if they were independent of God and independent of other people. God's vision of a community of love was shattered.

When God called, "Where are you?" Adam reluctantly emerged from his hiding place and confessed, "I was afraid . . . so I hid."[10] As God probed further, Eve tried to shift the blame for her action to the stranger, and Adam resentfully blurted out, "The woman you put here with me—she gave me some fruit from the tree, and I ate it."[11]

We can almost hear the plaintive accusation in Adam's voice:

"The woman *you put here with me* . . ." Reading between the lines, we can imagine Adam's thoughts as he sought to wriggle off the hook of responsibility: *God, you must have known what she was like. It wasn't my fault. I ate the fruit, sure—but God, ultimately you're the one to blame.*

Because God had created Adam and Eve in his image, they possessed the ability to choose to love him, freely and responsively. But that very same ability meant they were also able to choose *not* to love God. The stranger's lies and innuendos may have influenced Eve's decision, but it did not *cause* her to choose what she chose. Nor did God's having placed Eve in the Garden with Adam cause the undeceived man to repudiate God's love on that fateful day.

The fear, the shame, the excuses, the resentment, and the blaming we now see in Adam and Eve are all evidence that something terrible happened *to* and *in* them. They are no longer the same people they were before they chose independence over remaining steadfast in God's love.

Evening in Eden

Adam's decision put into motion the inevitable outcome he'd been warned of by God: "When you eat from it you will certainly die."[12] Scripture's concept of death is complex. On the one hand, it refers to the end of biological life. The bodies of living things die, and the elements return to the earth. But Scripture also treats death as far more than a biological phenomenon. "Mankind's problem, and God's great challenge, has to do with the grim darkness of a living death that . . . shrouds human existence for time as well as for eternity."[13] In repudiating God and declaring their independence, Adam and Eve stepped out of the shelter of God's love into a world where they would have to find their way without him. They still bore his image and likeness; they were still persons, with minds that could reason and hearts that could feel; but their thoughts and emotions were now twisted in ways they could not have imagined.

Years ago, I took my two sons and a neighbor boy out on Arizona's Saguaro Lake for a nighttime fishing trip. After traveling the length of the lake, the boys got out of the boat to explore. A few minutes later, I heard a cry and saw my younger son, Tim, limping toward me. He'd tripped on a strand of barbed wire and had opened a great gash on his leg. The wound needed stitches, so we clambered back into the boat and headed for home. But as I piloted the boat back up the canyons, I found myself disoriented. Nothing looked the way it had in daylight. The cliffs and islands were unrecognizable, and I had no idea where I was or which way to go.

The effects of spiritual death are something like that night on Saguaro Lake, except that the darkness is within us. Human beings were created to live in relationship with God and with each other, loving and being loved. But when we're apart from God, insisting on our independence, everything we see is disfigured, twisted out of shape, and unrecognizable. In the apostle Paul's letter to the Ephesians, he comments on the deadly spiritual and psychological effects of abandoning God: "As for you, you were dead in your transgressions and sins, in which you used to live when you followed the ways of this world and of the ruler of the kingdom of the air, the spirit who is now at work in those who are disobedient. All of us also lived among them at one time, gratifying the cravings of our flesh and following its desires and thoughts."[14]

In declaring their independence, Adam and Eve stepped out of the shelter of God's love and out of community with each other. Instead of finding freedom, they found themselves in bondage to their fears, their cravings, and their sinful desires.

The world of possibilities that now opened up to Adam and Eve was very different from what might have been if they hadn't repudiated God's love. Eve would now experience terrible pain in childbirth, and even more pain when her first two sons, who were born as flawed as Eve and Adam had become, came into conflict with each other, resulting in death, just as God had foretold.

Eve's daughters later discovered the significance of "you will certainly die" while living in societies ruled by men, in which women were no longer equal partners but property. Yet they would still search desperately to find meaning in life through relationships with the very men who devalued them.

Adam would toil all his life, and his sons would search for identity and meaning in their work rather than in their relationship with the Creator. In the grip of the cravings that now drove them, their once-intimate connection with God now broken, humans would be filled with unmet longings, never realizing that what they longed for was a return to Eden and to God.

Wise Men Know

One book in the Old Testament—Ecclesiastes—powerfully sums up the emptiness of life apart from God. Tradition tells us it was written by Solomon, among the wisest of men in the ancient world. In his early years, Solomon seems to have been committed to God. But in his old age "his wives turned his heart after other gods, and his heart was not fully devoted to the LORD his God."[15] Like Adam and Eve, he lost contact with the Creator. Sensing an inner void despite all his activity, Solomon set out on a search for life's meaning.

In Ecclesiastes, Solomon states both his goal and his methodology: "I applied my mind to study and to explore by wisdom all that is done under the heavens."[16] Solomon would rely only on what he could personally see and feel. He would not consult history, turn to any Scripture, or listen to any of God's prophets. What's more, he relied completely on his ability to reason (wisdom). And so Solomon probed his own experience as well as all that he'd observed during his lifetime and drew his conclusion: "'Meaningless! Meaningless!' says the Teacher. 'Utterly meaningless! Everything is meaningless.'"[17]

Few of us expect to reach this conclusion when we start out in life.

We begin optimistically, hoping to make it through college, get a good job, get married, own our own home, and have a family. We expect we'll save enough money to ensure a comfortable retirement. And we assume that this kind of life, what most of us would call "the good life," will provide happiness and satisfaction. We don't realize that we are spiritually dead and that spiritual death means our thoughts and desires are warped and twisted. We don't realize that what is "under heaven" simply can't satisfy our deepest longings.

Life Outside the Garden

In eating the forbidden fruit, Adam and Eve turned their backs on the God of love in favor of what must have seemed like an exciting independence. But they also began to experience the effects of spiritual death. From the moment they repudiated God's love, death distorted their relationships and their desires. Their sons and daughters were born still reflecting the image of the Creator, but now the true image was distorted.

It's clear from Adam and Eve's actions after they ate the fruit—the hiding, the fear, the shame, the excuses, the resentment, and the blaming—that the first couple could no longer be called *good*. Yet the Creator kept on loving them. In the story, God entered the Garden to search for them, despite their repudiation of his love. Though he banished them from the Garden and drove them out, there was a reason for that.[18]

Genesis 3 tells us that along with the tree bearing the forbidden fruit, Eden contained a *tree of life*. God determined that the man "must not be allowed to reach out his hand and take also from the tree of life and eat, and live forever."[19] If this sounds cruel, think what it would have meant for Adam and Eve to witness all the pain, all the suffering, all the injustice, all the tragedy that has befallen human beings throughout history. That would have been cruelty beyond cruelty. And that God would not permit. So in driving them out of the Garden, God protected them from a fate that truly would have been worse than death.

Just before banishing Adam and Eve from the Garden, God provided them with another gift, a gift that foreshadows a major theme in God's unfolding story. The text tells us, "The LORD God made garments of skin for Adam and his wife and clothed them."[20]

The provision of skins to cover Adam and Eve must have made a deep impression. It seems to have anchored itself in the consciousness of all humanity, for peoples and tribes from around the world and throughout history have shared a tradition of blood sacrifice. Whether it's the white bull sacrificed to Jupiter by the ancient Romans or the chickens sacrificed in contemporary Haitian voodoo, humans seem to sense that blood is required when approaching deity. The beliefs have differed across times and places, but the tradition of blood sacrifice seems deeply rooted in the human psyche.

God did not explain why he took the lives of two animals to provide a covering for Adam and Eve. He simply provided the clothing made of skins. Much later in the story, when God designs a system of sacrifices for the people of Israel, we'll catch a glimpse of the necessity of blood sacrifice. God will tell Israel through a man named Moses, "The life of a creature is in the blood, and I have given it to you to make atonement for yourselves on the altar; it is the blood that makes atonement for one's life."[21]

How strange it is that on the very day when death entered the world through Adam and Eve's sin, God took an animal's life to symbolize a then-unknown truth. Rejecting the love of God may result in spiritual death, but the dead can be revived—if only at the cost of another's life.

The shed blood of the animals on that day in Eden could not fully restore the relationship that Adam and Eve had rejected. They remained committed to their independence. Their natures remained warped and twisted. But God's act in providing the covering that Adam and Eve required was a silent promise. A promise that would be fulfilled when the proper time had come—and only after death seemed to have established an unbreakable grip on the post-Edenic world.

Discussion Questions

1. In order to be able to choose to respond to God's love, humans had to be able to choose to reject God's love. How important to God do you think it was to grant human beings freedom of choice?

2. What impact would you expect spiritual death, experienced by Adam and Eve and passed on to their children, to have on the Bible's narrative?

3. What does God's response to Adam and Eve after they rejected his love tell you about him? About his attitude toward people who reject his love today?

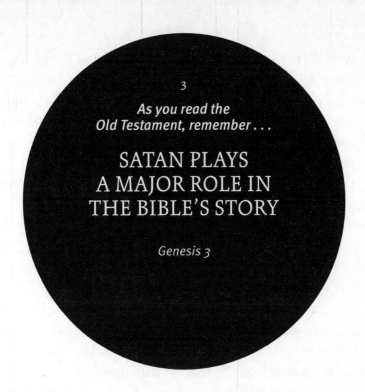

*As you read the
Old Testament, remember . . .*

SATAN PLAYS A MAJOR ROLE IN THE BIBLE'S STORY

Genesis 3

The Pivotal Event

When evening fell and the Creator came in search of Adam and Eve, I imagine the serpent still lurking in the Garden. Sensing danger, he began to slip away but felt himself constrained. As the Creator questioned Adam, the serpent was a silent witness, unable to leave. Then, just as suddenly, he felt himself drawn into the clearing and found himself beside the human couple, facing the Creator.

Digging Deeper into Genesis 3

A good novel has strong characters. There's always a protagonist—the good guy. And if there's any real dramatic development, the novel also has an antagonist—a bad guy. Even comic books pit good against evil. Can you imagine Batman without the Joker? Or Superman without the evil Lex Luthor?

If we fail to recognize the bad guy, the Bible may not seem to be a unified story. Instead, it might appear to be simply a series of dos and don'ts, a compendium of good advice, or a collection of stories with morals. Without an understanding of the struggle between protagonist and antagonist, many parts of the Bible don't make sense as elements in an interconnected story.

On the one hand, it's hard to fault people for ignoring the antagonist in the Bible. References to the evil one and his activities are scattered throughout the books of the Old and New Testaments. No single writer or passage of Scripture provides all the information we'd like to have. On the other hand, there are plenty of clues for anyone who reads the Bible with an active curiosity.

Take the stranger in Genesis 3, for example, whom the Judeo-Christian tradition identifies as Satan. When he appears in the guise of a serpent, there are many peculiar things about his emergence that should make us intensely curious. For starters, when Genesis gives us a day-by-day account of how God fashioned our planet and placed it in its setting in the universe, it doesn't mention Satan. So . . . *who* or *what* is Satan?

If the Bible's description of God's fashioning of our planet and the origins of biological life is a complete account of beginnings, and yet there is no mention of the creation of Satan, *where did he come from?*

And if Satan was not created during the seven days depicted in the Bible, and yet he shows up on Earth shortly after Adam and Eve . . . *when* does he come from?

Reading on in the early chapters of Genesis, we are compelled to ask the same questions about other beings mentioned in the text. For instance, Genesis 3:24 tells us that God "placed on the east side of the Garden of Eden cherubim and a flaming sword flashing back and forth to guard the way to the tree of life." *Who* or *what* are cherubim? Where did the cherubim come from? And *when* do cherubim come from?

If you grew up going to Sunday school, as I did, you may know the standard response: Satan and the cherubim are angels. Satan is a bad angel, and cherubim are good angels. Everybody knows that. But the appearance of Satan and cherubim in the early chapters of Genesis has a significance we shouldn't overlook.

Modernism's Worldview

For the past two or three hundred years, the worldview of most Westerners has been shaped by certain beliefs and attitudes, which in turn are built on the self-confident assertion that *science* has the potential to deal with all human concerns. As people have learned more and more about the way the universe works, they've come to believe that *knowledge* can be harnessed to rid the world of poverty, to provide abundant food and energy, and even to reach the stars.

Science provided us with the theory of evolution, which professes to explain the origin of the universe and of life. And science has now decoded the human genome, raising hopes that we might one day eradicate disease. In this brave new world, there is no need for God, and there is no such thing as the supernatural. Every phenomenon has a rational explanation, and the miracles of Jesus are tossed on the culture's garbage heap, along with belief in UFOs and little green men from Mars.

Though many Christians continue to contend for Jesus' miracles and to point out flaws in the theory of evolution, most of us cheerfully accept the basic assumptions of the modernist worldview. The material universe is what counts—the things we can see and touch and measure with the tools of science. So quite naturally—while still arguing, of course, that God is real and that God is important—Christians have by and large ignored the realm of the supernatural.

The trouble is that when we fail to understand Satan and the evil he represents, we simply cannot understand the biblical narrative, nor can we properly find our place within God's story.

Spiritual Beings in the Real World

Adam and Eve are enjoying life in Eden when a stranger, in the form of a serpent, unexpectedly appears. This stranger, Satan, has not been mentioned in the account of the seven days of creation of the material universe. Later, we will learn that he is from a different realm, a spiritual realm populated by angels and demons, but what is fascinating here is that Satan appears on Earth, in Eden, and he interacts with Adam and Eve. The world of spirits and what we think of as the *real world* interface!

Although Satan is a spirit being, apparently he can enter and can act in the material universe. We see the same phenomenon in the Bible's initial reference to the cherubim. God places angels east of Eden and gives them the task of guarding the way to the tree of life.[1] Commentators debate whether the angels' mission was to prevent Adam and Eve from returning to the Garden or to prevent Satan from closing the path to eternal life. But the point is that angels, beings from the spirit world, were commissioned to act in the material world.

The "Silence" of Scripture

At this point, curious and thoughtful readers are likely to object. If Satan and cherubim can pop out of the spiritual realm—whatever or wherever that is—to attack or defend humans, why aren't such supernatural creatures featured throughout the Bible? Oh, we know angels occasionally appear to make announcements from God. And there are stories in the Gospels about Jesus casting out evil spirits. But evil spirits aren't mentioned in the rest of the Old Testament or in the New Testament epistles, are they? So how can Satan and evil spirits be central to either God's story or our personal stories?

This would be a reasonable objection . . . *if* Satan and evil spirits were not major players in the Old Testament and the Epistles. But they are. For instance, in Leviticus 17 God instructs the Israelites to make sacrifices only at the Tabernacle. They were not to sacrifice on hilltops or in groves because that's what the pagan peoples around them did. The text says, "They shall no more offer their sacrifices to demons."[2] In Deuteronomy, God forbids sacrifices to pagan gods and goddesses, reminding a new generation of his people that their parents "sacrificed to demons, not to God."[3] Psalm 106 reminds God's people that under the influence of pagan religions they had "even sacrificed their sons and their daughters to demons."[4] We simply cannot understand Old Testament history if we fail to recognize that pagan religions were energized by demons who were intent on the corruption of Israel and on keeping men and women from responding to God. No demons in the Old Testament? Why, every time we meet a god or goddess of one of the peoples surrounding Israel, we come face to face with a demon.

But what about the New Testament epistles? The word *demon* hardly ever appears. But that is because the New Testament adopts terminology that was then current throughout the Roman Empire, where the people believed in spirits of every sort: gods, goddesses, ghosts, demons, familiar spirits, spirits of the dead, and so on. Though the term *daimonion* was used at times to describe such spirits,[5] the most common terms for spirit beings were drawn from power words, such as *rule, authority, power*, and *dominion*. In Ephesians 6:12, Paul makes it very clear that he recognizes the impact of evil spirits in the visible world: "For our struggle is not against flesh and blood, but against the rulers, against the authorities, against the powers of this dark world and against the spiritual forces of evil in the heavenly realms."

As Christians, when we read the New Testament epistles with awareness of first-century terminology, we discover that the writers portray an active spiritual warfare. Our enemies are demonic rulers, authorities, powers, and dominions.

The Expulsion of the Stranger

Ancient Jewish and Christian scholars agree in identifying Eden's stranger as Satan. Scholars in both traditions have viewed two Old

Testament passages as descriptions of Satan's origin. The clearest of these is Ezekiel 28:14-17. While prophesying against a human "prince of Tyre," Ezekiel suddenly shifts focus and begins to speak about a "king of Tyre," who is identified as a *cherub*:

> You were anointed as a guardian cherub,
>   for so I ordained you.
> You were on the holy mount of God;
>   you walked among the fiery stones.
> You were blameless in your ways
>   from the day you were created
>   till wickedness was found in you.

Here we meet someone besides Adam who was created blameless, and who also chose against love and turned to "wickedness." The passage goes on:

> Through your widespread trade
>   you were filled with violence,
>   and you sinned.
> So I drove you in disgrace from the mount of God,
>   and I expelled you, guardian cherub,
>   from among the fiery stones.
> Your heart became proud
>   on account of your beauty,
> and you corrupted your wisdom
>   because of your splendor.
> So I threw you to the earth.

Having rejected God's love out of pride, this anointed cherub was "filled with violence" and God "threw [him] to the earth."

The second passage believed to describe Satan's origin is Isaiah

14:12-15, which harmonizes perfectly with Ezekiel 28 and focuses on the motivation of the once-bright angel.

> How you have fallen from heaven,
>> morning star, son of the dawn!
> You have been cast down to the earth,
>> you who once laid low the nations!
> You said in your heart,
>> "I will ascend to the heavens;
> I will raise my throne
>> above the stars of God;
> I will sit enthroned on the mount of assembly,
>> on the utmost heights of Mount Zaphon.
> I will ascend above the tops of the clouds;
>> I will make myself like the Most High."
> But you are brought down to the realm of the dead,
>> to the depths of the pit.

This account is eerily similar to that of the fall of man. A being who was created blameless rejects the role assigned by his Creator in favor of independence. But whereas Adam simply claimed his independence, this cherub—a member of the highest order of angels—intends to push God off his throne! We sense the passionate intensity of his "I wills," culminating in "I will make myself like the Most High," which is to say, "I demand ultimate power."

Satan's rebellion failed. Isaiah tells us he has "fallen from heaven," and Ezekiel makes it clear that God "threw [him] to the earth." Yet it is also clear that God did not destroy the rebel. Nor did Satan rebel alone. References to "the devil and his angels"[6] and to "the dragon and his angels"[7] suggest that the beings we know as demons and evil spirits are angels who followed Satan when he rebelled against his Creator. In fact, Revelation 12 casts the rebellion as the beginning of a war. The text tells us that

War broke out in heaven. Michael and his angels fought against the dragon, and the dragon and his angels fought back. But he was not strong enough, and they lost their place in heaven. The great dragon was hurled down—that ancient serpent called the devil, or Satan, who leads the whole world astray. He was hurled to the earth, and his angels with him.[8]

Creation before the Creation

Earlier, I raised several questions about the stranger of Genesis 3. Who is he? Where did he come from? And *when* did he come from? To answer these questions, we need to note something else that seems peculiar about the text of Genesis.

Genesis opens, "In the beginning God created the heavens and the earth." This beginning is also pictured in the book of Job. There, we find God describing an original creation in which he "laid the earth's foundation . . . while the morning stars sang together and all the angels shouted for joy."[9] If angels were shouting for joy at the creation of the material universe, they must have been fashioned prior to what we think of as the creation story in Genesis 1.

What, then, *is* described in Genesis 1? One possible answer is that Genesis 1:1 refers to the original creation of the heavens and the earth, and that the next phrase—"Now the earth was formless and empty"[10]— depicts conditions that existed when God *refashioned* the earth as a home for humankind. This is known as the gap theory. In any case, "formless and empty" hardly conveys the image of an ordered universe. It sounds more like a barren landscape, cratered and void of life, with "darkness . . . over the surface of the deep."[11] Nothing moves, although the Spirit of God is "hovering over the waters."[12]

This is hardly the universe as God first created it. But it may very well be the condition of the universe following a devastating war in heaven.

This now becomes the backdrop for what we refer to as the six days of creation. Indeed there is a six-day account, but these six days were spent refashioning an earth and a universe devastated by a war in which Satan and his angels—the demons of Scripture—were thrown down from heaven.

On this restored planet, then, God planted a garden in Eden and placed Adam and Eve there with the commission to "fill the earth and subdue it."[13] The word for *subdue* is a strong one in Hebrew. Human beings, created in God's image, were to maintain the *good* of all that God had established in bringing order, consistency, and beauty to a once-ruined world.

It's no wonder that Satan was intent on subverting Adam and Eve. His strategy of undermining the humans' trust in their Creator was successful, but he failed to win mankind as an ally. God blocked that move of Satan when he pronounced the curse recorded in Genesis 3:15: "I will put enmity between you and the woman, and between your offspring and hers."

From that moment, Satan became the implacable enemy of humankind. He would not succeed in enlisting the human race in his war against the Creator, but he would do all he possibly could to prevent humans from returning to God's love and fulfilling God's purpose of fashioning an eternal community of love. Even so, the Creator's next words must have been like a dagger to Satan's heart: "He will crush your head, and you will strike his heel."[14]

Through the ages since, Satan has caused unbelievable pain and suffering to human beings. Yet in the end it will be a human being— the Son of Man—who crushes Satan's head and puts an end to the invisible war.

Satan is the antagonist in God's story, an evil presence intent on crushing all that is good. Wherever God seeks to bring order and consistency and to provide security, beauty, and peace, Satan seeks to create chaos and promote anxiety, ugliness, misery, and suffering.

Whenever God seeks to draw human beings into community, Satan sows discord and envy. Just as God is the measure of all that is good and right, Satan is the measure of all that is twisted and evil, a dark personage who seeks to stamp his values on the character of individuals and societies.

Satan was created as an angel, but then "wickedness was found"[15] in him. Like humans, Satan was created with the ability to love and the ability to reject love. The picture of Satan being thrown down to earth fits well with Scripture's characterization of the great fallen angel as the "god of this age,"[16] the "prince of this world,"[17] the "ruler of the kingdom of the air,"[18] and the "prince of demons."[19] Satan maintains an invisible presence on the earth, a position from which he continues to battle against the Creator. It is from a very real spirit world, one that interfaces with the material world, that Satan and his demons continue to launch their attacks on humankind.

Whatever happened prior to the activity of the first day described in Genesis, by identifying the stranger we have established the framework within which the Bible's story unfolds.

We have God, the Creator, who is committed to fashioning a universe filled with sentient beings who love him and whom he loves completely, beings who will live out that love in community.

We have human beings, who have declared their independence and rejected God's love, yet who retain a freedom of will that enables them to choose good over evil or evil over good.

We have angels, spirit beings who are loyal to God and committed to his purposes. And we have Satan and his demons, spirit beings who have rebelled against God and who are dedicated to overthrowing God and doing evil.

It is within the context of this invisible war that God's story unfolds and must be understood. And it is within this structure that we discover how our individual stories fit into God's story.

Playing Navy

When I was about six, someone gave me a set of metal toy ships. I had tiny, two-inch-long submarines, slightly larger cruisers, a toy battleship, and an aircraft carrier. I used to lie on the floor in our small living room, playing navy, conducting mock battles with my ships. I'd tuck a submarine behind one of the legs of the sofa, and as a cruiser or aircraft carrier sailed past, I'd slip the submarine out from its hiding place. Sometimes I'd pretend to be the captain of the sub. Other times, I'd be the captain of the cruiser. But in this game of mine, no matter which vessel I captained, I was never taken by surprise. Nothing ever took place that I didn't choose to have happen. I was in total control.

Like others, I believe in a sovereign God whose ultimate triumph is guaranteed. But does that mean that God exercises his sovereignty by controlling every decision made by human, angelic, and demonic agents? It seems that God has given his created beings—humans, angels, and demons—freedom of choice. It's true that the choices they are free to make are limited. Nevertheless, when we decide between two or more courses of action, it is *our own* choice. We are free to choose. At least, it *seems* we're free.

There's a story in Scripture that suggests that Satan has a freedom similar to ours. In the opening passage of the book of Job, Satan reports to God. In the conversation, when God mentions "my servant Job,"[20] Satan challenges the Creator. Job, he insists, serves God only because God has blessed him and has not allowed Satan to harm him. Remove the blessings, Satan challenges, and Job "will surely curse you to your face."[21] God removes the hedge of protection, and Satan mounts devastating attacks on the innocent Job. Within the new limits that God sets, Satan chooses the tragedies he inflicts upon Job.

The story of Job raises a question that all of Scripture, in fact, raises: Does God "play navy" with the universe? That is, is our freedom to choose *real* or only apparent? Is God actually making the decisions for us behind the scenes, while letting us imagine that we have free will? Was Satan responsible for the tragedies he perpetrated on Job, or was God ultimately the one who decided when and how Job would suffer?

God, man, and Satan. These are the characters in the Bible's grand narrative. As the story unfolds within the framework of a war between good and evil, with human beings challenged to choose sides and to play a part in the war, we need to know: Are the choices we make really our choices—or are they God's? And we need to know whether the evil that stalks us is initiated by Satan, or if God is ultimately responsible for evil as well.

Discussion Questions

1. How conscious have you been of the interface between the spirit world and the material world? How do you suppose a greater awareness would affect your daily life?

2. Why do Christians, by and large, fail to take the spirit world seriously? What other reasons can you think of?

3. What is the significance of the "playing navy" story in this chapter? Can you clearly state the issue that the story raises?

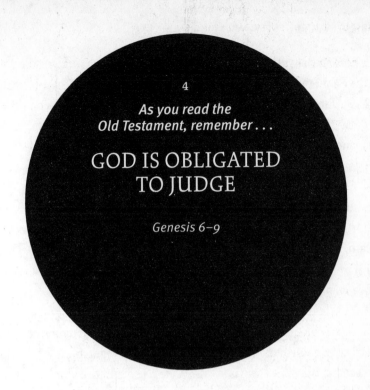

4

As you read the
Old Testament, remember . . .

GOD IS OBLIGATED
TO JUDGE

Genesis 6–9

The Pivotal Event

Noah wasn't expecting a visit from God. Even so, he recognized the Creator's voice. The words that God spoke must have filled Noah with both fear and hope. God said, "I am going to put an end to all people, for the earth is filled with violence because of them. I am surely going to destroy both them and the earth. So make yourself an ark."[1]

Digging Deeper into Genesis 6–9

There's a rhyme that's been running through my mind the past few days. I first heard it from my dad, who liked to break out unexpectedly with poems he'd memorized. This little verse can hardly be called a poem, but I can't seem to get it out of my mind. It goes like this:

There was a little girl,
And she had a little curl
  Right in the middle of her forehead.
When she was good
She was very, very good,
  And when she was bad she was horrid.[2]

When we look at the two young men we meet in Genesis 4, I suspect most of us would classify Abel as "very, very good," and his brother, Cain, as "horrid." Certainly what Cain did in murdering Abel *was* horrid. But we ought to pause before we dismiss Cain merely as a horrid, hateful person.

The text tells us, "In the course of time Cain brought some of the fruits of the soil as an offering to the LORD."[3] A rabbinic tradition accuses Cain of bringing rotting fruit and vegetables. When God rejects his offering, Cain is insulted. He'd brought the best he had. Yet God says to Cain, "If you do what is right, will you not be accepted? But if you do not do what is right, sin is crouching at your door; it desires to have you, but you must rule over it."[4] Adam's sons understood the lesson of the animal skins that God had used to clothe their parents. There was a decision to be made, and decisions have consequences.

Human beings are not born horrid. Nor are we born "very, very good." We are all born bearing the image and likeness of our Creator, and something within us knows and desires what is good; but at the same time, sin is crouching at the door, and we must *choose* to rule over it by choosing the good.

In Romans, Paul reminds his fellow Jewish countrymen that while God has given Israel a written law, non-Jews are not ignorant of right and wrong. "Indeed," he writes, "when Gentiles, who do not have the law, do by nature things required by the law, they are a law for themselves. . . . They show that the requirements of the law are written on their hearts, their consciences also bearing witness."[5]

We can wander through time and across continents, but we will not find a society devoid of a moral sense. The rules that govern societies will differ in specifics, but every society has moral codes, and it makes a difference whether you "do what is right" or "do not do what is right."

The Old Testament features three primary words for sin. Each depicts sin as a violation of an established standard. Within the Bible's narrative, that standard is God himself. God created human beings in his image and likeness, and anything that falls short of his image is *sin*.

In the shadows of Cain's nature, there was something crouching, something lurking, eager to spring and fasten its claws deep into his soul; something that desired to master Cain and *would* master him if he did not choose to do what is right. What God told Cain was, "*You must master it.*"

That's why I think it would be a mistake to dismiss Cain as simply a horrid person, just as it would be a mistake to credit his victim, Abel, with being very, very good. Cain and Abel lived in a world where the future was in doubt. When their parents chose to step outside of their love relationship with God in favor of independence, they discovered that the flip side of independence is *responsibility*. From now on, they and their offspring—including Cain and Abel and you and me—would have to live in a world of "if you do what is right." And all the while, crouched at the door of our hearts and minds, will be sin—a distortion of the likeness of God that, if not mastered, will surely master us.

We Christians tend to have a naive view of what it means to be sinners. On the one hand, we know that falling short of God's glory means there is nothing we can do to make ourselves acceptable to him or to earn his approval. The New Testament quotes King David's verdict on our spiritually dead humanity: "There is no one righteous, not even one."[6]

Apart from the grace of God and the active prompting of the Holy Spirit, there is no possibility that any individual will turn in trust to the God of love. On the other hand, when it comes to the lives we live here on earth, falling short of God's glory means we are faced daily with Cain's choice: doing right versus not doing what is right. And those little daily choices we make between right and wrong shape more than our future. They shape *us*.

C. S. Lewis describes the process in his book *Mere Christianity*:

> Every time you make a choice you are turning the central part of you, the part that chooses, into something a little different from what it was before. And taking your life as a whole, with all your innumerable choices, all your life long you are slowly turning this central thing either into a heavenly creature or into a hellish creature.[7]

We don't know the innumerable little daily choices that led to Cain's refusal to go to his brother to bargain for an animal to sacrifice. But we do know that he hardened his heart, not just against God but also against Abel. Cain's anger burned against his brother, and the sin that crouched at the door of his heart mastered him.

Surrendering to the hurt of rejection and driven by anger, Cain struck out against Abel in a premeditated act. Cain invited Abel to go with him into the fields, and there he murdered him and buried his body. Later, when the Lord asked Cain, "Where is your brother Abel?" Cain challenged the Creator, "Am I my brother's keeper?"[8]

My Brother's Keeper

One of the things that should trouble us about our independence is its impact on others. Cain was free to choose. Yet the choice he made robbed Abel of *his* freedom.

That's the risk involved in granting humans independence. If a person is to be free to choose what is good and right, he or she must also be free to choose what is evil and wrong. And every choice we make has an impact on ourselves and on others. We can choose what is right, and others will be blessed—and so will we. Or we can choose what is wrong, and others will suffer. And so will we.

There's another word group in the Old Testament that makes this important point. The verb is *ra'a*, which means "to be evil, to be bad" or, more often, "to act wickedly" or "to harm." Constructed on the same root, the feminine noun *ra'ah* means "evil," "misery," or "distress." The point is that when a person chooses to *do* evil, the result is an experience *of* evil. Wrong choices, *acting wickedly*, lead inexorably to misery and distress.

This is one of the ways in which God, in his mercy and kindness, sets limits on human freedom. We cannot continue to make wrong moral choices without ultimately injuring ourselves.

Evil and a Good God

The prophet Habakkuk had a theological problem. He lived during the reign of King Josiah, a godly king who led a spiritual revival in Judah. Under Josiah, pagan worship centers where child sacrifice had been practiced were destroyed, and worship of the Lord at the Jerusalem Temple was revitalized. But despite the flourishing of religion in Judah, injustice still pervaded Jewish society. In Habakkuk's words, "There is strife, and conflict abounds. . . . The wicked hem in the righteous, so that justice is perverted."[9]

Knowing God's commitment to good, Habakkuk cries out to the Lord, "Why do you tolerate wrongdoing?"[10] God answers the prophet by revealing that even then, in far-off Babylon, a "feared and dreaded people"[11] was preparing to invade little Judah. At first, Habakkuk is satisfied with this response. God intends to discipline his people after all. But then Habakkuk has second thoughts. The Babylonians were even more wicked than the people of Judah. How would God deal with the Babylonians?

Deeply troubled, Habakkuk left Jerusalem and headed up into the surrounding hills. There God revealed a secret. No one gets away with doing evil. We may be free to act wickedly, but we are never free from the consequences of our wicked actions.

As for the Babylonians, their hunger to possess more and more would never bring them satisfaction. Instead each success would inflame their desire and drive them to desire more and more.[12] Their treatment of their victims would create a hostility that would ultimately bring them down.[13] They believed that power and wealth would provide security, but no realm built on unjust gain can "escape the clutches of ruin."[14] All that they had built would collapse on history's ash heap, for the earth is destined to be filled with the glory of the Lord.[15] In the end, the violence they perpetrated on others would overwhelm them, and they would be destroyed.[16]

We live in a moral universe. We have been given the freedom to choose to do what is right and the freedom to choose to do what is not right. But we cannot choose the consequences of our actions.

The Great "Or Else"

In God's invitation to choose between what is right and what is not right, we sense implied consequences. If we fail to master sin in our daily lives, we turn "the central part" of ourselves, in C. S. Lewis's terms, "the part that chooses, into something a little different from what it was before."[17] We are on our way toward becoming not very, very good, but horrid.

In the fact that God steps in to curse Cain, taking away his gift for farming and turning him into a wanderer,[18] we sense that our freedom has limits. This is the first time we see God in an unexpected role. We've seen that God is our lover, the one who made us in his own image, the one who searches for us even after we repudiate his love. But God is also our judge. As judge, God has woven into the fabric of human experience consequences that limit our freedom to do wrong. Genesis clearly establishes that the God who gives us freedom is himself free to terminate that freedom.

After the time of Cain and Abel, we're given a glimpse of a human civilization that has tamed animals, that works with bronze tools, and that enjoys music played on a variety of instruments. The genealogies in Genesis 5 emphasize the passage of long periods of time, with generation after generation expanding and populating the earth.

As individuals continue to exercise their freedom and make choice after choice, they turn "that central part of themselves into something a little different from what it was before," and their society is transformed as well. In Genesis 6:5, we're given a description of the society of Noah's time: "The LORD saw how great the wickedness of the human race had become on the earth, and that every inclination of the thoughts of the human heart was only evil all the time."

Human beings don't start out in life as very, very good, and they don't start out as horrid. Neither do peoples and nations. But the humans who populated the ancient world, humans whose "every inclination" was "only evil all the time," had truly become horrid. The text tells us God's response: "The LORD regretted that he had made human beings on the earth, and his heart was deeply troubled. So the LORD said, 'I will wipe from the face of the earth the human race I have created.'"[19]

God provides human beings with the freedom to choose. But he remains free to limit the damage that human freedom is allowed to do. The people who lived prior to the Genesis flood reached that limit.

As God looked at what the world had become, his heart was filled with grief. In giving humans the freedom to choose love, he had also given them freedom to reject love—with everything that rejection entails. But now the pain had become too much. In witnessing the anguish and misery inflicted by human beings on one another, God saw that humanity had become utterly horrid. It was time for him to act.

We all know the story of the Genesis flood. In an inconceivable cataclysm, raging waters scoured the human race from the surface of the planet. To visualize the God of love and justice standing over a trembling planet as millions, and perhaps billions, of people died is a frightening thing. Even with all the wars, genocides, and acts of terror we have seen in the modern world, we can scarcely imagine the horrors that the people of that day must have perpetrated on each other to make such a radical cleansing necessary.

God the Judge

Flash forward to about 1400 BC. Moses stands on the side of a hill, exhorting his people, who are straining with eagerness to invade Canaan. Forty years earlier, the parents of these people were slaves in Egypt; for four decades now, the people have been wandering in a barren wilderness, waiting for all their parents to die. Now they are about to be unleashed on a verdant countryside, a countryside dotted with cities and villages.

As we listen, Moses speaks words that shock us: "When the LORD your God has delivered them over to you and you have defeated them, then you must destroy them totally. Make no treaty with them, and show them no mercy. . . . This is what you are to do to them: Break down their altars, smash their sacred stones, cut down their Asherah poles and burn their idols in the fire."[20]

We can hardly believe our ears. Mount an attack on a seemingly peaceful land? Defeat the inhabitants and *destroy them totally*? These Israelites that Moses leads may be God's chosen people, but how can God command them to do such terrible things to the people who have made their home in Canaan for centuries?

To understand this, we must go back some four hundred years and listen in on another conversation, a conversation between God and Abraham, when God says,

Know for certain that for four hundred years your descendants will be strangers in a country not their own and that they will be enslaved and mistreated there. But I will punish the nation they serve as slaves, and afterward they will come out with great possessions. . . . In the fourth generation your descendants will come back here, for the sin of the Amorites has not yet reached its full measure.[21]

Imagine it! God is willing to allow his chosen people to settle in a land where they will be oppressed for four centuries, rather than dispossess a people, the Amorites, who already are moving down a sinful path, simply because their sin "has not yet reached its full measure."

In Abraham's time, the people of Canaan were already making sinful choices. But God withheld his hand of judgment four hundred more years, until the character of the Amorites and their culture had truly become *horrid*.

We know quite a bit about the people of Canaan who lived about fifteen centuries before the time of Christ. We have snatches of their hymns and religious poetry. We know they practiced a nature religion, worshiping gods and goddesses thought to control the forces of nature. We know they encouraged religious prostitution and believed that sexual orgies excited their deities and made the land fertile. We know that the Canaanites practiced child sacrifice, sorcery, and witchcraft.[22] God was not about to violate the freedom of the Canaanites, but he would judge them for the choices they made with that freedom. And he used Israel as his chosen instrument of judgment.

God does not revoke our freedom to choose. But when our innumerable, lifelong choices turn the central part of us into hellish creatures, in C. S. Lewis's terms, God has no choice left but to judge.

The truth is, meeting God as judge in Scripture's narrative should comfort us rather than shock us. How terrible it would be if the horrid, hellish consequences of our choices went on and on, world without end. Not that we can expect immediate relief from the pain and suffering that the sinful choices of others may cause us. Immediate relief might come only at the cost of robbing others of their opportunity to choose what is right and turn back in the direction of God's love. But a day is coming when God will cleanse the universe and set all things right. As the apostle Paul reminded the persecuted believers in Thessalonica, "God is just: He will pay back trouble to those who trouble you and give relief to you who are troubled, and to us as well."[23]

Leaving the Ark

When the floodwaters receded, Noah and his family emerged from the ark onto a fresh, new landscape. God spoke to this family from which he would again seed the world and gave them this commission: "Whoever sheds human blood, by humans shall their blood be shed; for in the image of God has God made mankind."[24]

This verse is widely understood to authorize the establishment of human government. God promised that never again would he destroy humankind, "as long as the earth endures."[25] But to keep that promise, it was necessary to place an external limit on human freedom. The unintended consequences of doing evil would not be enough to keep humanity from becoming horrid once again. Instead, in the new world that Noah's family entered, human authorities would serve as "agents of wrath to bring punishment on the wrongdoer."[26]

Within the new limits imposed by government and the limits imposed by the unintended consequences of evil actions, people remain free to choose. And the words that God spoke to Cain remain true for you and me: "If you do not do what is right, sin is crouching at your door; it desires to have you, but you must rule over it."[27]

Discussion Questions

1. Most scholars believe that Job is the oldest book in the Bible. Read Job 31 and discuss: Based on Job's defense, before the Bible was even written, how clear of an idea did people have of "doing what is right" versus "doing what is not right"?

2. How aware are you that you are responsible for the choices you make daily? What kind of person do your daily choices suggest you're on course to become?

3. What does God do to encourage people to "do what is right" without in any way violating their freedom to choose? Why do you suppose God doesn't do more?

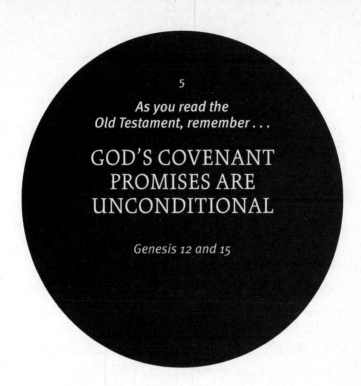

*As you read the
Old Testament, remember...*

GOD'S COVENANT PROMISES ARE UNCONDITIONAL

Genesis 12 and 15

The Pivotal Event

Abram was bent over, working on his accounts, when the Lord said to him, "Go from your country, your people and your father's household to the land I will show you."[1]

The command—for it *was* a command—was simple, but its implications were overwhelming. Along with the commandment to leave, God told Abram what he intended to do for and through him.

Digging Deeper into Genesis 12 and 15

I hope the government never gets rid of pennies. True, a penny costs more to produce than it's worth. And I hate to carry pennies as much as I hate to think of making up fifty-penny rolls to take to the bank. But despite the irritation, I have affection for pennies. Pennies motivated my young children to master addition, subtraction, and the multiplication tables. Pennies served as "clean plate club" rewards, teaching the kids that vegetables aren't as bad as they had imagined. Pennies provided rides on the mechanical ponies that once stood outside Meijer grocery stores. And then there were penny trips.

Penny trips always intrigue children, especially if you let them flip the coin. On a penny trip, you drive along a street or road until the person with the penny decides it's time to turn. Before the next intersection, he or she flips the penny. If it comes up heads, you turn right. If it comes up tails, you turn left. You travel along the new road until the person with the penny decides it's time to turn again, and you repeat the process.

Penny trips give children a sense of control—something they largely lack in an adult world. And there's always intrigue. No one knows what lies ahead after the next random turn.

Adults typically don't share a child's enthusiasm for penny trips. When we get in the car, we usually have a destination in mind. The randomness of the penny trip can be unsettling. Will the next flip of the coin take us into a bad neighborhood? What if we're low on gas and can't find a service station?

We live in a world awash with both good and evil. The news media constantly report events that remind us of how dangerous the world really is. As we examine the chaos around us, it seems that history itself is on a penny trip, taking turn after random turn.

The early chapters of the Bible might lead us to see chaos as normal. According to Genesis, when human beings declared independence from the Creator, each individual, in effect, chose to function as his or her own deity, driven to satisfy personal needs and passions. Added to this is Scripture's revelation of the stranger in Eden, Satan. He and his fellow fallen angels are committed to producing and enticing evil. Human history, churning with anguish and uncertainty, depicts just the kind of world we might expect, given the effects of constant demonic activity and mankind's sinful bent. Our world often seems to be on a cosmic penny trip, with every turn leading to greater chaos and meaninglessness.

Abram

Around 2160 BC, a child was born in lower Mesopotamia (present-day Iraq). His name was Abram. Abram grew up in one of the several mature cultures of the ancient Middle East. As an adult, he lived in the city of Ur, a strong city-state featuring libraries, sewers, and two-story houses, many of which had running water. Like other citizens of Ur, Abram was a pagan. Modern excavations of the city provide a picture of a people who worshiped idols and who looked to occult sources to help them make choices and manipulate the gods.

Abram was already an old man when God spoke to him.[2] The message was brief: "Go from your country, your people and your father's household to the land I will show you."[3]

Along with this message, the Lord told Abram what he firmly intended to do. In a series of "I will" statements, God established the direction of human history and set in motion the fulfillment of what he had told the stranger in Eden: A descendant of Eve was destined to crush Satan's head, even though Satan would strike his heel.[4] Right from the outset, even in the earliest chapters of Genesis, we sense that the Creator *knows* and—at least to some extent—*shapes* the future.

What are these "I will" statements, and what do they tell us?

- "I will make you into a great nation."[5]
- "I will bless you."[6]
- "I will make your name great, and you will be a blessing."[7]
  Later, in a foreshadowing of his plans for the future, God would change Abram's name (which means *exalted father*) to Abraham (which means *father of many*).[8]
- "I will bless those who bless you, and whoever curses you I will curse."[9] "All peoples on earth will be blessed through you."[10]

- After Abram traveled to Canaan, God appeared to him again and said, "To your offspring I will give this land."[11]

These statements of God's intentions assured Abram—and assure us—that despite appearances, history is proceeding along a path that God marked out beforehand. Despite the seeming randomness of many events, human history has both a purpose and a goal.

History records the fulfillment of God's promises to Abram, who was both protected and blessed during his lifetime. Today three major world religions—Judaism, Christianity, and Islam—honor Abraham as their patriarch. His offspring through Isaac and Jacob were rescued from slavery in Egypt and founded a nation. Under King David, the nation of Israel became a great power in the ancient Middle East.

In addition, the peoples of the earth truly have been blessed through Abraham's descendants. The nation of Israel became the channel for God's written revelation, and the Savior of the world—that descendant of Eve's who would crush the head of the serpent—was born to a young Jewish maiden.

Though God's statements to Abram do not fully reveal the course of the future, those ancient "I will" statements have nonetheless served as landmarks designating a path along history's way.

There's another important aspect of these statements that we need to understand: *They are essentially eschatological statements.* That is, they primarily reveal what God intends to accomplish at history's *end*. The ultimate blessing on all people awaits the return of Jesus Christ.

At times down through the ages, chaos and evil have seemed to win: the Jews are forced from their homeland, their enemies triumph, the revelation given to them is either rejected or ignored. But time and again, as history seems to veer off course, the landmarks reappear, and we're reminded that the flow of events is moving toward a time when the "I will" statements will be fully realized.

Promise

Ten years pass after God's initial appearance to Abram. He has converted his wealth to herds and flocks and has traveled to Canaan. Now eighty-five years old, he and his seventy-five-year-old wife are still childless.[12] When God speaks to him again, Abram boldly confronts the Creator. Despite God's statement of intent for Abram's offspring, the old man points out, "You have given me no children."[13]

In response God directs Abram's gaze to the night sky. "Look up at the sky and count the stars—if indeed you can count them. . . . So shall your offspring be."[14]

That night, God directs Abram to select five animals, cut them in two, and place each half opposite the other. Then, as a dreadful darkness surrounds Abram, a smoking firepot with a blazing torch passes between the animal halves. The text interprets the significance of these events, saying, "On that day the LORD made a covenant with Abram."[15]

Three things in this scene are vitally important. First, in setting his "I wills" within a covenant context, God transforms them from statements of intent into promises. They become commitments made to Abram and his offspring, who now have a special relationship with the Lord because of the covenant. Abram and his offspring have truly become God's chosen people.

Second, while Abram slept, God alone passed between the animal halves. Ancient covenants required all parties to the covenant to commit to the relationship. But God caused Abram to fall into a deep sleep, and then God alone passed between the halves of the divided animals. *Only God committed himself in the covenant with Abram that night, making that covenant an unconditional commitment.* God would do everything that he promised, no matter what Abram or his offspring did or failed to do.

Looking back at Genesis 12 and 15, the writer of Hebrews confirms God's commitment:

People swear by someone greater than themselves, and the oath confirms what is said and puts an end to all argument. Because God wanted to make the unchanging nature of his purpose very clear to the heirs of what was promised, he confirmed it with an oath. God did this so that, by two unchangeable things in which it is impossible for God to lie, we who have fled to take hold of the hope set before us may be greatly encouraged.[16]

The unconditional covenant that God entered into that night established forever the basis of his relationship with Abram's offspring.

The third thing to note is recorded in Genesis 15:6. God responded to Abram's complaint about still being childless by promising that his offspring would be as numberless as the stars in the sky. The Bible tells us, "Abram believed the LORD, and he [God] credited it to him [Abram] as righteousness."

Even before the statements of God's purpose were transformed into promises by the establishment of the covenant, Abram responded to God's word with faith. In the apostle Paul's letter to the Romans, he highlights the significance of this faith response:

Against all hope, Abraham in hope believed and so became the father of many nations, just as it had been said to him, "So shall your offspring be." Without weakening in his faith, he faced the fact that his body was as good as dead—since he was about a hundred years old—and that Sarah's womb was also dead. Yet he did not waver through unbelief regarding the promise of God, but was strengthened in his faith and gave glory to God, being fully persuaded that God had power to do what he had promised. This is why "it was credited to him as righteousness." The words "it was credited to him" were written not for him alone, but also for us, to whom God will

credit righteousness—for us who believe in him who raised
Jesus our Lord from the dead. He was delivered over to death
for our sins and was raised to life for our justification.[17]

Abram's personal relationship with God was based not on the covenant or the covenant promises, but on his belief that God could and would do what he promised. It's important to remember this as we read the Old Testament.

Corporately, the Jewish people are God's covenant people. As a people, the Jews have a covenant relationship with the Lord. But *individual* Jews—whether of the Old Testament era, the time of Christ and the apostles, or today—can have a personal relationship with God only by responding as Abram did, with unwavering faith in God's word to them personally. For Abram, that word took the form of an invitation to trust that his descendants would be as numberless as the stars. For us, that word takes the form of God's invitation to us to trust the Savior who died for our sins and rose again to give us eternal life.

Some four hundred years after Abram, the generation of Israelites that succeeded those who had been freed from slavery in Egypt approached the Promised Land. The ruler of Moab, a country the Israelites had to pass through to reach Canaan, was terrified of the marching Israelites, so he enlisted the help of Balaam, a man with recognized occult powers. Offered great riches to curse the Israelites, Balaam found he could utter only blessings—much to his chagrin. As the Moabite king fumed, Balaam tried again and again. Finally, against his will, he was forced to acknowledge, "There is no sorcery against Jacob, nor any divination against Israel."[18] Balaam could not curse the people whom God had committed himself to bless.

Even Balaam's efforts to cause the Lord himself to curse his chosen people failed. Moabite women were sent to the Israelite camp, and they enticed many of the men into sexual sin and idolatry. "In this way, Israel joined in the worship of Baal of Peor, causing the

LORD's anger to blaze against his people."[19] Yet God did not curse his people for abandoning him, as Balaam had expected. The guilty individuals were punished, but God remained faithful to his covenant promises.

God's refusal to repudiate Israel is a theme we see over and over in the Old Testament. God's people display stunning faithlessness, abandoning the Lord in favor of pagan gods, who are nothing but Satan's demons in disguise. God disciplines his people to turn them back to him, yet he does not reject them. The covenant God made with Abram remains an unconditional covenant. God keeps his promises, no matter what a particular generation of Israelites may do.

Conditionality

Not every statement of divine intent in Scripture should be read as a promise. It was the weaving of the divine "I will" statements into a covenant that transformed God's stated intentions into unconditional promises. In cases where God states his intentions outside of a covenantal framework, we should normally see such statements as contingent on human action.

In the eighth century BC, the kingdom of Israel, then ruled by Jeroboam II, was both prosperous and powerful. But the prophet Amos predicted disaster, warning that God would judge his people for the many sins identified in Amos's sermons.[20] Another prophet of the time, Jonah, was a patriot who had predicted Jeroboam II's victories.[21] Unexpectedly, God spoke to Jonah and told him to go to Nineveh, the capital of Assyria. He was to enter the city and "preach against it," stating, "Forty more days and Nineveh will be overthrown."[22]

There could hardly be a clearer statement of God's intentions. The powerful empire that posed the greatest threat to Israel was destined to fall in just forty days. One would think that patriotic Jonah could hardly wait to join the first caravan heading north and east, to proclaim the coming judgment against Nineveh. Instead, he hurried to Joppa and took a ship headed west, toward Tarshish, eager to get as far away from Nineveh as possible. Why?

We all know the story of the violent storm the Lord caused, of Jonah being swallowed by a great fish and carried in its belly, and then being vomited onto dry land.[23] We remember that the reluctant prophet then delivered the message of what God intended to do. But after the forty days passed, Nineveh was not destroyed. God did not do what he had said he intended.

As the text explains, "the Ninevites believed God. . . . When God saw what they did and how they turned from their evil ways, he relented and did not bring on them the destruction he had threatened."[24]

Jonah had fled because as a patriot, he *wanted* God to destroy the Assyrian capital. Jonah understood that many of God's statements of intent are contingent on human response. God fully intended to overthrow Nineveh, but when the people "turned from their evil ways," God changed his mind.

The book of Jonah reminds us of one of the implications of human freedom. Even fallen human beings who have no personal relationship with God have the ability to choose between good and evil. And the choices they make may affect what God chooses to do.

We see something similar in the life of Joel, another prophet who ministered in the northern Hebrew kingdom of Israel. Joel warned his generation of impending judgment. But along with the warning, Joel offered hope:

> Return to the LORD your God,
>   for he is gracious and compassionate,
> slow to anger and abounding in love,
>   and he relents from sending calamity.
> Who knows? He may turn and relent
>   and leave behind a blessing.[25]

God has stated his intention to judge a sinful generation. But whether or not that judgment falls will depend on how the people of the northern kingdom respond. Israel may return to God. And if they do? Who knows? Maybe God will change his mind.

In a later chapter, we'll examine more fully the idea that God can and does change his mind, depending on how humans respond to him. The freedom we seem to experience is real, and the choices we make either draw us closer to God or distance us further from him. Best of all, this characteristic of God, which we might call his *flexibility*, gives us great confidence in prayer. If everything that happens in this world has been determined before the Creation, as some believe, what is the use of prayer? But if God is flexible and responds to us as we respond to him, prayer truly can make a difference.

This is why it's so important to identify the statements of God's intentions that have been set in a covenant context and thus are fixed and certain. Such statements of intent are transformed into unconditional promises. Because they are unconditional, nothing we do or fail to do can alter God's commitment to accomplish what he has promised. The unconditional covenants, with their statements of what God is certain to do, are the bedrock of God's story, a firm foundation for our faith, and fixed landmarks by which to navigate as history unfolds.

The Promise Covenants

Promise covenants meet four criteria: (1) They state what God intends to do, (2) they are specifically set in a covenantal framework, (3) they are unconditional and thus cannot be canceled or superseded, and (4) they have an eschatological focus (that is, their complete fulfillment awaits history's end).

The foundational promise covenant is God's covenant with Abraham. God's "I will" statements provide an overview of where history is going. Each of the other promise covenants provides added insight into how God firmly intends to accomplish his purposes in and through human history.

The second promise covenant is found in 2 Samuel 7 and is expressed by the prophet Nathan, who conveys God's words to King David, "Your house and your kingdom will endure forever before me; your throne will be established forever."[26] This statement of divine intent is identified as a covenant in Psalm 89:3-4.

Based in part on this unconditional covenantal promise by God, the Jews of Jesus' day believed firmly that a Messiah would one day be born from David's family line. Christians understand that the birth, life, and death of Jesus fulfill the biblical prophecies about the Messiah. The Jews, however, do not acknowledge Jesus as the Christ because they have not understood that the Abrahamic covenant is *eschatological* and that the kingdom over which Christ will rule lies ahead, awaiting his return.

The third promise covenant is introduced in Jeremiah 31:31, where the prophet looks into the future and declares that God will "make a new covenant with the people of Israel." This covenant contrasts with the Mosaic covenant.

"It will not be like the covenant
    I made with their ancestors
when I took them by the hand
    to lead them out of Egypt,
because they broke my covenant,
    though I was a husband to them,"

            declares the LORD.

"This is the covenant I will make with the people of Israel
    after that time," declares the LORD.
"I will put my law in their minds
    and write it on their hearts.
I will be their God,

and they will be my people.
No longer will they teach their neighbor,
    or say to one another, 'Know the LORD,'
because they will all know me,
    from the least of them to the greatest,"

declares the LORD.

"For I will forgive their wickedness
    and will remember their sins no more."[27]

Like the Davidic covenant before it, the New Covenant is a revelation of the way in which God intends to keep his promise to Abraham, that through a descendant of his "all peoples on earth will be blessed."[28] That blessing includes forgiveness of sin and an inner transformation, and the inscription of God's righteousness not on stone tablets but on the hearts of his people.

This new covenant was *cut* (executed, put in force) by the death of Jesus. Though it, too, is an eschatological covenant, it promises full forgiveness and the possibility of progressive transformation by God's Spirit to all who trust Jesus now.[29]

If we are to read the Bible from *within* the story, it is essential that we understand the promise covenants. They underline the role of the Jews as God's chosen people, God's goal of establishing his Kingdom on earth, and the centrality of the Cross as the focus of a faith that offers forgiveness of sins and ultimate transformation.

That said, we must also remember that not every statement of God's intentions is unconditional or a covenant promise—and that's what can make so much of human history seem like a penny trip.

God created men and angels with freedom of choice that they might freely respond to his love and be loved in return. But freedom of choice means that men and angels might choose to reject God's love and repudiate God's ways. It is this capacity of ours, and of the demons, to choose evil that makes this world such an uncertain and chaotic place. All too often, we humans have exercised our free will to rebel against God, and Satan and his demons have focused their efforts on turning generation after generation from God's path.

Despite the chaos, however, God's ultimate purposes will be achieved. His unconditional promises, enshrined in the biblical covenants and supported by prophecies describing the landmarks along the way, guarantee it.

I no longer take any penny trips. Instead, I decide where I intend to go and enter the address into my Garmin GPS. It directs my route, and should I make a wrong turn, a voice says, "Recalculating," and the device guides me back to the road I should take.

Likewise, when we stray from the path in life that we should be on, God responds by recalculating our routes and redeeming our failures. He exercises his power and his grace to put history back on its predetermined course. Because we see the landmarks established in the promise covenants, waypoints that assure us that history is moving along God's appointed path, we know that he will triumph in the end.

Discussion Questions

1. One thing that makes the promise covenants so special is that they are unconditional. Why might understanding the unconditional nature of God's covenant commitments be important to anyone who has a personal relationship with him?

2. In this chapter, we suggest that God is *flexible*; that is, that a statement of his intentions in Scripture may be conditional, dependent on our human response. How does this fit with your idea about the sovereignty of God? If God is flexible, how does this affect your intention to live within the biblical narrative, allowing your perspective of life and your experiences to be shaped by Scripture's revelation?

3. We looked at several *promise covenants* that meet four specific criteria for covenant agreements. What are these criteria, and what are the promise covenants that meet these criteria? How does understanding them help you live within God's story?

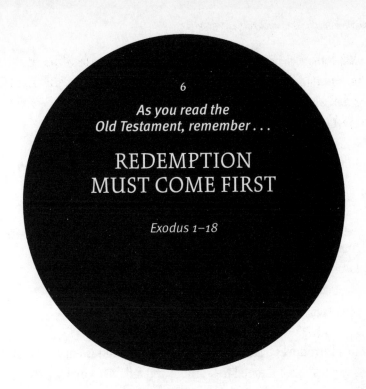

6

*As you read the
Old Testament, remember . . .*

REDEMPTION MUST COME FIRST

Exodus 1–18

The Pivotal Event

Moses straightened up, peering at a strange sight just over a nearby ridge. A bush was burning, but it was not consumed. Curious, Moses left his flock and approached the burning bush. As he drew near, he was confronted by the angel of the Lord, visible within the flames, and he heard the voice of God say, "I have indeed seen the misery of my people in Egypt. . . . I have come down to rescue them from the hand of the Egyptians."[1]

Digging Deeper into Exodus 1–18

When I read the early chapters of the book of Exodus, I'm reminded of the opening lines of the 1961 hit song "Stand By Me," performed by soul singer Ben E. King:

When the night has come
And the land is dark
And the moon is the only light we'll see,
No, I won't be afraid
Oh, I won't be afraid
Just as long as you stand, stand by me. . . .

If the sky that we look upon
Should tumble and fall,
And the mountain should crumble to the sea,
I won't cry, I won't cry
No, I won't shed a tear
Just as long as you stand, stand by me.[2]

Exodus introduces a time when, clearly, "the land is dark" and even the sky must have seemed to "tumble and fall." Originally welcomed in Egypt as guests, the Hebrew people have since been enslaved and forced to undertake great building projects. The rapid growth of the Hebrew population has alarmed the Egyptians. Fearful that if Egypt were invaded, the Hebrews might turn on their masters, Pharaoh orders that every male baby be killed at birth. In this hopeless situation "the Israelites groaned in their slavery and cried out, and their cry for help because of their slavery went up to God."[3]

The rest of the story is well known. Moses, a Hebrew infant adopted into Pharaoh's own family, grew up to identify with the Jewish people. After a forty-year exile, he returned to Egypt, demanded that Pharaoh release his slaves, and called on God to perform crushing miracles that devastated Egypt. Moses then led the Israelites out of the land of bondage and brought them to the land God had promised to Abraham's descendants.

What you may not know is that this particular section of the Bible's narrative is critical to our understanding of God's story and our own.

It introduces a theme—*redemption*—that is woven throughout both the Old and New Testaments.

Redemption

The Bible frequently introduces doctrine through stories. It seems we're better able to grasp the truth when it is dressed in narrative form. This is certainly the case with the Exodus story and the doctrine of redemption.

In the early chapters of Exodus, we're forced to confront the utter hopelessness of the Israelites' situation. Pharaoh and his people intend to murder the male infants born to the Hebrews, such that in time, the people will cease to exist. There is nothing the enslaved Israelites can do to save themselves. All they can do is cry out in their anguish.

Those of us who know the story well from Sunday school, with its emphasis on the rescue of baby Moses, might not feel the awful sense of hopelessness that shrouds the early verses of Exodus. Yet if we consider the plight of the Israelites in Egypt, we can hardly miss the despair. Night has come, and the land is dark indeed.

Thus the foundation for the doctrine of redemption is laid in the hopeless condition of a people who are enslaved, with freedom but a distant memory in their culture.

The narrative then introduces the baby Moses. Though he, too, is born a slave, he is adopted into the royal family. At the age of forty, Moses identifies with his people, sensing that he is called to deliver them.[4] But his efforts are rejected by the Israelites, and he spends the next forty years as a shepherd on the Sinai Peninsula. Then he receives a call from God. His earlier dream is to be fulfilled. God, who is concerned for his people, will send Moses to lead them to freedom.

Here, another story element with implications for God's own story is introduced: God will bring redemption through one who is both royalty and the closest of kin to the slaves he is destined to free.

As the narrative unfolds, Moses returns to Egypt and confronts Pharaoh, demanding that the king let God's people go. When Pharaoh refuses, God intervenes. In a series of miraculous judgments, he crushes all opposition, leaving the fruitful land of Egypt in ruin and its people weeping over their dead. The Israelites, carrying with them the plundered wealth of Egypt, exit their servitude and set out for a land of their own.

Three major elements in this story give shape to the doctrine of redemption: (1) The people are enslaved and helpless; (2) God commissions an agent to act on their behalf; and (3) through God's mighty acts, the evil power that has held the Israelites in slavery is defeated and the captives are set free.

This story incarnates—fleshes out—our understanding of the underlying doctrine, providing us with vivid images that illustrate truths deeply embedded in the word *redeem*.

In the Old Testament, there are two Hebrew words that are translated *redeem*. Each is a word that was used in daily life in ancient Israel. The first, *padah*, is a commercial term, commonly used to express transfer of ownership from one person to another. Through *padah*, God's miracles win Israel's release from servitude and establish God's claim on the allegiance of the freed people. Ownership of the Israelites is transferred from their Egyptian slave masters, and they become God's possession. Deuteronomy 7:6-8 reminds Israel that "the Lord your God has chosen you out of all the peoples on the face of the earth to be his people, his treasured possession. The Lord . . . brought you out with a mighty hand and redeemed [*padah*] you from the land of slavery, from the power of Pharaoh king of Egypt."

This transition from slavery to being God's treasured possession is viewed in the Old Testament as more than a historical event. When faced with difficulties or danger, Israel can look back and "remember his power—the day he redeemed them from the oppressor, the day he displayed his signs in Egypt."[5] The nation of Israel "had the assurance that God had established ownership of [them] through redemption and would continue to act to deliver them as they trusted him."[6]

A second Hebrew term referring to redemption, *ga'al*, means "play the part of a kinsman." In its common usage, *ga'al* reflects a distinctive element in Hebrew culture: the right and duty of a close relative to act on behalf of another who is in trouble or danger. As with *padah*, *ga'al* speaks to a situation in which an individual (or his or her property) is held in the power of another and is helpless to change the situation. But *ga'al* places the emphasis on the requirement that the rescuer must be a close kinsman. Only a near kinsman is eligible to make the payment necessary to win the release of the individual or the return of his or her property.

Through the covenant promises he made to Abraham and his offspring, God has adopted Israel as his own people. He has become their nearest kinsman, who is able and willing to act on their behalf. Thus God says through Moses, "I will free you from being slaves to them, and I will redeem [*ga'al*] you with an outstretched arm."[7]

When we view the Old Testament doctrine of redemption through the lens of the events in Exodus, we see that God acted on Israel's behalf "because they were his family. Love and duty combined as God stepped into history to meet the needs of a people who were helpless without him."[8]

The New Old Story

When we turn to the New Testament epistles, we discover that once again story is used to communicate the concept of redemption. The story aspect of the Epistles is often missed by readers, who view the letters as merely doctrinal expositions. However, we can see how the Epistles can be understood as *story* by looking at what Paul tells us in the first chapter of his letter to the Romans. Genesis tells us how sin entered the human race. In Romans, Paul carries the story further, showing how sin has corrupted humankind's soul and culture. Here's the story Paul tells:

> At one time, human beings knew God. In fact God continues to speak to them through the creation. Yet humankind has failed to respond. They have not been thankful, nor did they even acknowledge his existence. As a result their "foolish hearts were darkened." Humans tried to satisfy their hunger for relationship with God by worshiping images of humans, birds, and animals. They became morally corrupt and degraded. Soul and culture became "filled with every kind of wickedness, evil, greed and depravity."[9]

This story is repeated again and again in the New Testament epistles, such as in Ephesians, where Paul portrays humankind as "dead in [our] transgressions and sins . . . gratifying the cravings of our flesh [our sinful nature] and following its desires and thoughts. Like the rest, we were by nature deserving of [God's] wrath."[10]

Thus the New Testament's redemption story also begins with a vision of an enslaved people. Just as Israel was helpless in ancient Egypt, today we all are helpless, enslaved by sin and evil.

There is another parallel between the New Testament and Old Testament stories. In the Exodus narrative, God works through an agent, Moses. Although Moses was a member of the royal family, he was also *kin* to the enslaved people with whom he identified, and thus was qualified to act as kinsman redeemer to win their redemption. In the New Testament story, God's agent is Jesus. Though he, too, is royalty, the very Son of God, he became an authentic human being in the Incarnation. As a true human being, Jesus is qualified to act on behalf of helpless humanity.

In both stories—Exodus and the Gospels—God intervenes in history. He permits his Son to die on a Roman cross, knowing that Christ's death serves as payment for humanity's sin and restores our relationship with himself, our Creator, which we had abandoned. Then, in the ultimate miracle, Jesus is raised, transformed, from the dead. Now, through our faith in Jesus, God's resurrection power flows to us, breaking death's grip and infusing us with power so that we might live godly lives (see Romans 8:11; Ephesians 2:4-6).

The New Testament's story is supported and enhanced by two Greek words that are translated as *redeem* or *redemption*. The first word is built on the root *lytro*, and the verb means "to ransom or redeem." Words constructed on this root emphasize the *nature* of the release won and the *means* by which release is accomplished.

Though words based on *lytro* are found only ten times in the New Testament, the context in each instance makes it very clear that our redemption is accomplished through "the precious blood of Christ," a price paid to release us from "the empty way of life" inherited from our forefathers.[11] As a result, New Testament redemption promises to "redeem us from all wickedness"[12] so that we "may serve the living God."[13]

The second Greek term, *exagoraz*, is an intensive form of a word that simply means "to purchase." The root, *agoraz*, is often used to describe the purchase of a slave at a slave market. This intensive verb, though found only four times in the New Testament (Galatians 3:13; 4:5; Ephesians 5:16; and Colossians 4:5), emphasizes the once-for-all transfer of believers from the dominion of evil to the family of God.

The New Testament applies the Old Testament concept of national redemption to the issue of personal salvation. "Each person in our world is in the grip of sin. Sin's bondage can be broken only through Christ's blood. Redeemed, the believer is given a place in the family of God and is called to live a life that reflects his new standing."[14]

The Antagonist

In the time of Moses, the religion of the Egyptians featured many deities, an elite and educated priesthood, and magnificent temples.

The temples were viewed as the homes of the gods or goddesses to whom they were dedicated. Pharaoh, who was viewed as a god himself and as a relative of the gods, was charged with maintaining good relations between Egypt and her deities. This responsibility was especially important because each deity was thought to make his or her contribution to the well-being of Egypt, tending to the floods that made the land along the Nile the best cropland in the world, providing the sunlight that nurtured the crops, and ensuring the birth of many calves to Egypt's herds.

We can imagine how the young Pharaoh must have felt when an elderly Moses approached him and demanded, in the name of the God of Pharaoh's slaves, that the king release the Israelites. How dare he demand anything from Pharaoh! Who was this God of slaves anyway?

Up to this point, we've looked at the human face of the stories that define the biblical concept of redemption. We haven't yet looked *behind* the stories. When we do, we discover a player who is too often ignored. We discover Satan, God's great adversary. Though he pales in comparison to God, Satan is nonetheless someone we must never overlook; indeed, we must never forget that the Bible's story is, in essence, the story of an invisible war in the spiritual realm, with earth as a key battleground.

The first indication that spiritual forces of evil are deeply invested in the events in Egypt appears in Exodus 7. When Moses renews his demand that Pharaoh release Israel, Pharaoh responds, "Perform a miracle."

It is not surprising that Pharaoh demanded a sign from Moses. Moses claimed to speak on behalf of God. So was the God that Moses represented powerful enough to perform a miracle? The Lord had prepared Moses for precisely this challenge. Moses told his brother, Aaron, "Take your staff and throw it down before Pharaoh."[15] When Aaron did, the staff became a snake.

Pharaoh responded by calling for his "wise men and sorcerers,

[who] also did the same things by their secret arts."[16] Even though Aaron's serpent then ate the serpents produced by the priests of Egypt's gods, "Pharaoh's heart became hard and he would not listen."[17]

It's easy to skim over this event and ignore its implications. Yet throughout the Old Testament, many references are made to the occult practices of sorcery, magic, witchcraft, divination, and spiritism. For many people, the idea of a spirit world whose denizens can (and do) affect what happens in the world is pure fantasy. But within Scripture's grand narrative, we see a spirit world that parallels our own and in which there are beings whose actions affect the world that we can see.

This interpretation is confirmed by God's statement of purpose in devastating Egypt: "that you may know that I am the LORD."[18] This phrase is repeated several times in Exodus.[19] A similar purpose declared in Exodus is so that "the Egyptians will know that I am the LORD."[20]

A third purpose for the plagues is stated in Exodus 12:12, with special reference to the final plague: "I will bring judgment on all the gods of Egypt." Here God refers not to the mute idols of wood and stone that the priests of Egypt dressed and pampered but to the spiritual forces of evil that exercised control over the Egyptian people through their deities. In the devastation caused by the plagues, God demonstrated the powerlessness of the Egyptian deities. In the final plague—the death of every firstborn in every Egyptian household—God showed that he and he alone has authority over life and death.

When we turn to the New Testament story of redemption, we once again find Satan the antagonist. In Ephesians 2, his role is emphasized. Humankind "followed the ways of this world and of the ruler of the kingdom of the air, the spirit who is now at work in those who are disobedient."[21] The New Testament indicates that human beings, apart from God's intervention, are fully in the grasp of the antagonist. Paul reminds us that those outside the narrative "cannot see the light of the gospel that displays the glory of Christ"[22] and are instead caught in "the trap of the devil, who has taken them captive to do his will."[23]

Satan is one who "leads the whole world [*oikoumene*, humankind] astray,"[24] and all human culture [*kosmos*, the whole world] is "under the control of the evil one."[25]

Helpless before the "powers of this dark world and . . . the spiritual forces of evil in the heavenly realms,"[26] those outside the Bible's narrative fall victim to "the devil's schemes."[27]

Purpose

Whenever I see a copy of Rick Warren's popular book *The Purpose Driven Life*, I'm reminded of the author's central theme that the purpose of our lives "fits into a much larger, cosmic purpose that God has designed for eternity."[28] I can't help but wonder whether anyone has ever asked, "What is *God's* purpose in life? What cosmic purpose drives him and gives his existence meaning?"

If we follow Warren's advice and turn to revelation rather than speculation, it would seem that these questions are asked—and answered—in Scripture. The creation story points toward a readily understood purpose. God created beings in his own image and likeness that he might build an eternal community of beings he would love and who would love him. He gifted these beings with the freedom to reciprocate or reject his love. As the grand narrative unfolds, we learn that many of the first-created beings, the angels, rejected God's love and rebelled against him, launching an invisible war against the Creator.

We've seen that God then created humans in his own image and likeness, gifting them with the same freedom to choose that he had given to the angels. Then Satan, the leader of the rebellious angels, influenced the first humans to declare their independence from God, corrupting them and their offspring. But God never stopped loving humankind.

Genesis describes how the Creator entered the Garden in search of

Adam and Eve. Exodus shows God actively intervening on behalf of a helpless humanity. He works through a human agent to redeem his enslaved covenant people, and he transfers ownership from the slave masters to himself. And it is out of this redeemed people that God will build the community of love for which he created humankind.

Scripture's vision of an eternal community of love is eschatological, to be realized at history's end, when all his covenant promises are fulfilled. Along the way, the hope of building a community of love is held out to the redeemed and engraved in Scripture's story. During the New Testament era, that community is the church. Like ancient Israel, the contemporary church falls far short of God's ideal. Yet that ideal is destined to be realized, and we are called to live in hope that we might experience much of the community of love in our present day.

My Name Forever

The familiar story of Moses and the burning bush introduces us to a defining conversation between Moses and the Almighty. When God tells Moses to return to Egypt and confront Pharaoh, Moses objects. He doesn't even know the Lord's name. What will he tell the people of Israel when they ask the name of the God who sent him? God's answer is, "Tell them, 'Yahweh sent me.'"

In Hebrew, the name *Yahweh* contains four letters and is constructed on the root of the verb *to be*. Most modern English versions translate it "I AM WHO I AM," and the essential meaning is clear: God simply *is*—not only in the past but also in the present and the future. We might translate the name *Yahweh* as an affirmation: "The One Who Is Always Present." As the Lord told Moses, "This is my name forever, the name you shall call me from generation to generation."[29]

No longer will God be known primarily as the God of Israel's forefathers, as if he were somehow locked up hundreds of years in the past. Israel's God is the God who invades space and time on behalf of his beloved people. Israel's God moves through time with them, taking his stand by their side, always present for them.

This special and very personal name of Israel's God appears more than 6,800 times in the Old Testament. It is a vivid affirmation of God's intention to stand by his people whatever their situation. The night may be dark, and the mountain may crumble into the sea, but I know that God, ever, always, will stand by me.

Discussion Questions

1. In the biblical stories that convey the meaning of *redemption*, what seems to be the most important element? What in your own experience makes this element stand out?

2. How aware have you been of attacks by Satan in your own life? Why must we take him seriously if we are to live within the Bible's narrative?

3. What is your response to the idea that fashioning an eternal community of beings whom he can love, and who can love him, provides God with a sense of meaning and purpose? What direction for your own life might understanding God's purpose provide?

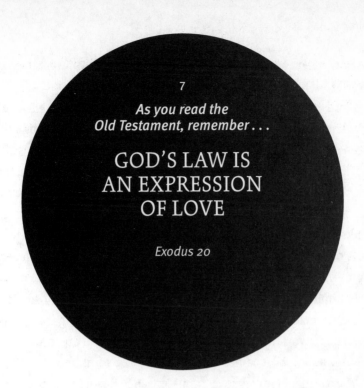

7

*As you read the
Old Testament, remember . . .*

GOD'S LAW IS
AN EXPRESSION
OF LOVE

Exodus 20

The Pivotal Event

As Moses climbed slowly up the side of Mount Sinai, the people looked on in fear mixed with awe. The peak of the mountain was concealed by dark, roiling clouds. Bolts of lightning flashed continually, bathing the mountain's sides in their light. Behind the clouds, God waited for Moses with a gift for the people below.

Digging Deeper into Exodus 20

When I was a young teen, I read as many as eight books a week. I'd go to our little public library, upstairs over the firehouse on Main Street, and exchange one stack of books for another. I even read on the way home, balancing a book on the handlebars of my bicycle. On Sundays, I read while listening to Detroit Tigers games on the radio; at night, after my parents called up to my room to tell me it was time to go to sleep, I read under the covers by flashlight.

I read everything our town's library had to offer. But I liked novels best. The stories captivated my imagination, and I raced through the pages, eager to trace the plot and see how the story turned out.

Thus far, the Bible has seemed like one of those adventure books I used to love. The story has moved quickly and is filled with excitement. Humankind declares independence, with terrible and tragic results. A grief-stricken God scours the planet with a terrible flood and starts over with Noah and his family. Humanity clings to independence, with predictable results. Then God announces what he intends to accomplish for and through a human family, and he transforms that announcement into an unbreakable promise by placing it in a covenant framework. As the story unfolds, the promises are transmitted to Isaac and Jacob (renamed Israel) and to Jacob's children.

The covenant family moves from Canaan to Egypt in search of food during a famine. Abraham's descendants, now known as Israelites, multiply and are enslaved. The tension becomes almost unbearable as the entire family is threatened with extinction when the ruler of Egypt orders the murder of every male infant born to the Israelites. But then, in an unexpected twist, an Israelite infant named Moses is adopted into Egypt's royal family.

What a story! So filled with disappointment, despair, and hope. What will happen next in this fascinating story that God tells in the Bible?

Everything?

In 1996, David Shibley wrote a book titled *Everything I Need to Know I Learned in Sunday School.* I have to take exception with the title. As a one-time editor and writer of Sunday school curriculum, I can assure you that we need to know much more than what we learned in Sunday school.

If you were brought up in church, you've heard the story of baby Moses and the basket in the river. You've learned about Adam and Eve, and the great ark that Noah built to save the animals. You've heard about the miracles that God performed in Egypt, and how the sea opened to save the Israelites. Most Sunday school curriculum is built around Bible *stories* rather than around the Bible's *story*.

This focus on Bible stories contributes to the jolt we feel when we reach Exodus 20 and suddenly find ourselves in strange territory. It's as if we were reading an exciting novel, then turned a page and found ourselves in the middle of a physics textbook or instructions on how to set up our new iPad. The rest of Exodus and all of Leviticus and Deuteronomy simply don't tell stories. They contain what Scripture calls the law of Moses, a rather dense set of rules that the Israelites were to follow. The average Sunday school Christian knows almost nothing about the law of Moses. Yet there is so much more to the turn our story takes with the arrival of the Israelites at Mount Sinai.

The Torah

In many English translations of the Old Testament, we find the word *law* where the original text has the Hebrew word *torah*. That's unfortunate. For most of us, *law* implies the exercise of coercive power to enforce conformity to a standard. That's why many people mistakenly view the Ten Commandments as harsh edicts—when they read "Do not," they seem to hear a stern voice in their heads add, "or else!" But the basic meaning of *torah* is not *law*; it is *instruction* or *teaching*. All five books of Moses are considered *torah*, which may refer in a general way to God's revelation as a whole or to specific regulations within that revelation.

The stern voice of authority we think we hear when we read the Old Testament is at odds with Scripture's affirmation of human freedom and with its reliance on the power of love to bring human beings into harmony with God. The "law" enshrined in the Hebrew Torah (the first five books of the Old Testament) is far more *gift* than *requirement*, more *invitation* than *demand*, more *gracious warning* than *threat*. What we call God's law is actually comprehensive instruction designed to shape a community here on earth that will reflect God's eternal community of love.

Israel as a Community of Love

As the Israelites emerge from the Exodus, God's story is about to be advanced and his purposes achieved through a faith community that will also be a nation. The instructions that God gives Moses at Mount Sinai (Exodus–Leviticus), and later as the Israelites are poised on the border of the Promised Land (Deuteronomy), are intended to mold the nation-state into a loving community. Strikingly, the divine instruction covers every aspect of the lives of the people of Israel.

There is moral instruction (*torah*), exemplified in the Ten Commandments (Exodus 20) and in the case law that immediately follows (Exodus 21–23). There is instruction on diet (Leviticus 11) and instruction on dealing with infectious skin diseases (Leviticus 13–14). There is instruction about when an individual must offer sacrifices, what to offer, and how the priest is to present the offerings to God (Leviticus 1–7). There is instruction on the Sabbath and on annual religious festivals (Exodus 23; Leviticus 23; Deuteronomy 16). There is instruction on how to treat the poor, widows, and orphans (Exodus 23; Leviticus 19). There is instruction on sexual practices (Leviticus 18) and instruction on the treatment of employees (Leviticus 19). There is instruction on bringing up children (Deuteronomy 6). There is instruction on acceptable worship, along with the prohibition of pagan worship practices (Deuteronomy 18:9-13).

All these instructions and many, many more are *torah*. God's instructions to Israel lay out a lifestyle that, if adopted, will provide

Israel with a resting place; a place on earth where God's people can live together as a true community of love.

Community Breakdown

"I want you parents to watch this closely," Dr. Phil says as a clip from YouTube flashes on the TV screen. Two girls are fighting, arms flailing. Then one is on the floor with the other girl on top, pounding her, her head bouncing again and again on the hard tile. We can hear the voices of the girls who've gathered to watch, excited, calling out.

"That's only twenty seconds."

"Hit her again!"

"Twenty-eight seconds!"

"Hit her! Hit her!"

The battering continues, the girl on the bottom no longer resisting.

"That's forty-five seconds."

"Don't stop!"

The scene flickers and goes black, and the TV camera now focuses on a slight, thirteen-year-old girl sitting next to Dr. Phil, her face expressionless.

"Were you the one down on the floor, getting your head banged into the tile?" Dr. Phil asks.

The girl nods.

"Did you want to do this?"

The girl shakes her head.

"Why did you do it?"

"Because I didn't want to be called a snitch or a punk."[1]

As Dr. Phil explained, these girls were playing a "game" called the Thirty Seconds Game. In recent years, it was all the rage in middle schools across the country. Two kids hit each other as hard as they can for thirty seconds, while a crowd watches and someone videotapes the fight to put up on the Internet. The two girls whose fight was shown on *Dr. Phil* were fighting in the girls' restroom while about twenty other girls watched.

The news programs on TV, the headlines in local papers, and the experiences of family and friends make it clear that no one in our society is truly safe. One of every four girls born in America today will be sexually molested before she is out of her teens—and researchers suspect that the true number is higher than that. For boys, the number is one out of six. Millions live below the poverty line, and most have little prospect of achieving the American Dream. Our prisons are filled to overflowing, and minorities make up a disproportionate number of the incarcerated. The moral fabric of America is being eroded, with the media glorifying blatant sexuality as more than 60 percent of young people suffer from pornographic or other Internet addictions.

No, our society is hardly a safe place for human beings to live and grow and prosper. Neither was the culture of the land into which the Israelites were moving. Religious prostitution was common. Infants were burned alive in an effort to gain favors from pagan deities. A rigid class system protected the wealthy and powerful. If God's people were to live and grow and prosper in Canaan, they would need to create a society in which every individual was protected. They would need a loving community.

This is exactly what the Mosaic law, the Torah, was designed to provide. Israel was to become a resting place, a safe haven, for every citizen and foreigner living there. Israel would witness to the surrounding nations, "who will hear about all these decrees and say, 'Surely this great nation is a wise and understanding people.'"[2]

What Does Love Look Like?

When asked to identify the greatest commandment in the Torah, Jesus gave this answer: "'Love the Lord your God with all your heart and with all your soul and with all your mind.' This is the first and greatest commandment. And the second is like it: 'Love your neighbor as yourself.' All the Law and the Prophets hang on these two commandments."[3]

In two simple statements, Jesus summed up both tablets of the Ten Commandments—the first four commandments governing our relationship with God, and the second six governing our relationships with others.

THE TEN COMMANDMENTS

Relationship with God	Relationship with Others
1. No gods before me	5. Honor father and mother
2. No idols	6. Do not murder
3. Do not take my name in vain (that is, do not treat my name as an empty or meaningless word)	7. Do not commit adultery
	8. Do not steal
	9. Do not give false testimony
4. Keep the Sabbath holy	10. Do not covet

The commandments were designed to answer the question "What does love look like?" Love is easy to see when we look at some of the issues every society must deal with. For instance, what does the Torah say about treatment of the poor, about sexual attitudes toward women, and about the justice system?

The Torah protects the poor and the powerless. As many as seven social mechanisms designed to protect the poor are woven into Old Testament law. The Torah specifically prohibits favoritism in settling disputes between the rich and the poor. Judges were told, "Do not show partiality to the poor or favoritism to the great, but judge your neighbor fairly."[4]

The Torah gives the poor access to necessities. At harvest time, landowners were to reap their fields just once. Anything that was missed, or that fell to the ground, was to be left for the poor to glean.[5] Every seventh year, fields were not to be plowed or planted. Whatever grew naturally that year was to be gathered by the poor.[6] In this, the Torah shows a unique sensitivity to the poor, who are allowed to maintain their dignity. They are not given handouts; they earn their food by working in others' fields.

The Torah also provided for interest-free, forgivable loans.[7] Though the borrower was expected to repay the loan, personal loans were to be forgiven every seventh year. No individual was forced to endlessly carry an unpayable or growing debt.

What the Torah prescribes is essentially an apprenticeship program. People who found themselves deeply in debt might contract their services to a fellow Israelite for a six-year period, during which the purchaser would pay off the debts. For six years, the debtor lived in the more successful person's household as a bondservant. In the seventh year, the debtor was set free. And even then, the Torah gave specific instructions: "When you release them, do not send them away empty-handed. Supply them liberally from your flock, your threshing floor and your winepress. Give to them as the LORD your God has blessed you. Remember that you were slaves in Egypt and the LORD your God redeemed you. That is why I give you this command today."[8]

In addition, the Torah called for organized collections to benefit "foreigners, the fatherless and the widows."[9] Every third year, a tenth of the produce of the land was to be set aside and stored locally to provide a safety net for those who were helpless and unable to provide for themselves.[10]

A seventh social mechanism was designed to preserve each family's capital, which in Israel's agricultural society was land. When the Israelites conquered Canaan, each family was given acreage of its own. This land was to remain in the family to which it was originally given. If members of one generation became heavily indebted, they might sell the *use* of their land, but they could not sell the land itself. Every fiftieth year, called the Year of Jubilee, use of the land reverted to the original family.

How a society deals with the poor is a critical indicator of its values.

The Torah of Moses lays out a unique system that, if followed, would make Israel truly a community of love and a safe haven for the poor.

The Torah affirms respect for women. Immediately after the Fall, God warned Eve of the consequences of Adam's and her decision. Husbands, God warned, would "rule over" their wives.[11] Most ancient societies were oppressively patriarchal. Women and girls were treated as chattel. Israelite society was also patriarchal. Legally, women were defined by their relationship to their father or their husband. Yet the Torah affirmed and protected a woman's status as a person rather than an object. The practice of ritual prostitution, a major component of Canaanite culture, was strictly forbidden in Israel.[12] The book of Proverbs, reflecting the attitude toward sex ingrained by the Torah, both encourages men, "Rejoice in the wife of your youth"[13] and warns, "The prostitute reduces you to a piece of bread"; that is, she sees you as nothing more than the bread she'll gain from you.[14] Within their families, women were protected from sexual exploitation: "No one is to approach any close relative to have sexual relations," which forbids one of the most common types of sexual abuse found in our own culture.[15]

Despite the patriarchal orientation of the society, women were respected, and any sexual intercourse outside of marriage was prohibited.[16] From childhood, the young were taught, "Honor your father and your mother,"[17] creating a context within which women (and girls) were respected and valued as persons.

By affirming sex within the marriage union and by discouraging all other sexual expression, the Torah fashions a safe place within which boys and girls can grow up free from the damage caused by sexual abuse, and it creates a safe environment for women, who can live without fear of sexual exploitation by men.

The Torah establishes a unique justice system, one that reflects God's concern with creating a safe, loving community that works to keep people from being either victims or violators.

Every society develops systems and structures to deal with civil violations and criminal acts. America's justice system, for example, views crime as an offense against the state. The justice system is designed to punish those who commit crimes. Perpetrators are generally sent to prison. After serving their terms, ex-convicts receive little or no support to enable successful transition back into society.

The Torah's justice system differs in significant ways. Crimes are viewed as wrong primarily because they harm the victim, not primarily because they violate laws of the state. The goal of justice is to make the victim whole, not to punish the perpetrator. Just as important, the Torah emphasizes restoring the relationship between perpetrator and victim, and reintegrating the perpetrator into society.

> The OT justice system relied more on restitution than on imprisonment. A person who was responsible for another's loss was to reimburse the value of the property destroyed (Exodus 22:1-15). Property that was stolen or obtained illegally had to be restored and a penalty of one to four times its value was added. Murder and accidental homicide were special cases with a distinct code to govern how they were to be judged.[18]

In the justice system prescribed by the Torah, we again sense a concern that the community be a safe haven for all. The underlying value is love, and in the Torah's prescriptions we discover what true love looks like.

Loving God

It is relatively easy to see what love looks like as the commandments in the Torah flesh out a picture of the community that the nation of Israel is intended to become. It is not as easy to see love for God in the many ritual (as opposed to morally rooted) instructions in the Torah.

Many of the practices specified in the Torah seem peculiar to us, such as these instructions found in Deuteronomy 22:11-12: "Do not wear clothes of wool and linen woven together. Make tassels on the four corners of the cloak you wear." There is clearly no moral component to such instruction, and though violating a ritual instruction made a person ceremonially unclean for a time, it could hardly be classified with sins that called for the offering of a blood sacrifice.

The Torah included many purely ritual requirements that seemed to have no purpose other than to remind the Israelites that they were different from their neighbors—that is, to continually remind them that they were the people of a God who was deeply involved in every aspect of their daily lives.

A Community of the Redeemed

The Torah was given to Israel, a people "chosen . . . out of all the peoples on the face of the earth to be . . . [God's] treasured possession."[19] The Torah is a gift to the redeemed, in the sense that it is comprehensive instruction designed to shape a community here on earth that reflects God's eternal community of love. To the extent that the Israelites lived by the Torah, they would become a resting place, a *haven*, and God could and would bless them.[20]

But here we have a problem. Both the Old and New Testament portray human beings as flawed and fallen creatures. It's not that we *can* sin and fall short of God's instruction, but that we *will* sin and fall short. Living by the Torah proved to be a far greater challenge than the Israelites realized. So God made provision in the Torah for those who would fall short.

For those who violated the ritual (nonmoral) instructions, the Torah provided ceremonial washing for cleansing. For those who violated a moral instruction, the Torah provided a priesthood and blood sacrifices. Though individual sacrifices covered only unintentional sins, an annual Day of Atonement was built into the calendar, when the high priest would offer a sacrifice that covered all the sins—intentional and unintentional—of all the people. Cleansed and restored, the people of God were then to recommit themselves to a holy life and to worship God at the annual festivals as an expression of their intimate relationship with him.

The flow of the Torah in Exodus and Leviticus lays out this pattern of instruction, obedience, disobedience, restoration, and recommitment, ushering in renewed fellowship with God. This pattern is enacted again and again throughout the history of God's people.

PROVISION IN THE TORAH FOR A REDEEMED PEOPLE

Exodus 20: The Ten Commandments Foundational Principles

Exodus 21–24: Case Law Application of Principles

Exodus 25–27: Tabernacle Design: A Holy People Worship

Exodus 28–31: Priesthood Intermediaries Ordained

Exodus 32–34: Golden Calf Incident: The People Sin

Leviticus 1–6: Offerings for Unintentional Sins

Leviticus 11–15: Cleansing for Ritual Offenses

Leviticus 16–17: The Day of Atonement: Atonement for All Sins

Leviticus 18–22: Instructions on Holiness: Recommitment

Leviticus 23–25: Worship Calendar: Renewed Fellowship with God

Even as God spoke to Moses, with Sinai shrouded in dark clouds and thunderbolts, the people on the plain below brought gold to Aaron so he could fashion an idol for them to worship. How clear it is that these people had no idea how to live in a relationship with God, or even with each other. But nothing they did could alter God's determination to accomplish his covenant commitments through them. God yearned to bless each generation of his people as the centuries flowed by. So he gave Israel the Torah, instruction on how to live in relationship with him and with each other, so they might experience in their own time some of the blessings guaranteed for history's end.

Looking back, the apostle Paul writes in Galatians 3:24, "The law was our guardian until Christ came." That is, the authority of the Torah was in force from the time of Moses until Christ appeared. And, Paul continues, "Now that the way of faith has come, we no longer need the law as our guardian."[21]

God has a new and better blueprint for us to follow, a blueprint we'll discover as we trace God's story into the New Testament. What is important for us to grasp now, if we are to understand the story of the Old Testament, is that God's story is always about *relationships*.

God confirmed his relationship with Israel when he brought them out of slavery in Egypt. Then he showed them how to live within that relationship by giving them the law, the Torah, of Moses. If God's people would commit to live by the Torah, they would experience a resting place, a community of love that would mirror the eternal community of love that God will establish at history's end.

Discussion Questions

1. How safe do you feel in today's world? What are some of the major things you worry about?

2. In this chapter, we suggest that most people place too much emphasis on the Ten Commandments. What do you think that means, and how valid do you believe the point is?

3. From what you know of the Bible, how successful were the Israelites in living as a "safe haven" community? What evidence can you cite to support your view?

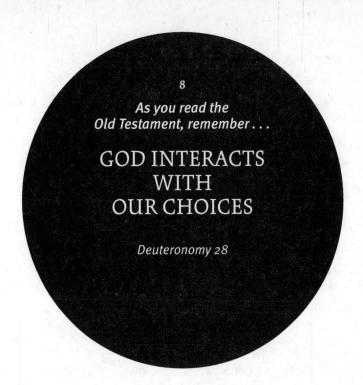

8

*As you read the
Old Testament, remember...*

GOD INTERACTS WITH OUR CHOICES

Deuteronomy 28

The Pivotal Event

As Moses peered into the confident faces of the new generation, he was assailed by doubt. Would these young up-and-comers be any more committed to the Lord and the Torah than their parents had been? Moses had experienced how stiff-necked a people could be, how prone to complaint and rebellion. Still, he felt constrained to provide one last warning. Taking a firmer hold on his staff, the aged leader leaned forward and began to speak.

"If..."

Digging Deeper into Deuteronomy 28

In 1964, when Lady Nancy Astor was on her deathbed, she awoke briefly, and upon seeing all her children gathered around her, said, "Is it my birthday, or am I dying?"

It seems that many people are fascinated by last words. Not that most final statements are all that significant. When convicted murderer Christopher Emmett was executed in 2008, after an unsuccessful appeal, his last words were, "Tell the governor he just lost my vote." The famous economist John Maynard Keynes's last remark was, "I wish I'd drunk more champagne." General William Erskine is supposed to have asked, after jumping out a window, "Now why did I do that?" Perhaps Winston Churchill's last words answered his question: "I'm bored with it all."

As we come to the end of the book of Deuteronomy and Moses contemplates his impending death, we find some truly remarkable last words. As the great deliverer and lawgiver stands before the Israelites, he declares:

> This day I call the heavens and the earth as witnesses against you that I have set before you life and death, blessings and curses. Now choose life, so that you and your children may live and that you may love the LORD your God, listen to his voice, and hold fast to him. For the LORD is your life, and he will give you many years in the land he swore to give to your fathers, Abraham, Isaac and Jacob.[1]

In the Torah, God provided a blueprint for a society that would reflect the eternal community of love that he intends to establish for the redeemed beyond history's end. But whether the generations to come would experience life or death, blessings or curses, depended on *them*.

Looking back on centuries of Israel's experience, the prophet Isaiah lamented the choices God's people made. It was the people of Israel "to whom [God] said, 'This is the resting place, let the weary rest'; and, 'This is the place of repose.'"[2] The Torah invited Israel to become a safe haven—a community that would truly be a resting place, a place of peace and tranquility. "But," Isaiah continues, "they would not listen."[3]

Israel's failure to listen would prove to have many consequences, including one graphically portrayed in the next verse in Isaiah: "So then, the word of the LORD to them will become: Do this, do that, a rule for this, a rule for that; a little here, a little there—so that as they go they will fall backward; they will be injured and snared and captured."[4]

In the Torah, God extended an invitation to a blessed and bountiful life. Instead, Israel's sages tore apart the fabric of the Torah, misunderstanding its true nature and treating it as lists of isolated rules that God required his people to follow. By the time of Jesus, an "oral Torah" had been developed, representing additions made by rabbis (the teachers of the law) and resulting in a deadening legalism. As Isaiah had predicted, God's people fell backward and were injured, snared, and captured.

Invitations and Warnings

Moses' last words to Israel echo a theme developed in Deuteronomy 28. The blessings and curses listed there serve equally as invitations and warnings.

The invitation (Deuteronomy 28:1-14): Moses has given God's *torah* to Israel. He now invites God's people to enter into its blessings. "If," he begins, "you fully obey the LORD your God and carefully follow all his commands I give you today, the LORD your God will set you high above all the nations on earth."[5] Then he lists the earthly blessings that will follow: a life of plenty, victory over foreign enemies, success in "everything you put your hand to," and a powerful witness to the nations that will generate profound respect.[6] "The LORD will grant you abundant prosperity . . . if you pay attention to the commands of the LORD your God that I give you this day and carefully follow them."[7]

The warning (Deuteronomy 28:15-68): Like the invitation, the warning is conditional. "If," Moses continues, "you do not obey the LORD your God and do not carefully follow all his commands and decrees I am giving you today, all these curses will come upon you and overtake you."[8]

The consequences this passage warns of are terrible indeed. There is more than the loss of prosperity. There are also plagues, drought, defeat, and oppression.[9] The nation will be uprooted and the people driven to a foreign land, to become a "thing of horror . . . and an object of ridicule."[10] The passage then concludes with a powerful portrait of the Diaspora:

> Then the LORD will scatter you among all nations, from one end of the earth to the other. . . . Among those nations you will find no repose, no resting place for the sole of your foot. There the LORD will give you an anxious mind, eyes weary with longing, and a despairing heart. You will live in constant suspense, filled with dread both night and day, never sure of your life.[11]

Looking back on the choices given to Israel in Deuteronomy 28, it's no wonder that Isaiah wrote that God had said of the Torah, "'This is the resting place' . . . and, 'This is the place of repose.'"

"But You Would Not . . ."

Isaiah is not the only prophet to express frustration at Israel's refusal to respond to God's invitation. Throughout the Old Testament's kingdom years prophet after prophet pointed to disasters described in Deuteronomy 28, interpreting current events as a call to return to the Lord and to the Torah.

In the eighth century BC, the prophet Amos, a prosperous rancher in the southern kingdom of Judah, was sent to the northern kingdom of Israel with a message from the Lord. At that time, the people of the northern kingdom had abandoned the God-ordained Temple in Jerusalem and had set up golden calves at Bethel and Dan. The society was rife with injustice. Amos writes, "There are those who oppress the innocent and take bribes and deprive the poor of justice in the courts."[12]

The nation that the Lord invited to experience rest and repose had become a land of chaos and crime. Amos harks back to Deuteronomy 28 to explain the troubles then being experienced by the nation:

> "I gave you empty stomachs in every city
>> and lack of bread in every town,
>> yet you have not returned to me,"
>
>> declares the LORD. . . .

> "I sent plagues among you
>> as I did to Egypt.
> I killed your young men with the sword,
>> along with your captured horses.
> I filled your nostrils with the stench of your camps,
>> yet you have not returned to me,"
>
>> declares the LORD.[13]

Each of these disasters was predicted in Deuteronomy 28. Each was embedded in God's warning of what would happen if the Israelites abandoned God and forgot his law. And each disaster was a reminder of the invitation to blessing that the Lord had given Israel at that same time.

Choosing Life

Israel was a redeemed people, a nation possessing covenant promises given to Abraham by God himself. For individuals who respond to God's revelation with faith, as Abraham did, that faith is credited as righteousness.[14]

But in Deuteronomy 28, the people are confronted with a new and different choice. God has given them a plan for a just and moral community, a place of rest and repose, within which all the people can experience something of the coming eternal community of love. The people standing before Moses, and each succeeding generation of Israelites until the time of Christ, must choose between life and death, between blessings and curses. As Moses stands beside the Jordan River, opposite the Promised Land, he says, "I have set before you life and death, blessings and curses. *Now choose life*."[15]

Even as we understand the role of human independence in God's unfolding story, we must understand the role God has chosen for himself. He will not manipulate or coerce human beings. He will permit us to choose. This has tremendous implications for our understanding of God and for our relationship with him. Many who affirm God's sovereignty assume that sovereignty implies control—in other words, everything that happens is ordained by God. Ultimately, however, this position leaves no room for real human freedom. If we hold this view, Moses' words make little sense. If Israel isn't free to choose between life and death, Moses' appeal to the people to *choose life* is pointless. But Moses doesn't speak as one whose words are meaningless.

Make no mistake, I believe entirely in the sovereignty of God. He is absolutely in control of his universe. The covenant promises he made to Abraham and the covenant promises he makes to us in Christ are altogether sure. The paradox of divine sovereignty and human free will can be resolved only if we understand the distinction between *sovereignty* and *control*. Sovereignty must mean that God knows every possible choice that every individual might make, and that he is great and powerful enough to weave every choice we make into his plan. Though God is outside of history, in a sense he is moving through history with us, waiting for us to choose and ready to respond by weaving our choices—whatever choices we make—into the fabric of his plans and purposes. In other words, God does not need to *control* our choices in order to work them into his plan.

Our Interactive Relationship

An interactive relationship is one in which a person's words or actions have a real impact on what another person says or does. And that impact is reciprocal. We can find many passages in Scripture that depict the interactive relationships between God and individuals and nations. That is, not only do God's words and actions affect people and nations, but what those nations or people do affect what God chooses to do.

One illustration of this reciprocal, interactive relationship on a national level is found in Jeremiah 18:7-10, where God explains his ways through the words of the prophet:

> If at any time I announce that a nation or kingdom is to be
> uprooted, torn down and destroyed, and if that nation I
> warned repents of its evil, then I will relent and not inflict
> on it the disaster I had planned. And if at another time I
> announce that a nation or kingdom is to be built up and
> planted, and if it does evil in my sight and does not obey me,
> then I will reconsider the good I had intended to do for it.

In other words, the future is not irrevocably *fixed*—even when God has announced what the future will be! In fact, the future is contingent on the free choices of human beings. God, individuals, and nations *interact*.

Here's another example, one that illustrates God's relationship with individuals. When Saul, Israel's first king, officiated at a sacrifice after being told to wait for the arrival of Samuel the prophet, Samuel told him, "You have not kept the command the LORD your God gave you; if you had, he would have established your kingdom over Israel for all time."[16] And when Saul continued to disobey, the Lord told Samuel, "I regret that I have made Saul king, because he has turned away from me and has not carried out my instructions."[17] The thought is repeated in 1 Samuel 15:35: "The LORD regretted that he had made Saul king over Israel."

Did God make a mistake in selecting Saul to be Israel's king? Not at all. He had foreseen all the possible choices that Saul might make. Once Saul made a choice, God responded, interacting with Saul on the basis of that choice. When Saul was disqualified as the founder of a dynasty, the Lord experienced grief (anguish, deep pain), rooted not only in the decision Saul made but also in the choice he himself had made in selecting Saul to be king.

We must never view God as a disinterested observer of our lives. He is deeply invested in us and in the choices we make. He yearns to bless us, and he feels real pain when we go down the wrong path. Yet God has chosen to limit himself by his decision to give human beings free will.

Jonah was sent to announce that Nineveh would be destroyed in forty days. But in response, the king and people of Nineveh repented, and the city was preserved.[18] The prophet Isaiah informed King Hezekiah that his illness was terminal. But Hezekiah prayed, and in response to his prayer, the Lord added fifteen years to the king's life.[19] God interacts with us. The Lord responds to our prayers and to the choices we freely make.

When a great swarm of locusts descended on Israel, the prophet Joel understood the plague in light of the warnings in Deuteronomy 28 and urged the people to change their ways.

> "Even now," declares the LORD,
> > "return to me with all your heart,
> > with fasting and weeping and mourning."
>
> Rend your heart
> > and not your garments.

Return to the LORD your God,
   for he is gracious and compassionate,
slow to anger and abounding in love,
   and he relents from sending calamity.
Who knows? He may turn and relent
   and leave behind a blessing.[20]

Another prophet—this time, Jeremiah—seems to include the Lord himself in the question of "who knows?" When God tells Jeremiah to "speak to all the people [and] . . . tell them everything I command you; do not omit a word," the Lord adds, "Perhaps they will listen and each will turn from their evil ways."[21] Could it be that God knows every possible choice his people *may* make, but not the actual choices they *will* make? What God knows for certain is his own response: If "they will listen and each will turn from their evil ways . . . I will relent and not inflict on them the disaster I was planning because of the evil they have done."[22]

Each generation of God's people soon learned that their choices shaped what happened to them in their lives.

The Antagonist

Deuteronomy 28 lays out principles governing interaction between God and his people. God sets before them life and death, blessings and curses. Their choices will determine how God will interact with them—to bless them or to impose judgment.

Still, we would be wrong to see this as an interaction involving only God and Israel. Throughout Scripture, there is another being lurking behind the scenes, one who leads a host of fallen angels who are hostile to God and his chosen people. When Moses, in Deuteronomy 28:14, warns the people not to turn aside from God's commands—that is, not to forsake or abandon the Lord—in order to follow other gods and serve them, he is referring to the corrupting influence of Satan. We know this because even at this early stage in the story, Moses refers to "foreign gods and . . . detestable idols"[23] and equates their worship with sacrificing to demons.[24] Both the Old and New Testaments reveal the existence of an ongoing struggle between angels and demons, between good and evil. In every instance, that struggle centers on the redeemed people of God.

Demons, acting through the gods of Egypt, were behind the suffering of God's people there and were judged in the plagues the Lord sent on Egypt.[25] Demons, acting through the gods and the people of Moab, were behind Balaam's plot to turn the Lord against Israel by seducing them to worship idols.[26] As God's story continues to unfold, we'll see again and again how the Israelites' decisions to worship foreign deities precipitated national disasters.

Repeated disaster and deliverance is the theme of the book of Judges, which is a record of the four hundred or so years that preceded the unification of the Hebrew tribes into a single nation. In the time of the judges, the tribes of Israel experienced seven cycles in which history repeated itself. In each cycle, the Israelites rejected God in favor of idols and then were dominated by foreign invaders. With each successive cycle, Israelite society seemed to sink lower and lower, until, as the final chapters of Judges portray, the people lost their religious identity and moral compass.

Each cycle is initiated in the same way, as described in Judges 3:7: "The Israelites did evil in the eyes of the LORD; they forgot the LORD their God and served the Baals and the Asherahs [the pagan deities of Canaan]." Satan's demons, acting through the pagan Canaanite people and their deities, actively sought to seduce God's people and turn their hearts from God.

Jeremiah, by asking a question, implies the demonic source of Israel's persistent turning aside to worship foreign deities: "Has a nation ever changed its gods? (Yet they are not gods at all.) But my people have exchanged their glorious God for worthless idols."[27] The answer to Jeremiah's question is *no*, the nations of the ancient Middle East did not change their gods, even though their deities were not gods at all. Yet Israel persistently turned away from the one true God, who was their glory, in favor of worthless idols. The best explanation for the loyalty of pagans to deities who "are not gods at all," and for Israel's abandonment of the only true God, is the supernatural influence of evil spirits.

What about Me?

Deuteronomy 28 is addressed to the entire nation of Israel. It describes the blessings that will accrue as Israel remains committed to the Lord and the Torah, and it describes the curses the nation will experience if the people abandon the Lord and violate the Torah. The blessings and the curses are *national* rather than *individual*. And so an Israelite man or woman might well have asked, "What about *me*? If I love the Lord and live by the Torah, and yet the rest of the nation turns to idolatry and sin, what can I expect to happen to *me*?"

The deeply disturbing answer to this question is that an individual's choice to live a godly life provides no immunity to suffering caused by the sins of others and of the nation. This is one of the most troubling implications of our free will. In the days of Amos the prophet, many godly poor were defrauded by the wealthy, who were able to bribe judges.[28] Today, as in ancient Israel, personal righteousness is no guarantee that we will avoid injustice or suffering. Only in a truly just society, in which everyone is committed to loving God and others, can an individual find the rest and repose that God promised to Israel. Though the Torah lays the foundation for just such a society, the ideal has never been truly realized.

The Torah describes what could have been. The books of history describe what was. Yet there is more to God's story than is recorded in the accounts of kings and nations.

The book of Ruth immediately follows the book of Judges in the Old Testament. This is appropriate, for the text introduces Ruth's story by setting it "in the days when the judges ruled."[29] The same verse tells us that "there was a famine in the land" (another one of the curses foretold in Deuteronomy 28), which makes it very clear that in Ruth's day, the Israelites had rejected the Lord and abandoned the Torah.

The book of Ruth traces the experiences of a family of four who abandon their home in Canaan and move to Moab. There the husband/father and two grown sons die, leaving the mother and two Moabite daughters-in-law as widows. The mother, Naomi, decides to return to her homeland, and one of the daughters-in-law, Ruth, determines to go with her. In a poignant moment, Ruth commits herself to Naomi, Naomi's people, and Naomi's God.[30]

Back in Canaan among the Israelites, the two women are poor and powerless. So Ruth goes out at harvest time to gather fallen kernels of grain in a relative's fields. Naomi's relative Boaz is kind to Ruth and encourages her to return the next day. Naomi is thrilled at Boaz's invitation. The Torah has a provision that allows a near relative to marry a widow and thus enable her to recover the land that was her husband's inheritance. Should the two have a male child, the title to the recovered land would revert to the son.

Ruth follows Naomi's instructions and invites Boaz to take on the role of kinsman redeemer. Boaz accepts. The two are married; Ruth has a son, who brings joy to Naomi; and that son becomes the grandfather of David, Israel's greatest king and an ancestor of Jesus.

This story illustrates a second answer to the question, *What about me?* Naomi and Ruth lived at a time when Israelite society was unjust and dangerous. Yet even in this corrupt society, it was possible to find godly individuals, and to establish godly homes, within which children could be brought up to live godly lives.

When we first read the curses outlined in Deuteronomy 28, we are likely to be horrified. But really, like the promised blessings, the curses are words of grace. God is speaking to a people who have free will, people who can (and must) choose. Even though the Torah is addressed to the entire nation of Israel, and obedience and disobedience have national implications, God also interacts with individuals. God responds to our individual choices. We may live in an unjust society, under constant threat from the choices of others, but God is walking with us. When we suffer because of the sins of others, God does not desert us. He will use even the evil that befalls us for good.[31]

Discussion Questions

1. According to this chapter, why is Deuteronomy 28 such a significant passage? What seems most significant about it to you?

2. This chapter looks at several Bible stories and passages that illustrate God's interactive relationship with human beings. What does "interactive relationship" mean? Can you think of additional illustrations from Bible stories you've read?

3. Are there any principles developed in this response to Deuteronomy 28 that help you understand aspects of your own story? What are they, and how do they relate to your story?

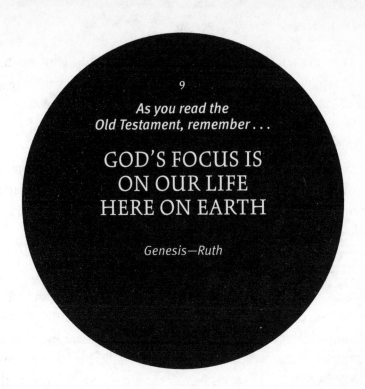

*As you read the
Old Testament, remember . . .*

GOD'S FOCUS IS ON OUR LIFE HERE ON EARTH

Genesis—Ruth

The Pivotal Event

Ruth shook off the doubts that often troubled her. Today she would gather all the grain she could and trust Naomi's God to provide enough to feed the two of them until another opportunity arose. After all, that was the way almost everyone lived, seeking daily bread. Still, as Ruth lifted to her head the basket she hoped to fill with grain and set off toward the field of Boaz, she couldn't help but be slightly apprehensive. Like anyone, she had no idea what lay ahead that day or the next.

Digging Deeper into Genesis—Ruth

The first funeral I conducted after finishing seminary was my mother's. She and my dad were in a car accident, and her leg was broken. On the morning of the day she was supposed to come home from the hospital, a blood clot broke loose in her leg, traveled to her heart, and killed her.

I drove to Michigan from Illinois with my son Paul, who was then about eight years old. That evening, we went to the funeral home for the visitation. The next day, as I preached my mother's funeral, I was flooded with the joyful realization that my mother was with the Lord she loved.

No wonder the apostle Paul encourages the Thessalonians to comfort each other, reassuring them that "the Lord himself will come down from heaven . . . and the dead in Christ will rise first. After that, we who are still alive and are left will be caught up together with them in the clouds to meet the Lord in the air. And so we will be with the Lord forever."[1]

Reading the first seven books of the Bible, we find no such encouragement. Oh, the doctrines of resurrection and eternal life are there. When Jesus encountered some Jewish scholars who questioned these teachings, he rebuked them by pointing to Exodus 3:6 and reminding them that God had said, "*I am* the God of Abraham,"[2] (not *I was*). The tense of the verb makes it clear that "he is not the God of the dead but of the living."[3] Daniel 12:2 says that "multitudes who sleep in the dust of the earth will awake: some to everlasting life, others to shame and everlasting contempt." Still, there is no doubt that in the Old Testament, the focus is squarely on the significance of a person's relationship with God in *this* world, not in the next. Psalm 33:18-19 is in harmony with this perspective:

> The eyes of the LORD are on those who fear him,
>   on those whose hope is in his unfailing love,
> to deliver them from death
>   and keep them alive in famine.

The Great Divide

In AD 644, a gathering of bishops was held at Whitby, a small town on the northern coast of England. The topics under consideration included the date on which Christians should celebrate Easter and the shape of the tonsure (the style of clipped or shaven hair) to be worn by monks. But far more was at stake than holidays and haircuts. The true question was whether the Roman Church or the Celtic Church would shape the future of Christianity. After listening to presentations from the two sides, the Irish King Oswiu decided in favor of Rome. By 670, all Celtic monastic communities on the continent had been forced to adopt the Roman model.

The decision had both theological and practical ramifications. The Roman Church, which reflected—and to some extent distorted— the views of Augustine of Hippo, emphasized the utter sinfulness of humankind. The Celtic Church, which reflected the views of its first great theologian, Pelagius, emphasized the goodness of God's original creation, the potential in human beings, and an evangelism based on welcoming seekers into the faith community and loving them into a personal relationship with Jesus. The Romans tended to intellectualize and ritualize their Christian faith. They were comfortable with rigid hierarchies and generally suspicious of women (as the source of temptation). The Celts tended to personalize their faith, took great delight in God's creation, emphasized community and prayer, and affirmed the gifts of women in church life and leadership. However we may come down on the central theological dispute between Augustine and Pelagius, I think most would agree that the lifestyle that characterized Celtic Christianity was far more biblical than that which characterized Roman faith.

Thinking Through the Bible

One of the flaws in the traditional approach to theology is our tendency to reorganize biblical material into categories. That is, we go through the Bible in search of teaching on a particular subject, such as humankind (anthropology), salvation (soteriology), or end times (eschatology). We then extract this biblical material and file it according to our categories. In stripping this information from Scripture, we lose the context in which it appears. In effect, we isolate truths from the role they play in the unfolding of God's story in the Bible. We then compound the problem by taking our created categories and using them as lenses through which we read the rest of the Bible. As a result, our theology defines for us what "the truth" is, and when we read the Bible, we see only that which supports our theology.

It isn't wrong to have theological convictions. But we must realize the extent to which our theology distorts as well as illumines what we read. It is also important to remember that although Scripture is divinely inspired, our theological systems are not. So we must approach the Bible humbly. As God's story unfolds and as we apply his story to our own lives, fresh insights will constantly emerge. These insights will both enrich and challenge our dearly held beliefs. But rather than threaten us, reading the Bible as story should broaden our understanding of God's Word and deepen our relationship with the Lord.

This World

In reading the Bible as story, I discover that God's story places a stunning emphasis on the significance of life in this world. The first chapter of Genesis sets the stage on which the story will take place. God fashions the world in which we live. He sets our planet spinning in the vastness of space, molds it, and seeds it with life. The result of each creative act is called *good*; and in a culminating act, the Creator fashions human beings in his own image and likeness, calling this *very good*.

Human beings were created to live in this world. Yet by creating humans in his image, God also created us for a relationship with him— a relationship that must first find expression within our temporal setting, as it did for Adam and Eve in Eden.

By the time we reach Genesis 3, a stranger has intruded upon God's story. Later we discover that this stranger is the story's antagonist, and his goal is to disrupt the relationship between God and human beings. Adam and Eve declare independence from God, but God "puts enmity" between humans and the antagonist. Almost immediately, we see the impact of the first pair's choice of independence. We can hardly imagine Eve's anguish as she learns that one of her sons, Cain, has murdered his brother. As generation follows generation, sin and suffering are woven so tightly into the fabric of human society that ultimately "every intention of the thoughts of [their] heart[s] was only evil continually."[4] God weeps with and for the suffering multitudes. Eventually, he sends a great flood that scours the earth clean.

Ages later, God tells a man named Abraham what he intends for history's end, and he promises to accomplish his purposes through Abraham's descendants. As the story continues to unfold, the chosen family leaves Canaan and moves to Egypt.

Meanwhile, the antagonist has been at work establishing his influence over the rest of humanity. Evil angels, who followed Satan in a great rebellion set before the Genesis 1 story, have seduced human beings into worshiping demonically inspired counterfeit deities. In the hearts of the Egyptians, the demon gods infuse fear of the Israelites, who are enslaved and then threatened with extinction. With the Israelites utterly helpless and suffering intensely, God acts.

God sends one of their own, Moses, who was adopted into the royal family and later exiled, to win the release of his people. In a series of miracles that execute judgment on the gods of Egypt and expose the limitations of the antagonist's powers, God wins the Israelites' freedom. This Exodus event vividly portrays one of the dominant themes in God's story and our own: *redemption*.

The story then shifts to Mount Sinai, where the Lord provides the Israelites with the Torah (law). The Torah gives precise instructions on how to live in relationship with God and with one another in this world. If followed, the Torah will shape a society in which every person can live in rest and repose.

But Moses' last words to the Israelites remind them that they, and each succeeding generation of Israelites, face a life-or-death choice. They can remain loyal to God, follow the Torah, and be blessed. Or they can repudiate God, ignore the Torah, and be cursed. Every blessing and curse listed is a description of what Israel can expect to experience in this world.

What is striking is that in each of these books, from Genesis through Ruth, the focus is squarely on the significance of relationship with God in the here and now. Up to this point in God's story, the Lord and the human beings who have a relationship with him are primarily concerned about what is happening to them in the present world. They are not concerned with "eternity."

The Celtic Way

In *The Celtic Way of Evangelism*, George G. Hunter III points out that much of the teaching and preaching in our churches focuses on what are called *ultimate concerns*. Religion as a system is designed to answer questions about the origins, purpose, and destiny of the individual, society, and the universe. While Scripture surely weighs in on these issues, fascination with the big metaphysical (top level) issues hardly drives most people in our postmodern world.

Building on anthropologist Paul Hiebert's concept of "the excluded middle," Hunter notes that most churches today attend to "top-level" issues—such as origins, purpose, and destiny—while tending to ignore middle-level, or "real-life," issues. He writes,

> What are the middle-level issues of life? Many people live
> much of their life anxious about the near future, the crises

of their present life, and even the unknowns of the past. To be specific, the mother whose son faces a court trial, the laid-off father who cannot make the mortgage payment, the teen who experiences new hormones surging within him, and the woman who still struggles with the memory that a parent loved her sibling more are primarily driven at this middle level.[5]

Reading the early chapters of God's story reminds us that it was just such real-life issues that God seemed most concerned with when he created the universe and designed the community we see in the Torah.

- Cain struggles with anger, and God warns him of sin crouching at the door. "You must master it," God says.[6]
- Eve gazes in horror at the dead body of Abel, and then looks into the eyes of her son Cain. How will she—how can she—deal with her loss?[7]
- Jacob slips into his father's tent, intent on stealing the blessing that Isaac intends to bestow on Esau. Later, his mother urges him to run, as a furious Esau talks of murdering him.[8]
- Leah, ignored by the husband who loves her sister so deeply, gives her children names that express her own desperate hopes and longings.[9]
- Dinah, the daughter of Jacob, is raped. The rapist then begs Jacob to let him marry Dinah. Her brothers demand revenge.[10]
- Joseph, sold into slavery by his jealous brothers, determines to honor God and do the best he can in his circumstances.[11]
- An Israelite mother and father look at their newborn son and glance toward the Nile. What will happen to them if they fail to obey Pharaoh's command?[12]

- Moses, frustrated by the Israelites' failure to trust God, angrily strikes a rock that God has commanded him only to speak to.[13]
- Rahab hesitates. Will she hide the Israelites who have come to spy out Jericho, or will she turn them over to the authorities?[14]
- Achan is tempted to disobey Joshua. Why shouldn't he take some of the wealth of Jericho?[15]
- Samson, now a blinded victim of his own selfishness, rests his hands on the pillars of his enemy's temple and begs for strength to bring the structure down.[16]
- Ruth and Naomi, destitute, travel to Bethlehem, seeking to rebuild their shattered lives.[17]

These are just a few of the many personal stories embedded in the early books of the Bible. Each book, and each individual's story, is about the middle-level issues, the challenges we all face while living in this world.

A Visit to the Psalms

David fastens his cloak more tightly about him. Head down, the fleeing king lengthens his stride. His son Absalom, his dearly loved son, intends to kill him.

David thinks, *I should have seen it coming.* For well over a year, Absalom had intercepted groups from the northern tribes coming to ask the king to settle this or that dispute. "If I were king," Absalom told each group, "I'd decide in your favor." Gradually, support for Absalom grew among the northern tribes, until now he had raised an army and was marching on Jerusalem.[18]

As the sun dips lower, David shivers, his mind full of doubt. He is deeply aware of his sins and failures. He had taken—raped, actually—Bathsheba, the wife of one of his military men. God would surely be justified in turning against him now.

Finally night falls. David finds a sheltered place to lie down, and his thoughts turn to his relationship with the God he loves. Later, he would capture those thoughts and feelings in Psalm 3:

> LORD, how many are my foes!
>> How many rise up against me!
> Many are saying of me,
>> "God will not deliver him."

> But you, LORD, are a shield around me,
>> my glory, the One who lifts my head high.
> I call out to the LORD,
>> and he answers me from his holy
>>> mountain.

> I lie down and sleep;
>> I wake again, because the LORD sustains me.
> I will not fear though tens of thousands
>> assail me on every side.[19]

Another of the psalmists, Asaph, struggled with a different one of life's middle issues—*envy*. He shares his experience in Psalm 73:

> As for me, my feet had almost slipped;
>> I had nearly lost my foothold.
> For I envied the arrogant
>> when I saw the prosperity of the wicked.[20]

As Asaph compares his experience to the carefree lives lived by those who scoff at God, he can't resist the self-pity that floods his soul:

> Surely in vain I have kept my heart pure
>> and have washed my hands in innocence.

All day long I have been afflicted,
    and every morning brings new
        punishments.[21]

Asaph kept the bitterness inside. After all, he was a worship leader at the Temple in Jerusalem. Nevertheless, the feeling that he had been betrayed by God oppressed him. Then, one day at worship in God's sanctuary, everything suddenly became clear. The wicked had no relationship with God. And without God, they had no future. Quickly Asaph wrote:

Yet I am always with you;
    you hold me by my right hand.
You guide me with your counsel,
    and afterward you will take me into glory.
Whom have I in heaven but you?
    And earth has nothing I desire besides you.
My flesh and my heart may fail,
    but God is the strength of my heart
    and my portion forever.[22]

David and Asaph both dealt with life's middle-level issues. Though they experienced the inner turmoil that middle-level issues create, they also freely expressed their emotions to the Lord. In the process, each found perspective and the strength to go on.

The poetic books of the Old Testament are similar to the books of Moses and to Joshua, Judges, and Ruth in that they focus our attention on life in this world. The book of Proverbs is filled with brief aphorisms containing advice on the practical choices everyone must make in life. Work, parenting, friendship, and the other topics addressed in Proverbs are all about life in this world.

The book of Psalms has been described as a handbook on worship.

Perhaps it is better described as a guide to a deeply personal relationship with God. And as we've seen in sketching the stories of David's flight and Asaph's inner turmoil, Psalms is also a middle-level issues book. We can't read Psalms without wondering at the freedom the psalmists experience in their relationship with the Lord. These powerful poems are filled with anger, frustration, guilt, shame, fear, depression, grief, joyfulness, thanksgiving, relief, and delight. The psalmists seem so sure that God is eager for them to share with him, so certain that he stays deeply involved in every aspect of their lives in this world.

Surely this is part of what it means to live within God's story. We are called to immerse ourselves in life's joys and sorrows, to drink deeply of its delights and its griefs. We are called to share our life in this world with God and to find in our relationship with him both perspective and comfort. Whatever small role we might have in the grand narrative, our personal stories reflect the quality of our relationship with the Savior. It is in this world, in this time, in the middle-level issues of our lives, that our stories and God's story are being written.

Sunday Church

It's strange. One morning a week we dress in our Sunday best, put on our public faces, and go to a building where we celebrate God. We attend a class, sing hymns, and hear a sermon. And then we go home. Chances are, no one has spoken to us about the middle issues that are driving their lives, and we have shared nothing significant about our own lives. We keep our stories close to the vest or locked away.

Yet as we've seen, the early books of the Old Testament, and the poetic books as well, are essentially middle-level issue books. They are about the lives that God's people live in this world.

Someone might argue that we're a New Testament people, and thus we emphasize New Testament truths. But if we read the New

Testament epistles carefully, we're struck by the realization that these books, too, focus our attention on life's middle-level issues.

Romans is rightly characterized as a carefully reasoned theological treatise. Yet in Romans, Paul also writes about the exercise of spiritual gifts in the Christian community, about the importance of love, about showing hospitality, and about how to live in harmony with one another.[23] He advises us about how to respond to persecution, calling on us to "overcome evil with good."[24] He writes of the believer's responsibility to the government.[25] And he even devotes a chapter and a half to dealing with the differences that often divide Christians, spelling out principles for maintaining unity even with those with whom we disagree.[26]

All these instructions are about living in this world in relationship with God and others, about the middle-level issues of life.

In fact, every New Testament epistle deals with middle issues as well as with transcendent truths. In one fashion or another, each epistle writer applies "New Testament truths" to the middle-level issues of life. As with the early Old Testament books, the New Testament's focus is on the issues that drive the thoughts, hopes, and fears of individuals in our postmodern world. The writers acknowledge that life in this world is difficult and hard. There's an antagonist at work, seeking to poison our relationships. As fallen creatures, we are subject to self-deception and to the grief we are sure to bring upon ourselves. Living in a world where freedom of choice rules, we are also vulnerable to victimization by wicked and thoughtless people.

Yet we do not live our lives alone. We have a God who goes adventuring with us. He shares our todays, is attuned to our every emotion, and stands ready to step with us into tomorrow. He gifts us with freedom and interacts with us as we choose. We know that our ultimate future lies in the eternal community of love that God will establish for the creatures he made in his image. Yet God's unfolding story teaches us that *today*, here in this world, is the most important day of our lives.

Discussion Questions

1. Our theological convictions function like a lens that often determines what we *see* when we read Scripture. Has looking at the Bible as God's story helped you see anything new or view anything differently? If so, what?

2. What are some of the "middle-level issues" that drive your present concerns? How do you see the relationship of these issues to your Christian faith?

3. What is the most important insight into prayer that you gain from the psalms of David and Asaph quoted in this chapter? Try writing a prayer in which you openly share your emotions and thoughts with the Lord.

10

*As you read the
Old Testament, remember . . .*

THE MEN AND WOMEN OF THE BIBLE ARE OUR MENTORS

*1 and 2 Samuel, 1 and 2 Kings,
1 and 2 Chronicles*

The Pivotal Event

David's arrival—alone, disheveled, and exhausted—aroused the priests' suspicions. But he was the king's son-in-law and a commander in the king's army. When David claimed that he'd been sent on a mission for Saul so urgent that he hadn't had time even to arm himself, the priests believed him. David was given food, and when he asked for the sword of Goliath, he was given that, too. But as David buckled on the sword, he noticed one of Saul's men, Doeg, watching from the shadows.[1]

Digging Deeper into the Books of Kingdom History

In the 1840s, the Scottish writer Thomas Carlyle popularized what's known as the "great man" theory of history. According to Carlyle, "The history of the world is but the biography of great men."[2] Carlyle even wrote a book, *On Heroes, Hero-Worship, and the Heroic in History*, to demonstrate how human history has turned on the actions of such great men as Muhammad, Luther, Shakespeare, and Napoleon.

Carlyle's theory was popular throughout much of the nineteenth century. But by the 1870s, sociologist Herbert Spencer had dismissed the great-man theory as hopelessly primitive and unscientific.[3]

Anyone who reads the historical books of the Bible might be tempted to agree with Carlyle. Although Saul was Israel's first king, it took a man like David to meld the tribes together as one nation. David's genius as a military leader multiplied by ten times the territory the Israelites controlled. David reorganized the army, structured a national government, and established Jerusalem as the political and religious capital of the united nation. He wrote numerous psalms and poured his own wealth into assembling the materials for the temple that his son Solomon would build. David even designed the Temple and defined the roles of the priests and Levites who would serve there. Throughout the Old Testament era and into the New, the covenant promises that God made to David fanned the hopes and expectations of God's people.

If this were a history book, we might look at the biblical kings and the events of their reigns, and evaluate each king's influence on the nation's history. But this isn't a history book, and although the Bible gives an account of the history of God's covenant people, the Bible itself is not, essentially, a history book either. Yet as the story unfolds, Scripture introduces us to individuals who are fellow members with us of the community of faith. Through these individuals, God speaks to us and seeks to shape our own stories.

The Trouble with Sunday School

In the 1960s, I spent three years as an editor of preschool Sunday school lessons at Scripture Press. Much later, I revised Scripture

Press's first-through-third-grade and fourth-through-sixth-grade lessons. I appreciate the value of Sunday school, but I'm very aware of the weaknesses in every curriculum out there.

Typically, Sunday school lessons tell a story from the life of a Bible man or woman and use it to encourage a desired behavior. David trusted God when he faced Goliath.[4] By analogy, boys and girls are encouraged to trust God when they face "giants" in their own lives. Hezekiah prayed when he was sick, and he got well.[5] We need to pray when we're sick so we can get well too. While our Sunday school lessons encourage students to trust God, too often they focus on instilling acceptable behavior, rather than on developing a close relationship with God in our daily lives.

There are so many problems with this approach. Learning theory and experience tell us that there's little transfer of learning from such stories to actual behavior. But our primary concern should be that the reason these stories of individuals are included in Scripture is not to promote acceptable behavior. Nor is the saga of David's rise to royal power a case study over which to debate the great-man theory of history.

This leads to a rather important question: In a book that tells God's story, how are we to interact with and understand the stories of the men and women who lived their lives within that larger story?

When I graduated from Dallas Theological Seminary, I was chosen to speak for the future pastors of my class. Two weeks later, much to my surprise, I found myself in Wheaton, Illinois, as the newly appointed editor of preschool lessons at Scripture Press. My years at Scripture Press were far from easy. I worked for a boss who was inclined to keep an overly tight rein on everyone, and I never got used to that level of control. Before long, I found myself sick to my stomach every time I drove to work. The stress was overwhelming.

During the three years I worked at Scripture Press, I found great comfort in David's story. He'd been anointed king but was outlawed and pursued by King Saul. What terrible pressure he must have felt. Yet even as a fugitive, David continued to honor Saul, the Lord's anointed. Then, at last, God delivered David and brought him to the position for which he was destined.

I had no idea what God intended for me. I certainly was no David. But I, too, could honor the person the Lord had placed over me and could wait for God to act. During the years I worked at Scripture Press, David was my mentor and constant companion. I not only understood his feelings, I experienced them. I knew that I was called to something different, as David had been. But like David, I sensed that I was to endure the pressure until God acted on my behalf. So although my stomach hurt every time I drove to work, I endured.

Then God intervened and a new opportunity presented itself. My totally unexpected stint at Scripture Press led to a teaching position at Wheaton College's graduate school and eventually evolved into a writing career that has produced more than 250 books. Looking back, I realize that those first painful years at Scripture Press were critical in my maturing as a person.

I'm not suggesting there's anything wrong with studying David's role in the rise of Israel a thousand years before Christ. I'm not suggesting we should ignore the continuing significance of David as the rest of God's story unfolds. What I am suggesting is that it is important for us to look more deeply into the stories of the men and women who, like us, were called to live within God's story. God speaks to us not so much through what these people did and said as through who they were.

In 1 Corinthians 10:13, the apostle Paul writes, "No temptation has overtaken you except what is common to mankind." In both Testaments, a *temptation* is "a difficult situation, a pressure that brings a reaction through which the character or commitment of the believer is demonstrated."[6] In reminding his readers that their difficult situations are "common to mankind," Paul makes a powerful statement: Because we are human, we are all vulnerable to the same pressures, the same fears, the same doubts and uncertainties. I'm no David, and neither are you, but because we share a common humanity with David, we can gain insight, through his life, into how to live our own lives within God's story.

A Visit to Nob

Saul attempts to kill David. David slips away to his own home. That night, David's wife (who happens to be Saul's daughter Michal) helps David escape. Later, David meets up with Saul's son Jonathan, who tells him that Saul is determined to see him dead. Alone and without any weapons to protect himself, David hurries to Nob, where the clan of the priest Ahimelek serves at the Tabernacle, the portable worship center constructed in Moses' time. The priests are surprised that David is alone and unarmed. David tells the priests he is on a mission for Saul and asks for food and weapons. He is given sacred bread from the Tabernacle and also the sword of Goliath. Before David leaves, he notices that Doeg, one of Saul's men, is watching.[7]

When Saul learns that David has been aided by the priests at Nob, he accuses them of treason and orders their execution. Eighty-five men are put to death, along with everyone else in town—men, women, and children. Later, David learns of the killings from Ahimelek's sole surviving son, Abiathar. David's response: "That day, when Doeg the Edomite was there, I knew he would be sure to tell Saul. I am responsible for the death of your whole family."[8]

We can imagine the shame and guilt that David must have felt when he learned from Abiathar that Saul had murdered the entire priestly family. Eighty-five priests and countless others perished because David ignored his conscience when he realized that Doeg would report to Saul what had happened.

We can also imagine how difficult it must have been for David to face his shame. It would have been so easy for him to say, "I had no idea Doeg would go to Saul" or "I can't believe Saul did that! How could I have known?" Instead, David tells Abiathar, "I am responsible for the death of your whole family."

It is difficult for me to read this story because I identify so strongly with what David must have felt at each point. And I must also face the fact that I failed a test that David passed.

When my wife and I were first married, I was still supporting the adult children from my first marriage. My wife and I agreed that I would continue to supplement them for a specified time; but when the time came to let go, I was torn. I remember standing in a filling station, putting gas in my vehicle and deciding to continue to give my kids money without telling my wife—and realizing that my decision was wrong.

David must have felt something like that as he lied to Ahimelek. Yet at the critical moment, he swallowed the shame of what he was about to do—just as I did in my own situation—and chose what he knew was wrong.

Later David learned the consequences of his decision: the death of eighty-five priests and an unknown number of other innocent people in Nob. I, too, learned some of the consequences of my decision—but not before I compounded my sin by conspiring with my children to keep my wife in the dark. When she found out, she was devastated. I had betrayed her, and the trust and joy she'd had in our relationship was shattered. It was a blow to our relationship from which we are still recovering. And it launched a pattern of deception that hurt her far more deeply than either of us can express.

When David learned of the consequences of his decision, he immediately took responsibility for what he had done: "That day, when Doeg the Edomite was there, I knew he would be sure to tell Saul. I am responsible for the death of your whole family."

I can sense how difficult it must have been for David not only to own the shame and fully acknowledge what he had done, but also to own its consequences. I can sense how difficult it was because when I was confronted by my wife and challenged to confess to my sons that my actions had been sinful, I was unwilling to own the shame. By refusing to do what I should have done, I robbed my wife of the healing that confession might have provided.

I share this not because I'm no longer ashamed, but because I don't know how else to communicate what I understand to be the way you and I are to read the stories of the Bible. We are to read them with empathy, identifying with the emotions of the men and women who struggled, as we struggle, to live lives of integrity in this world and in relationship with God. When I read of David at Nob, I understand something of who David was and of his relationship with God. I see what David did, and I know what I did. In the process, I learn more about how I can live my life better. I experience community with David and am mentored by him.

At first it might seem strange to think we can sense thoughts and emotions from the sparse accounts recorded in Scripture. But every novelist writes with the confidence that readers will be able to understand the characters in the book and to some extent identify with them. Authors intuitively grasp the truth of Paul's assertion that every difficult or challenging situation "is common to mankind." As human beings, we all know what it is to feel anxiety, hope, rejection, anger, affection, desire, appreciation—the whole host of emotions available to each of us. The very fact that we have our humanity in common gives us the potential to understand other people—from our contemporaries to those in ancient history—and to link our stories with theirs.

Thus, the stories of individuals in the Bible do more than invite us to read as observers, or to seek morals or principles to shape our behavior. These stories of people summon us, entice us, to identify moments in our own lives with moments in theirs. In each such moment, The One Who Is Always Present interacts with us. Each such moment has the potential to teach us much about God and about ourselves.

Abigail

Abigail was married to a fool. Even his name, Nabal, meant "fool," but he was a particular kind of fool, one with an inner disposition that is closed to reason and to God. The text describes Nabal as "very wealthy . . . but . . . surly and mean in his dealings."[9]

Already we have some idea of what life must have been like for Abigail, who is described as "an intelligent and beautiful woman."[10] More than likely, Abigail's parents had been eager to contract for their daughter's marriage to the wealthy Nabal. And Abigail was neither the first woman nor the last to find herself married to a man who wasn't worthy of her.

Then Nabal made a serious mistake. At the time, David was an outlaw, on the run from King Saul. He and his band of men had camped near Carmel, where Nabal kept his flocks and herds. David left the herds alone and never harmed Nabal's herdsmen. When it was time to shear the sheep, David sent men to Nabal to ask for his favor: "Please give your servants and your son David whatever you can find for them."[11] Nabal, responding like the fool he was, not only refused to give the messengers any supplies but also deeply insulted David.

Nabal's herdsmen were terrified. One just didn't insult the leader of a band of armed and dangerous men. So Nabal's servants urged Abigail to do something to avert the disaster they feared.

It would have been easy for Abigail to do nothing. She certainly knew that whatever she did would make her husband angry. Instead, she acted instantly. She ordered the men to load some donkeys with food, and she set off to meet David herself.

Meanwhile, David, who was furious, was on his way to Nabal's ranch with about four hundred warriors. But as David followed the path into a ravine, he came upon Abigail, who was hurrying to meet him.

Abigail quickly got off her donkey and knelt before David. She took responsibility for Nabal's insult. She acknowledged that her husband was a "wicked man" and a "fool," confirming that David was in the right. She presented the food she'd brought and asked forgiveness for her offense, even though it was Nabal who had insulted David.

Abigail then pointed out that as yet, David had not shed any "innocent blood" (i.e., killed Nabal's servants). Furthermore, she continued, when David became king, he wouldn't want "the staggering burden of needless bloodshed" on his conscience.[12] Implied in her words was a warning: A man who expected to become king could hardly afford to arouse the hostility of one of Israel's tribes by wiping out one of its families. David listened. He blessed Abigail for her "good judgment and for keeping me from bloodshed this day and from avenging myself with my own hands."[13]

The next day, Abigail told her husband what she'd done, and Nabal suffered a stroke. When Nabal died ten days later, David sent messengers to invite Abigail to become his wife.

Clearly Abigail was a victim of Nabal's surly and mean nature. She was trapped in a painful and demeaning marriage, yet she maintained her self-respect and was strong enough to take responsibility and act decisively in an emergency. Abigail won David's respect by her attitude and the shrewd advice she offered. There is so much in this simple story—so much to identify with, so much to learn about relationships, so much about courage. There is so much to learn about the choices we make, about God's interaction with us and with our choices. There are so many ways that the Holy Spirit might speak through Abigail to different individuals in different situations.

Paul reminds us, "All Scripture is God-breathed and is useful for teaching, rebuking, correcting and training in righteousness."[14] This is one of the wonders of God's story. Woven within the Scriptures are stories of individuals who are, essentially, like you and me. Through their stories, God the Holy Spirit can speak to us and shape the stories that our lives will tell.

Discussion Questions

1. In the context of this chapter, how did God speak through the stories of David? How has God spoken to you through the story of an individual whose life is recorded in Scripture? Share this story with your spouse or with friends.

2. According to this chapter, what is lacking in the "Sunday school" approach to the stories of individuals in the Bible? How should we approach these stories? How is this similar to or different from the way we would approach the history of the nation of Israel?

3. Pick one biblical character that you feel is most like you, or one whom you most want to be like. Tell your spouse, friends, or small group why you chose this character.

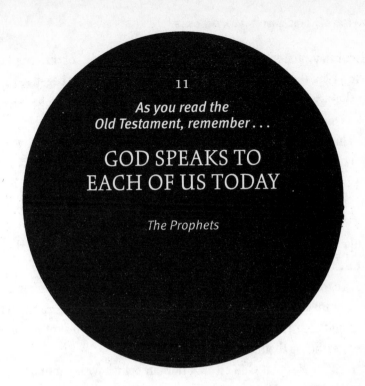

11

*As you read the
Old Testament, remember . . .*

GOD SPEAKS TO
EACH OF US TODAY

The Prophets

The Pivotal Event

Nathan was concerned. God had told him to go and confront the king. It was an uncomfortable mission, for Nathan's commission was to tell King David how greatly he had displeased the Lord. Kings in the ancient Middle East weren't used to being confronted about their sins and failures. With David's track record, Nathan had reason to believe the king might have him put to death. More than one messenger bearing bad news to David had been summarily executed.[1]

Digging Deeper into the Prophets

Pinocchio had a problem. In the little wooden marionette's quest to become a real boy, he realized that he lacked a conscience. Then he met Jiminy Cricket, who volunteered to serve as his conscience. In the Disney version of the story, whenever Pinocchio got into trouble, didn't know right from wrong, met with temptation, or began to slide off the straight-and-narrow path, Jiminy Cricket told him to "give a little whistle."

Though most of us don't have Jiminy Cricket handy when we get into trouble, we do have a conscience to be our guide. In the book of Romans, the apostle Paul takes note of that fact. He confronts those who call themselves Jews and who brag about being "instructed by the law."[2] Expressing what seems to have been a shocking point of view, Paul writes, "Indeed, when Gentiles, who do not have the law, do by nature things required by the law, they are a law for themselves, even though they do not have the law. They show that the requirements of the law are written on their hearts, their consciences also bearing witness, and their thoughts sometimes accusing them and at other times even defending them."[3]

Paul implies that God created human beings with a moral sense. As a result, the moral issues dealt with in the Torah (the law) are recognized as moral issues in every society. In this limited sense, "the requirements of the law are written in their hearts." We know this, for the universal existence of conscience demonstrates that those without the Torah have moral standards, for conscience exercises itself either by accusing humans of violating their standards or by making excuses for their violations.

Paul's argument in Romans 2 is helpful to those who worry that God might judge individuals who have no access to Scripture. Paul makes it clear that God's judgment will be fair. Those who have the standards revealed in God's law will be judged by those standards. Those without God's law will be judged by their own standards. In essence, it makes no difference whether one is a Jew or Gentile. No one lives up to even his or her own standards. Ultimately we all need a Savior.

Paul's argument is both narrow and specific. He believes that the

Jews have been set apart as God's covenant people and "entrusted with the very words of God" (Romans 3:2). But even having the Scriptures is not enough. The Jews, like the Gentiles, have fallen short.[4]

The Trouble with Scripture

Every now and then, Christians are accused of bibliolatry—that is, treating the Bible as an idol. I suspect there is more truth to the charge than most of us would like to admit—particularly if we understand bibliolatry not as worship of the Bible, but as confusion between the written Word and God himself.

When we look to the Ten Commandments, we're told specifically what *not* to do. Whatever you do, *do not* steal, *do not* murder, *do not* commit adultery, *do not* give false testimony, and *do not* act out of covetousness.

In my teens, I had an opportunity to sell encyclopedias. The first half-dozen homes I visited bought the expensive sets, which included a free bookcase (and a nice commission for me!). Then I began to feel uncomfortable. That bookcase wasn't really *free*, and the talking points I'd been told to use seemed a little deceptive. I realized that I was being dishonest. That ended my career as an encyclopedia salesman. The Ten Commandments' injunction against giving false testimony had done its job. But years later, when I graduated from seminary and was offered a job at Scripture Press, the Ten Commandments were of no help at all in making a decision about the job. "Do not" simply did not apply. And there was no text in the Bible that said "take it" or "don't take it." I needed a more robust strategy than simply adhering to the law of Moses.

In the 1960s, an Episcopal priest named Joseph Fletcher came up with a fresh approach to Christian decision making. He called it "situation ethics," which he identified as "the new morality."[5] Fletcher's starting point was Christ's teaching that the law is basically a matter of loving God and loving one's neighbor. He argued that one should simply assess the situation and then do the loving thing.

There are problems with situation ethics. In order to determine "the loving thing" in a given situation, one must first calculate the possible outcomes of every choice. This assumes that we are capable of rightly predicting outcomes. Even more questionable is Fletcher's suggestion that when "the loving thing to do" violates biblical precepts, we're to do the loving thing and ignore the rules. In other words, the end we hope to accomplish justifies the wrong we may be forced to do on our way to doing "the loving thing."

Even more problematic is that most choices we make in our lives don't involve ethics at all. For most decisions, neither the Ten Commandments nor situation ethics offers any help.

Let's examine the predicament in the life of King David.

He has finally been anointed king of the newly united Israelite tribes. The Philistines are concerned about this development and have assembled all their forces to find and kill David. The text says that David "went down to the stronghold."[6]

David has a decision to make. Should he gather his men and fight the Philistines? Or should he stay in the stronghold until the massive enemy army has dispersed? What is David to do?

What David does *not* do is call for a copy of the Torah. The Torah includes the Ten Commandments, along with additional instructions the Lord had provided to enable Israel to build a just and loving community. But there is not one word in the Torah that would tell David how to respond to the Philistine invasion. In this case, the Bible just doesn't help!

In fact, the Bible doesn't help with many, if not most, of the specific choices we make. We simply won't find a text that tells a young person whether or not to enlist in the military, or whether to apply to this college or that college. We won't find a Bible verse that directs us as to whether or not to propose to the person we're dating, or that defines how long our engagement should last before we marry. We won't find a passage that instructs us to take or to quit a job, to make an offer on a house, or even to go with a hybrid Toyota rather than a vehicle with extra safety features.

The trouble with Scripture, in spite of the fact that we, too, are "entrusted with the very words of God,"[7] is that the Bible just isn't enough. There simply isn't a proof text for every situation we will ever face.

David's Experience

The story of what David did while he was taking refuge in the stronghold, with a massive Philistine army camped in Israelite territory, is found in 2 Samuel 5 (and repeated almost verbatim in 1 Chronicles 14):

> Once more the Philistines came up and spread out in the Valley of Rephaim; so David inquired of the LORD, and he answered, "Do not go straight up, but circle around behind them and attack them in front of the poplar trees. As soon as you hear the sound of marching in the tops of the poplar trees, move quickly, because that will mean the LORD has gone out in front of you to strike the Philistine army." So David did as the LORD commanded him, and he struck down the Philistines all the way from Gibeon to Gezer.[8]

Facing his first critical decisions as ruler of Israel, David "inquired of the LORD." And the text tells us that the Lord answered! The answers described in this passage were not of a yes/no variety. God gave David specific guidance. *Circle around behind the Philistines. Wait to attack until the wind moving in the tops of the trees makes a sound like men marching.* David did what the Lord commanded, "and he struck down the Philistines."

Nearly four hundred years before David's time, God had revealed his personal name, *Yahweh*, to Moses. The name can be translated as

"The One Who Is Always Present." God told Moses, "This is my name forever, the name you shall call me from generation to generation."[9] Israel was never to forget that the Lord their God is *always present*. Thus, when David "inquired of the LORD," God responded and provided David with the guidance he needed.

We don't know exactly how God spoke to David on that occasion. The Bible describes at least five avenues through which God communicated directly with his Old Testament people, including dreams and visitations. Abraham was visited by the Lord himself in the guise of a human (Genesis 18). God communicated with Joseph and Laban in dreams (Genesis 31). Gideon was visited by an angel (Judges 6). Though such phenomena are recorded several times, we shouldn't assume that dreams or visitations were common experiences. However, two typical avenues of guidance are found in the Torah.

The first is explained in Exodus 28. The garments worn by Israel's high priest included a bejeweled "breastpiece for making decisions."[10] This breastpiece contained a pocket, which held the Urim and Thummim, which most scholars believe were stones symbolizing *yes* or *no*. We know that David used the Urim and Thummim on at least two occasions.[11] But by far the most common way in which God provided guidance for specific situations was through prophets.

In biblical times, when pagan rulers (and ordinary people as well) felt a need for supernatural guidance, they turned to their deities for help—gods and goddesses who were demons in disguise. Deuteronomy 18:9-12 describes some of the occult practices the peoples of Canaan used in their efforts to obtain help or guidance, practices that the Torah strictly forbids to God's people.

The fact that the deities of the pagans were demons meant that—to some extent at least—these occult practices *worked*. Pagan nations and individuals relied on help that evil spiritual forces were glad to provide in order to hold their worshipers in bondage.

Those living within God's story are forbidden to use occult means to access the supernatural. The occult brings humans under the influence of Satan, God's antagonist.

But God is The One Who Is Always Present with his people. To guide his people, God sent his personal spokespeople, called prophets. In the same passage that forbids the use of occult practices, the Lord promises, "I will raise up for them a prophet like you [Moses] from among their fellow Israelites, and I will put my words in his mouth. He will tell them everything I command him."[12]

For those who might question whether an individual was an authentic prophet or merely a pretender, the Torah provided tests. Not only must an authentic prophet come "from among their fellow Israelites" and speak in the name of the Lord, "if what a prophet proclaims in the name of the LORD does not take place or come true, that is a message the LORD has not spoken."[13] The authentic prophet will foretell events that actually happen.

The prophet Jeremiah urged the people of Judah to submit to Nebuchadnezzar of Babylon, warning that the remaining Temple treasures would soon be taken as plunder to Babylon. Jeremiah acted out his message by placing a yoke—representing submission—on his own shoulders.[14]

Hananiah, who also professed to be a prophet, contradicted Jeremiah. Claiming to speak in the name of the Lord, Hananiah predicted an early return of treasure that had already been taken and also the return of King Jehoiachin, then a captive in Babylon. Jeremiah responded, "Amen," but he also reminded the listening crowds that Hananiah's prediction of peace was contrary to the warnings of preceding prophets as well as to his own grim forecast.[15]

A short while later "the word of the LORD came to Jeremiah." Jeremiah then announced that the Lord would place an iron yoke on Judah and all Middle Eastern nations and would make them all serve Nebuchadnezzar.[16] And Jeremiah said to Hananiah, "The LORD has not sent you, yet you have persuaded this nation to trust in lies.

Therefore, this is what the LORD says: 'I am about to remove you from the face of the earth. This very year you are going to die, because you have preached rebellion against the LORD.'"[17]

Jeremiah 28 concludes with the report that two months later, Hananiah was dead.

The Old Testament includes one more test of the authentic prophet, a test that reminds us that Satan, God's antagonist, has supernatural powers. Deuteronomy 13 raises the case of a prophet or occultist who announces beforehand a miraculous "sign or wonder," but then urges Israel to follow other gods or to violate God's commandments. Despite the apparent supernatural confirmation, such an individual is a false prophet and is to be put to death.[18]

The Real Meaning of Prophecy

Years ago, in a book I wrote about the twelve "minor" prophets in the Bible, I argued that in order to understand the prophetic books, we need to see them primarily as messages to the people of the prophets' own times. Though a prophet's words might contain predictions to be fulfilled in the distant future, his primary role was that of God's spokesman in his own day. Each prophet's message provided divine guidance intended to shape choices that God's people were to make at that time.

What we might call the *todayness* of a prophet's message may not be easy to discern. But it is always there, always reminding us that God is present and that he is eager to provide the guidance his people need.

Let's examine *todayness* in the prophecies of Jonah, the patriotic prophet who predicted the military victories of Jeroboam II that made the northern kingdom of Israel a power in his time.[19] God sent Jonah to Nineveh, the capital of the great Assyrian empire that threatened Israel and the other nations of the region. Jonah was told to announce that God was about to destroy Nineveh.

Instead of obeying, Jonah took a ship going in the opposite

direction. We know from Sunday school the story of the great fish that swallowed Jonah and carried him back toward Nineveh. We remember that Jonah entered the city, announcing, "Forty more days and Nineveh will be overthrown."[20]

But Nineveh was not destroyed. The population "turned from their evil ways."[21] As a result of their repentance, the Lord "did not bring on them the destruction he had threatened."[22]

How was the story of Jonah's experience a *today* message for Israel? Jonah had initially run away from the mission because, as he later explained, "I knew that you are a gracious and compassionate God . . . who relents from sending calamity."[23] The prophet was afraid that Nineveh *would* repent and that God would change his mind! As a patriot, Jonah wanted this enemy of his people destroyed.

Jonah's insight into God's flexibility is the key to understanding the significance of the book of Jonah. During the forty-one-year reign of Jeroboam II, two other prophets—Hosea and Amos—were sent to the northern kingdom. Each denounced the people's sins and warned of coming judgment. Then Jonah went to Nineveh, and God's people were shown that God can change his mind. The Ninevites turned from their evil ways and were saved. How much more eager to relent would God be if his covenant people turned from *their* evil ways? This little book that testifies to God's flexibility had a powerful message for the people of Jonah's day.

I suggested earlier that Scripture isn't enough by itself. I do not mean to suggest that Scripture isn't important. Scripture tells God's story, and in the deepest sense, it tells our story too. As we read the Bible as God's story, we come to know God better. We begin to share his values and his priorities. Gradually, Scripture informs our consciences and shapes our understanding. Though we won't find proof texts that specify the choices we should make, the more our consciences are informed by Scripture, the more our perspectives will be transformed and the clearer the right choices will become.

Scripture also constantly reminds us of a vital truth. Even though the Bible contains "the very words of God,"[24] the Bible is not God. Our relationship is not with words printed on a page but rather with a living person. In Christ, the living God is committed to us for time and for eternity. He is The One Who Is Always Present, walking with us into every *today*. He interacts with us and responds to our choices. And he communicates with us.

What God knows about our life-shaping choices is hidden from us. We simply cannot know, cannot reason out, cannot find a proof text to reveal what God knows about the future. But the Spirit of God knows. The Holy Spirit is present within us, and it is he—not dreams, not Urim and Thummim, not even prophets—who provides the guidance we need.

Neither the promise of God's presence nor the provision of divine guidance is intended to turn us into puppets. He always preserves our freedom to choose. God's promise and provision do not cancel the risk involved in making decisions; nor do they release us from responsibility for the choices we make. God expects us to use our freedom and to make the best choices we can as we live our lives. Yet at the same time, God is committed to walking with us. When we need or want his direction, he will provide the guidance we need. You and I will hear and recognize the Spirit's voice.

Today

In Hebrews 3 and 4, the writer develops the theme of hearing God's voice in our todays, reminding us that God told the people of Israel to enter Canaan, where they would find rest. But that generation rebelled. Rather than finding rest, they wandered for forty years in the wilderness. So the writer of Hebrews says, "Today, if you hear [God's] voice, do not harden your hearts as you did in the rebellion."[25]

But the writer continues, "the promise of entering his rest still stands" as an open invitation.[26] We know this because in the time of David, the warning is repeated. "Today, if only you would hear his voice, 'Do not harden your hearts as you did at Meribah.'"[27] The writer goes on to tell us that in our "today," anyone who hears and responds to God's voice will rest "from their works, just as God did from his."[28]

This imagery carries us back to the first chapter of Genesis and the story of the seven days. Each day is marked by an evening and a morning. Each, that is, except the seventh day, the day on which God rested. That day has no evening or morning specified, and Jewish scholars have recognized the implications of that omission. It means that the seventh day has not ended! God is active throughout history, but he is *at rest*.

Still, the scholars did not recognize the full significance of their insight. God is at rest simply because there is no possible choice that human or demon might make for which God is unprepared. Without needing to control what each free agent will do, God is prepared with a response that will carry his purposes forward to their predestined end.

Applying this truth, the writer of Hebrews urges us to "make every effort to enter that rest."[29] In other words, we should stop guessing how this choice or that choice will turn out, and instead focus on our relationship with God and listen for his voice. We are to live our lives in freedom, rejoicing in the gift of choice the Lord has given us, yet tuned to hear his voice and committed to respond.

When Hebrews 4:12 tells us that "the word of God is alive and active," it is referring not to the words printed on the pages of our Bibles but to Christ, the *living* Word, as he works in our hearts. In 1 Corinthians 2:16, the apostle Paul tells us that "we have the mind of Christ." In Hebrews, the writer reminds us that God has *our* minds. God knows each of us perfectly, evaluating the "thoughts and attitudes of the heart."[30] God knows each of us so well that his solution to any problem we face is designed just for us, with our individual strengths, weaknesses, gifts, and talents all taken into account. "Everything is uncovered and laid bare before the eyes of him to whom we must give account."[31] And the account we must give is simply this: Today, when you heard his voice, did you open your heart to him, trust, and obey?

Time and again, as we read the Bible as story, we come face-to-face with the supernatural. There is no natural explanation for the timing and focus of the plagues that devastated Egypt before the Exodus. There is no natural explanation for the instructions given to David in his battles with the Philistines. There is no natural explanation for the death of Hananiah within the time frame announced by Jeremiah. Yet, living as we do in a material universe, we often stumble through life blind to supernatural realities. In the Bible's stories of supernatural guidance, of angels and Urim and Thummim, of prophets whose ministries are authenticated by fulfilled predictions or by signs and wonders, we're reminded that we are called to live supernatural lives in this present world. We who live within God's story are called to a relationship with The One Who Is Always Present; the God who has planted his Spirit deep within our hearts; the God who walks with us into our tomorrows, and who, by his Spirit, speaks to us in our todays.

Discussion Questions

1. What does it mean to say that the Bible isn't enough?

2. What role has Scripture played in your life? In your relationship with God? How might reading the Bible as God's story change the role of Scripture in your life?

3. Describe an experience in which you "heard God's voice" in one of your todays. How did you recognize God's voice? How has that experience helped you see that living within God's story involves taking the supernatural seriously?

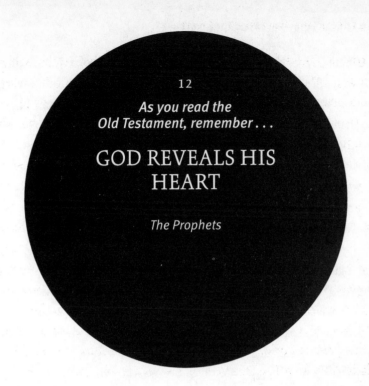

12

*As you read the
Old Testament, remember . . .*

GOD REVEALS HIS HEART

The Prophets

The Pivotal Event

Malachi could hardly stand it. "These people!" he muttered, shaking his head in frustration.

As the prophet continued to speak God's word, he shared a vision of a day in the future when God would act in judgment and then afterward would "pour out so much blessing that there will not be room enough to store it."[1] But most of the people in Judea laughed at him, ignored his warnings, and scornfully replied, "It is futile to serve God."[2]

Digging Deeper into the Prophets

In my large-print, New International Version "reading Bible," 324 pages of the Old Testament are devoted to the Pentateuch—the five books of Moses, or the Torah. It takes 447 pages to cover Old Testament history.

The next 278 pages are devoted to the poetical books: Job, Psalms, Proverbs, Ecclesiastes, and Song of Songs. Then there are 433 pages containing the messages spoken or written by the major and minor prophets. Yet with the exception of a few prophecies relating to Jesus—his virgin birth, his birthplace in Bethlehem, predictions relating to his death—the Old Testament books penned by the prophets are largely unexplored territory for many.

I can understand why. The prophetic books don't tell stories. We meet few interesting people there. And overall, the writings of the prophets are, one might say, *disturbing*. There is so much darkness, so much gloom. When we read the Prophets, a dark pall seems to hang over the Promised Land—and we wonder, *How can these writings be important enough to God's story to deserve so many pages?* (Seven more pages, in fact, than the entire New Testament!)

The Prophets' Ministry

To understand, we first must review a few things about the ministries of the Old Testament prophets. They were, in part, God's contemporary voice in those times, providing situational guidance to the nation and to individuals. They were also, in part, the conscience of the nation. Furthermore, they were part watchman—urging those who had abandoned the path of peace to return to the Lord—and part purveyors of hope, calling God's people to look ahead to the bright promise of history's end.

These roles were taken up again and again by the prophets, who then recorded their message for posterity. Three of the four roles are expressed in themes—conscience, warning, and hope—that are deeply embedded in the seventeen Old Testament books referred to collectively as the Prophets. The prophets' messages were directed to different people and different times, yet the themes are essentially the same, and the prophets' role as conscience, contemporary voice, watchman, and purveyor of hope remains constant.

As God's spokespersons, the prophets provided specific guidance in uncertain times. For instance, when a remnant of Jews returned from exile to their homeland in 539 BC and quickly fell on desperate times, the prophet Haggai explained that it was because they had failed to put their relationship with God first. In that case, the people responded and finished rebuilding the Temple, whereupon the prophet (declaring the word of the Lord) announced, "From this day on I will bless you."[3] Sadly, such responsiveness from God's people was unusual. During the era of the divided kingdom, messengers providing divine guidance were typically ignored.

As the conscience of the nation, the Old Testament prophets confronted the spiritual unfaithfulness of God's people and their violations of the Torah. Amos famously described conditions in his time, saying, "They sell the innocent for silver, and the needy for a pair of sandals . . . and deny justice to the oppressed."[4] Thus the prophet announces in God's name, "Therefore I will punish you for all your sins."[5]

As a watchman, Ezekiel cried out, "Turn! Turn from your evil ways! Why will you die, people of Israel?"[6] What the hearers did with the watchman's warning was their own responsibility. Yet the prophets were responsible to deliver the message as clearly and forcefully as they could.[7] Each individual must have the truth in order to make a choice for or against the Lord.

Still, when many people think of the prophetic books of the Old Testament, what they focus on are the visions of the future embedded in nearly every message.

Prophecy Conferences

The first prophecy conference I attended was while I was in the navy. I had made a conscious commitment to Christ and had started teaching a Bible class on the base. Then I found Bay Ridge Baptist Church, just a few blocks from where I was stationed at the New York Port of Embarkation in Brooklyn. I immersed myself in church activities, attended street meetings, went to rescue missions with the youth group, taught vacation Bible school, and attended the prophecy conference led by our pastor, the Rev. E. A. Lockerbie.

The conference was held in the church basement. A great white banner stretched across the front of the hall, filled with pictures and symbols and Bible references. I quickly realized I was looking at a time line, which was decorated with a picture of the statue described in Daniel 2 and with symbols for Media-Persia, Macedonia, Rome, and a revived Roman Empire. There was also a place for the 1948 establishment of modern Israel, pictures of dry bones from Ezekiel 37, and a picture of believers meeting Jesus in the air at the Rapture. At the far right, there was an image of the eternal state, with both heaven and hell represented.

Pastor Lockerbie's chart was like many I've seen since then. It was a serious attempt to harmonize Old Testament and New Testament prophetic visions. I have no problem with those who enjoy playing with prophecy, as long as we understand that our charts—with whatever sequence of events we come up with—probably aren't quite accurate.

The reason for that is simple. In the context of God's story, prophetic elements are not presented in time-line form. The timing of a particular prophesied event, or its relationship to other predicted events, is not explained in the Bible.

The prophet Joel realized that a locust plague prefigured an invasion of the Promised Land by an irresistible army on a coming Day of the Lord.[8] He then called on God's people to repent and change their ways.[9] But even though Joel then looked beyond the Day of Judgment to a time of restoration,[10] he made no attempt to link either the judgment or the blessing to events predicted by other prophets. What concerned Joel was that his listeners would realize that God *will* judge and that they must "return to the Lord," because, "Who knows? He may turn and relent and leave behind a blessing."[11]

When Paul describes the event we call the Rapture, he doesn't link it with the appearance of the Antichrist or with the Tribulation. He simply says that we need not grieve the death of loved ones as those who are without hope, because when Jesus appears, the dead in Christ will rise to meet the Lord in the air.[12]

The focus within God's grand narrative is on the significance of future events for our present experience. The future is in God's hands. You and I are to deal with the present.

This doesn't mean, of course, that prophecies should be ignored or viewed with suspicion. If we examine the Old Testament prophecies that have been fulfilled, we find consistent portraits of future history. Daniel's predictions concerning the great powers that would dominate the ancient Middle East are so stunningly accurate that skeptics still argue that the book of Daniel simply could not have been written in the sixth century BC. Yet it's impossible to dismiss Isaiah's prophecy of Jesus' virgin birth or Micah's prediction that the Messiah would be born in Bethlehem, though both were penned about seven hundred years before Christ was born. And it's impossible to dismiss the picture of the Messiah's death in Isaiah 53.

One of my friends in the navy was Gerson Megin. Gerson was Jewish, and one day I read Isaiah 53 to him. "Who is that passage about?" I asked.

Gerson didn't hesitate: "Jesus."

When I showed him that the description was in the Old Testament book of Isaiah, written some seven hundred years before Jesus was born, Gerson just shook his head.

Too Long

About seventy years ago, I sat on the porch of my family's little house in Milan, Michigan. Our planned vacation to the cabin in Oscoda was only two weeks away, but to a ten-year-old, it seemed an eternity. I ached for the promised day to come.

I remember that moment as I imagine what it must have been like for the people of the divided kingdom of Israel. Even though generations had failed through disobedience to experience the safety and blessing that God yearned to provide, the prophets urged the faithful few to look ahead expectantly. The blessed future God had in mind for his people lay just over the horizon.

Isaiah 11:11-12 introduces one of several repeated prophetic themes. "In that day," Isaiah writes, "the Lord will reach out his hand a second time to reclaim the surviving remnant of his people from Assyria. . . . He will raise a banner for the nations and gather the exiles of Israel; he will assemble the scattered people of Judah from the four quarters of the earth." The theme of a great regathering of the Jews to the Promised Land is found frequently in the prophets. We read about it in the writings of Isaiah, Jeremiah, Ezekiel, Hosea, Joel, Amos, Micah, Zephaniah, and Zechariah.[13] The land God promised to Abraham in Genesis 12:7 is to be occupied by Abraham's descendants as history comes to a close.

The prophets also describe a dark aspect to the future, in which the nations of the world will unite to exterminate God's people. Joel launches his description of that terrible time by calling it "a day of darkness and gloom, a day of clouds and blackness."[14] He concludes his description by saying, "The day of the Lord is great; it is dreadful. Who can endure it?"[15] This same theme is found repeatedly in the writings of the other prophets.[16]

Still, after the dark times a great spiritual conversion will sweep through Israel and extend even to the Gentiles. Then the promised Messiah, a ruler who springs from David's line, will establish an endless Kingdom and the promised eternal community of love. Prophecies of the national conversion of Israel and of the Messiah's glorious Kingdom also abound in the Old Testament prophecies. Isaiah describes God's gift of a Son and says, "Of the greatness of his government and peace there will be no end. He will reign on David's throne and over his kingdom, establishing and upholding it with justice and righteousness from that time on and forever."[17]

This vision, too, is held up by prophet after prophet.[18] Yet despite the prophets' emphasis on what God intends to do for his people, the citizens of both Israel and Judah failed to listen. Promises and warnings were ignored. By the time Malachi wrote the book that concludes the Old Testament, the people—and even the priests—had lost respect for God and his ways, cynically denying each charge the prophet brought against them. In describing this day, a day when "we call the arrogant blessed [and] evildoers prosper, and even when they put God to the test, they get away with it,"[19] Malachi can find only one note of comfort:

> Then those who feared the LORD talked with each other, and the LORD listened and heard. A scroll of remembrance was written in his presence concerning those who feared the LORD and honored his name.
>
> "On the day when I act," says the LORD Almighty, "they will be my treasured possession."[20]

After Malachi, the prophets fell silent for some four hundred years. No spokesman arose to speak for God. There was no one to serve as the conscience of the nation, as the prophets had done. There was no one to warn of impending judgment. And there was no one to dream of a future when the promises to Abraham would be fulfilled and one from David's royal line would rule a glorious, endless community of love.

Reading the Prophets

At the beginning of this chapter, I asked, "How can these writings be important enough to God's story to deserve so many pages?"

A Christian activist who is passionate about social justice might point to passages in which the prophets take on the role of conscience of the nation, such as Amos's call to "let justice roll on like a river, righteousness like a never-failing stream!"[21]

Evangelicals might look to the prophets' repeated warnings and their cry, "Turn to me and be saved, all you ends of the earth; for I am God, and there is no other."[22] We, too, are watchmen, and many in our world do not yet understand the gospel message.

Students of prophecy might point to prophecies that have been fulfilled to "prove" the supernatural origin of the Bible, and they delight in debating whether the Rapture will occur at the beginning, middle, or end of the Great Tribulation.

Personally, I find all of these answers unsatisfying. None seems to explain why the writings of the prophets are given so much space in the telling of God's story. I believe there is another reason entirely—one that now seems obvious to me, but that I failed to recognize until I approached the Bible as a love story.

The story begins in Genesis 1, as God fashions the world as a home for the human beings he will create in his own image and likeness. It is here we begin to sense God's strong desire to create an eternal community of love through which we can fully know him and be fully known by him. We sense the theme of love in God's response to Adam's fateful choice of independence. We see it in the covenant promises he makes to Abram and in the rescue and redemption of his people from slavery in Egypt. We see God's love in the gift of laws designed to help his people fashion a loving community here on earth. In all this, and in so much more throughout the Bible's story, we sense that God's actions are driven by love.

When we read the Psalms, we begin to understand something of the freedom created by an awareness of God's love. The psalmists are so open with the Lord. They unhesitatingly pour out their hearts to him. They express their doubts, their fears, their hopes, even the anger they sometimes feel toward him. There's no pretense; there are no masks.

The psalmists make themselves totally vulnerable to God, confident that he accepts and loves them as they are. In the Bible's telling of God's story, there's nothing quite like the book of Psalms—nothing that conveys as powerfully the truth that this story really is about love and about relationship.

There's nothing, that is, until we come to the Prophets. In the Prophets, we discover that God is as open and honest with us as the psalmists have been with him. The voices of the prophets throb with God's pain. They shout his anger at the arrogance of those who ignore him and oppress their fellow men. The voices of the prophets ache with God's passionate hopes for his people, his eagerness to bless, and his utter frustration when his people refuse to hear or respond. God cares for us so deeply that he becomes flushed with anger when we refuse to respond to his pleading. He struggles with the intensity of his love when we suffer, fighting his desire to intervene, committed to extending continued freedom in the hope that the evil will change their ways.

It is impossible to read the Prophets and imagine that God is a dispassionate observer of history. It is impossible to imagine that he stays coolly in the background, manipulating the choices of men and demons and angels. The God we meet in the Prophets is deeply, totally invested in the lives of every generation.

This, perhaps, is why it is so difficult for most of us to read the Prophets. We're not certain that we want a God who becomes angry. We're not sure we want a God who announces:

> They have rejected the law of the Lord Almighty
>> and spurned the word of the Holy One of Israel.
> Therefore the Lord's anger burns against his people;
>> his hand is raised and he strikes them down.
> The mountains shake,
>> and the dead bodies are like refuse in the street.[23]

We much prefer the God who says, "In the time of my favor I will answer you, and in the day of salvation I will help you."[24]

And yet the God who speaks judgment and the God who speaks comfort through the prophets is one and the same God. In the words of the prophets, God invites us to know him and accept him as he is. Not as we imagine him to be. Not as we'd like him to be.

Not long ago, I received a catalog from a publisher, featuring a book I had recently written. Yet it was another book in the same catalog that drew my attention. According to the description, "there is significant tension between Jesus' nonviolent mission and message and the apparent violence attributed to God and God's agents at the anticipated end."[25] The author "challenges the ready association between New Testament eschatology and retributive vengeance on christological and canonical grounds."[26]

I understand the author's perspective. Surely a gentle God is more comfortable for us than the God who reveals himself to us in the Prophets. But making himself vulnerable was a risk God was more than willing to take. Without the voices of the prophets and especially their exposure of God as a deeply emotional and passionate being, we would not know him as he is.

God doesn't ask us to understand him. He doesn't ask us to defend him. But he does want us to know him as a passionate person who is totally invested in each of our lives.

Perhaps the prophet who best communicates this is Hosea, who had an unfaithful wife. In this he was like God, who was united by covenant promises to an unfaithful Israel. We sense both Hosea's and God's pain as the prophet cries out, "Let her remove the adulterous look from her face and the unfaithfulness from between her breasts."[27]

Anger follows, along with a threat: "Otherwise I will strip her naked and make her as bare as on the day she was born."[28] Deeply humiliated, the husband intends to humiliate his wife, and God adds, "I will punish her [Israel] for the days she burned incense to the Baals."[29]

As the story unfolds, God lays out his charges against Israel: "There is no faithfulness, no love, no acknowledgment of God in the land. There is only cursing, lying and murder, stealing and adultery; they break all bounds, and bloodshed follows bloodshed."[30] We sense God's frustration as he says, "Whenever I would restore the fortunes of my people, whenever I would heal Israel, the sins of Ephraim are exposed and the crimes of Samaria revealed."[31]

Frustration turns to anger again as the prophet announces, "Woe to them, because they have strayed from me! Destruction to them, because they have rebelled against me! I long to redeem them but they speak about me falsely."[32] God then calls on his people to "throw out [the] calf-idol" and warns, "My anger burns against them. . . . They sow the wind and reap the whirlwind."[33]

Yet even though "a sword will flash in their cities; [and] it will devour their false prophets and put an end to their plans,"[34] God is unwilling to put an end to these people who are so determined to turn from him.

God loved Israel as a child when he called the people out of Egypt.[35] Now he cries, "How can I give you up, Ephraim? How can I hand you over, Israel? . . . My heart is changed within me; all my compassion is aroused. I will not carry out my fierce anger, nor will I devastate Ephraim again."[36] As the prophet concludes his message, God promises, "I will heal their waywardness and love them freely, for my anger has turned away from them."[37]

What we find exposed in Hosea, and in the writings of the other prophets as well, is God's revelation of himself as deeply passionate and totally involved with his people. God feels the pain of hurt and rejection, is furious over man's injustice to his fellow man, and can inflict terrible punishments. Yet through it all, he is driven by compassion and love.

It is in the words of the prophets that we discover the passionate heart of God.

Discussion Questions

1. Where in the Bible do you usually turn when you read Scripture? Have you spent much time reading the Prophets? Why or why not?

2. Why might we be doubtful of attempts to create prophetic time lines? What are the various roles the prophets played when acting as God's spokespeople? Which of these roles do you think is most important for our own time?

3. Open your Bible to any of the Old Testament prophets. Read one or more passages as if through the prophet's words God were opening his heart to you, inviting you to know him better. How valuable do you suppose reading the Prophets might be in deepening your personal relationship with the Lord?

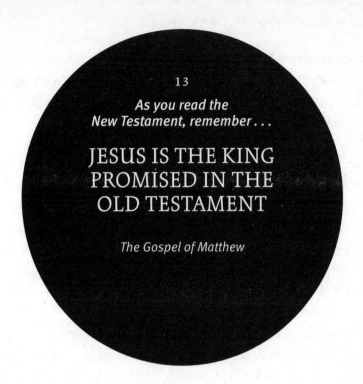

*As you read the
New Testament, remember . . .*

JESUS IS THE KING PROMISED IN THE OLD TESTAMENT

The Gospel of Matthew

The Pivotal Event

The young woman knelt before the grindstones and began to crush the barley kernels. She was startled when a shadow fell across where she was working. She looked up and was amazed to see a man standing there. *No!* she realized. It was an angel, one of God's messengers.

The angel, Gabriel, explained that she would have a child, a son, who would be the Son of God and not of her husband. "The Lord God will give him the throne of his father David, and he will reign over Jacob's descendants forever; his kingdom will never end."[1]

Digging Deeper into the Gospel of Matthew

George Washington is rightly known as the father of his country, so it didn't surprise me to discover twenty-four different contemporary portraits of George Washington on the Internet. Each image is similar, of course. Each shows the same strong jaw, overly large nose, white wig or hair, and weary-looking eyes. Some paintings show Washington's left side, some his right. Yet each portrait is unmistakably a representation of George Washington.

We might be surprised to find so many different portraits of the same man, each more or less the same. But we have to remember that in the decades following the American Revolution, George Washington meant much to the people of the nation he helped establish.

When we open the New Testament, we are immediately confronted with four Gospels—four portraits of Jesus Christ—each more or less the same, though seen from different angles. In God's story, the man Jesus is far more significant than George Washington is in the story of the United States.

The four portraits of Jesus in the Gospels exhibit significant differences. Matthew's Gospel is written with the Jewish people in mind. It answers questions that those steeped in the Old Testament were sure to ask. Too many, when reading the Gospels, fall into the trap of comparing and contrasting versions of the same or similar events reported in two or more Gospels. Granted, this is one way to study the Gospels. But it's best if we read each Gospel as a distinctive story, as a unique portrait introducing Jesus to a particular audience.

The Empty Years

The last book in the Old Testament, Malachi, was written at some point between 465 BC and 430 BC. The centuries that passed from Malachi's writing until Jesus was born were long, dark, and empty. No prophet's voice was heard. No divine spokesman appeared to confront the nation of Israel or offer guidance. Generations lived and died while God remained silent.

Not that he was inactive. Some 550 years before the birth of Jesus, the prophet Daniel laid out the course that history would follow in preparation for the next twist in God's story.[2] And history followed the course that Daniel predicted. The Babylonian Empire (605–538 BC) was succeeded by the Medo-Persian Empire (538–331 BC). That empire fell to Alexander the Great, who was passionately determined to plant Greek culture throughout the known world. Although Alexander died young, his generals divided up the lands he had conquered and fulfilled Alexander's dream. Greek language and culture were planted in the major population centers throughout the Mediterranean world.

The kingdoms established by the generals remained independent till about 146 BC. At that point, a fourth Mediterranean world power, Rome, gained control. By the time of Christ, barriers to travel and commerce had been removed, and with the entire Roman world speaking Greek, it was possible for the Good News about Jesus to spread rapidly.

There's scant evidence that the Jewish community in the Holy Land understood the significance of the events taking place around them. They were occupied with more immediate concerns. For 122 years, the tiny Jewish colony had been dominated by Egypt. Then, in 198 BC, the Seleucid (Syrian) Empire to the north wrested control of the Jewish homeland from the Egyptians. But when a Seleucid army occupied Jerusalem and made the practice of Judaism a capital offense, the Jews rebelled. Known as the Maccabean revolt, this struggle was a civil war as well as a clash of nations. It pitted those committed to the ancient faith against those who favored adopting the Hellenistic Greek culture. Though the Syrians were defeated, and a Jewish family (the Hasmoneans) maintained political power and provided the Jews with pseudo-independence for about a hundred years, in 34 BC power passed out of Jewish hands entirely and into the hands of the Romans.

Most Jews chafed under the burden of Rome's increasingly heavy taxes. As in the time of the Maccabees, the people yearned for freedom. That yearning took the form of dreams of the appearance of the Messiah. The Messiah, the ruler promised by the Old Testament prophets, would restore David's kingdom. The yearning was powerful. And as the time for Jesus' birth drew nearer, it intensified.

We can see why Matthew would craft a Gospel for a Jewish audience. Deeply invested in the Old Testament, the Jews dreamed of a day when their promised Messiah would appear and they would dominate their world as they had in the time of King David. After the Crucifixion, it was difficult for the Jews to accept the notion that Jesus of Nazareth was the promised Messiah. The prophesied King was assumed to be a powerful individual who would rule the kingdoms of this world. Then Jesus died on a cross, a victim of both the Jewish religious establishment and the Roman overlords. How could the victor portrayed in the Old Testament suffer as a victim? And what happened to the kingdom that the true Messiah was destined to establish?

Meet Matthew's Jesus

As soon as we begin to read Matthew's Gospel, we plunge into his argument that Jesus of Nazareth is truly the promised Messiah. The opening verse launches "the genealogy of Jesus Christ, the son [descendant] of David."[3] Matthew moves on to describe Jesus' miraculous birth in Bethlehem, the visit of the magi, Herod's attempt to kill the infant Jesus, the family's escape to Egypt, and their subsequent return to Nazareth in Galilee. Significantly, each of these events is linked to Old Testament prophecy, further enhancing Matthew's thesis that Jesus is the promised "ruler who will shepherd my people Israel."[4]

Matthew skips over Jesus' childhood to instead introduce John the Baptist, a man commissioned to "prepare the way for the Lord."[5] Like a prophet of old, John confronts his generation, calling on the people to confess their sins and repent. Here, on the banks of the Jordan River, we meet the adult Jesus, who insists on being baptized as an act of solidarity with John's message. And here, as Jesus comes up from the water, a "voice from heaven" identifies Jesus as "my Son, whom I love."[6] There is no doubt—this Jesus is special indeed.

The next scene Matthew describes harkens back to Genesis. In Eden, Adam and Eve enjoyed an idyllic life and an intimate relationship with the Creator. In contrast, Jesus is led by the Spirit into a desolate wilderness and goes without food for forty days. After the first few days of any fast, hunger pangs recede. But when the body's resources are exhausted, hunger returns. Thus Matthew's comment, "After fasting forty days and forty nights, he [Jesus] was hungry," is significant.[7] Unlike Adam in the Garden, Jesus in the wilderness is exhausted and weakened physically.

In both settings, Eden and the wilderness, our story's antagonist suddenly appears. But this time, although the tempter's words are again designed to undermine confidence in God's love, Jesus meets each of the adversary's challenges with a quote from God's Word. The antagonist's attempt to isolate Jesus from God the Father fails, and Matthew tells us, "the devil left him."[8]

We can't help but see a pattern in this weaving of God's story. Genesis begins with a victory for the antagonist, as Adam and Eve declare independence from the Creator. The Gospels begin with a defeat for the antagonist, as Jesus remains firmly committed to doing his Father's will. Is it possible that what Adam lost through disobedience Jesus regained?

Returning from the wilderness, Jesus selects a few disciples and begins to share God's love and wisdom with those who are interested. His healings and exorcisms draw crowds. And as the crowds gather, Jesus launches a major teaching ministry.

The Inward Shape of Jesus' Kingdom

The Old Testament law laid the foundation for a community in which God's people could experience safety and rest here on earth. A life lived according to the law embodied love for God and for neighbor, and an obedient Israel was intended to be a beacon of hope in a world corrupted by selfishness and sin. Yet century after century, despite the urgings of prophets and the examples of a few godly kings of Judah, the community envisioned in the Torah was never realized. Speaking now with royal authority, Jesus explains why Israel failed and what it means to live in the here and now as a citizen of his Kingdom.

First, Jesus challenges the values by which God's people had been living. Followers of Jesus must adopt new and radically different values, as reflected in the Beatitudes.[9] Jesus then turns to the law. What he says must not be taken as a rejection of the Torah. Yet, he tells the crowds, "Unless your righteousness surpasses that of the Pharisees," who were known for their scrupulous adherence to Old Testament law, "you will certainly not enter the kingdom of heaven."[10] Using a series of illustrations, Jesus shifts the focus of the Torah from *behavior* to *character*. The basic issues raised in the Torah's commandments are not acts of murder and adultery. The basic issues are the anger and lust that generate them.[11] Life in Jesus' Kingdom requires an inner transformation—a transformation so profound that a Kingdom citizen is to "be perfect . . . as your heavenly Father is perfect."[12]

What does a transformed life look like? Jesus uses various stories to illustrate that it's a life of independence from others' expectations, lived solely to please the unseen Father in heaven. It's a life free of anxiety over the concerns of this life, for we trust God as Father to supply our needs.[13] It's a life of total dependence on a Father who responds when we ask, is found when we seek, and opens the door when we knock.[14] Such an intimate relationship with God, hidden though it is from the world, will produce the visible fruit of a life of love.[15]

The crowd does not know what to make of Jesus. They are "amazed at his teaching," being used to leaders who quote each other to support their teachings. But Jesus spoke "as one who had authority."[16]

Jesus Demonstrates His Authority

It's no accident that the next three chapters of Matthew's Gospel (8–10) are packed with stories that demonstrate Jesus' authority. He heals a man with leprosy. He forgives the sins of a paralyzed man—and as evidence of his authority to forgive, tells the man to take up his pallet and walk. He casts out a legion of evil spirits from two demonized men, calms a violent storm on the Sea of Galilee, brings a dead girl back to life, stanches the flow of blood from a woman who has suffered for a dozen years, gives sight back to two blind men, and restores speech to a man silenced by demons. And then he extends his reach by giving his twelve disciples "authority to drive out impure spirits and to heal every disease and sickness."[17]

What right did Jesus have to explain the true intent of the Torah, exposing a hidden, inner Kingdom over which he was to rule? Matthew answers this question, which would have been in every Jewish reader's mind, with account after account of miracles that Jesus performed—miracles that authenticated Jesus as God's spokesperson.

Again we're told that "the crowd was amazed." No wonder. The people exclaimed, "Nothing like this has ever been seen in Israel."[18]

Then, unexpectedly, we're given a preview of the reaction of the religious establishment. Whereas the crowds were amazed, the Pharisees attributed Jesus' miracles to an evil power source: "It is by the prince of demons that he drives out demons."[19]

Growing Resistance

Matthew doesn't date the stories he tells. Neither do the other Gospel writers. So when we reach chapter 11 of Matthew's narrative, we don't know how long Jesus has been teaching and performing miracles. It's reasonable to assume, however, that Jesus has been a highly visible public figure for well over two years by this point in Matthew's account. The Jewish people have had plenty of time to acknowledge him as the promised Messiah, but they have not done so. Now Jesus cautions his disciples, "I did not come to bring peace, but a sword." Debate over Jesus' identity will indeed "turn 'a man against his father, a daughter against her mother.'"[20]

As we move along in the story, we learn that even John the Baptist has developed doubts about Jesus' identity. Jesus responds by quoting a messianic prophecy found in Isaiah 35:4-5, which he fulfills as John's messengers watch. Jesus is confident. Unlike others, whose initial enthusiasm has waned, John will not "fall away."

Jesus has harsh words for the cities in which most of his miracles have been performed, for there has been no mass repentance and turning to God.[21] Significantly, when Jesus concludes his denunciation of the cities, he extends an invitation to individuals. "Come to me," he says, "and you will find rest for your souls."[22]

Matthew's narrative moves quickly now. Jesus announces that he is "Lord of the Sabbath," an open claim to deity.[23] In response, the Pharisees plot how they might kill him.[24] When Jesus heals a demonized individual, the people are astonished and wonder, "Could this be the Son of David?"[25] The Pharisees insist that Jesus' miracles are counterfeit, empowered by Beelzebul, the prince of demons.[26] When the Pharisees demand another miraculous sign, Jesus refuses. The only sign these men will receive is the sign of the prophet Jonah, he says. Just as Jonah was three days and nights in the belly of a huge fish, Jesus will be buried in the earth for that same amount of time.[27] His victory over death will be the ultimate miracle, sealing his identity once and for all. But this lies ahead. As Matthew continues with the story of Jesus for his Jewish audience, he relates a turning point in Christ's ministry.[28]

Jesus had announced that the Kingdom of Heaven was at hand—and it was, in the person of the King. Yet for all their amazement at Jesus' teachings and miracles, the people have not acknowledged him as the Messiah. So now Jesus introduces a series of parables.

Kingdom Secrets

Today, we think of a kingdom as a geographic area with a distinct national identity. But in the Bible, "kingdom" is best understood as *reign* or *sovereignty*. A kingdom consists of the people or things over which one has authority or control. In this sense, the universe, and history itself, are viewed in Scripture as God's Kingdom, for he is ultimately in control. As Psalm 103:19 affirms, "The Lord has established his throne in heaven, and his kingdom rules over all." Yet the form that God's rule takes has varied through human history.

When Jesus came proclaiming that "the kingdom of heaven" was at hand, he was speaking of a particular expression of God's rule. It was natural for his Jewish audience to understand Christ's announcement as a reference to the messianic kingdom described in the Old Testament. But now Jesus tells a series of parables that describe the Kingdom, each introduced with the phrase, "The kingdom of heaven is like . . ."[29] And the Kingdom portrayed in Jesus' parables is very different from the kingdom pictured in Old Testament prophecy:

- In the prophesied kingdom, the Messiah turns *Israel and all nations* to himself. In the parable of the sower, Jesus describes a kingdom in which *individuals* respond differently to God's invitation.[30]
- In the prophesied kingdom, righteous citizens *rule over* the world *with the King*. In the parable of the tares, Jesus describes a kingdom in which citizens *live among* the people of the world until God's harvest time.[31]
- The prophesied kingdom is *initiated in splendor*. In the parable of the mustard seed, Jesus describes a kingdom launched in *insignificance*, its growth to greatness a surprise.[32]
- In the prophesied kingdom, *only the righteous enter*; sinners are excluded. In the parable of the leaven, Jesus describes a kingdom in which righteousness is *implanted in sinners* to gradually transform them.[33]
- The prophesied kingdom is *public and for all*. In the parable of the hidden treasure, Jesus describes a *hidden* kingdom that is for individual *"purchase."*[34]
- The prophesied kingdom *brings all valued things* to men. In the parable of the priceless pearl, Jesus describes a kingdom that *demands abandonment of all other valuables.*[35]

- The prophesied kingdom is *initiated with the separation* of the righteous and unrighteous. In the parable of the dragnet, Jesus describes a kingdom that *ends with a final separation* of the unrighteous from the righteous.[36]

In his Kingdom of Heaven parables, Jesus announces that *he is about to initiate a form of God's rule that is simply not a subject of Old Testament prophecy*. This is underscored by his reference to "secrets" of the Kingdom of Heaven.[37] Jesus' Kingdom parables introduce a totally unexpected twist into God's story. There is a form of God's Kingdom rule that has been kept secret from the very beginning. Jesus uses parables to describe it in order to keep those who have rejected him as Messiah from discerning God's intent before it is time.

Once again, Matthew's narrative moves along quickly. John the Baptist is beheaded by Herod.[38] Jesus continues to perform miracles.[39] The religious leaders continue to challenge him.[40] It seems the only person to trust Christ fully is a Canaanite woman whose daughter is demon possessed.[41] Even so, Jesus shows compassion for his own, miraculously feeding four thousand people.[42]

Despite all the signs and wonders that Jesus performs, the religious leaders still come to him and demand a miracle. Again Jesus refuses, and again he refers to "the sign of Jonah."[43]

The Identity Issue

We now come to another pivotal moment in Matthew's narrative.[44] Jesus asks who the people say he is. The disciples tell him the universal opinion. Jesus surely is one of the prophets, a great man. But the people don't recognize that he is the Messiah.

"Who do you say I am?" Jesus then asks the Twelve. Peter answers for them. "You are the Messiah, the Son of the living God."[45]

From this point on, there is no more proclamation of a Kingdom of Heaven at hand for the Jewish nation. Now the teaching focuses on preparing the disciples for a future in the new, secret form of God's Kingdom, in a community to be formed after the death and resurrection of Jesus. In chapters 18–20 of Matthew's Gospel, teachings and incidents are woven together to drive home the point that leadership in Jesus' Kingdom is to be rooted not in power, but in servanthood. Jesus "did not come to be served, but to serve, and to give his life as a ransom for many." Those who take the lead in Jesus' Kingdom are not rulers over God's people but servants among them.[46]

As we reach the last week of Jesus' life, Matthew describes what seems to be a breakthrough. When Jesus enters Jerusalem, the crowds acclaim him as "the Son of David."[47] But the next day, as Jesus is teaching in the Temple courts, the religious leaders again challenge his authority.[48] Jesus wins a series of verbal confrontations with the leaders[49] and publicly condemns them.[50] Failure to acknowledge his identity has doomed the nation.

What Happened to the Messianic Kingdom?

What happened to the messianic Kingdom? This is the question on the hearts of Matthew's Jewish readers. It is also on the hearts of Christ's disciples during the last week of his earthly life. When Jesus predicts the destruction of the Temple, his disciples privately raise a series of questions. When will his predictions come to pass? What will be the sign marking his promised return? And what will be the sign of the end of the coming age? Jesus answers the questions in reverse order.[51]

An event predicted by Daniel will mark the beginning of the end; there will be a long period of moral deterioration, culminating in "the abomination that causes desolation,"[52] which will be "standing in the holy place."[53] This event will usher in a time of unequaled worldwide distress, which will end when Jesus returns and the world sees "the Son of Man coming on the clouds of heaven, with power and great glory."[54] As for the timing, "About that day or hour no one knows . . . but only the Father."[55]

The rest of Matthew 24, along with chapter 25, is filled with stories exhorting Jesus' people to be ready for his return, whenever that occurs.

Christ's reference to Daniel's prophecy is the key to Matthew's understanding of what happened to the Kingdom predicted in the Old Testament. Israel's rejection of Jesus as the Messiah led to the introduction of an unexpected expression of God's universal rule, an expression we refer to today as the church age or the Christian era. With the rejection and crucifixion of Jesus, the flow of history as described in the Old Testament was diverted into an unexpected channel. Yet Christ's answer to his disciples' questions in Matthew 24 and his reference to Daniel's prophecy make one thing clear: Jesus will come again, this time in power and glory. And the kingdom envisioned by the prophets will be initiated here on earth.[56]

The Death and Resurrection of the King

Matthew devotes seven of the twenty-eight chapters in his Gospel to the final week of Jesus' life. As the dramatic events of the last day unfold, we realize that Matthew seems intent on fixing primary responsibility for Jesus' death on the Jewish leaders. They are shown plotting to arrest and kill Jesus, agreeing to pay Judas to betray Jesus, and sending an armed mob to arrest him.[57] The leaders condemn and mock Jesus at an illegal nighttime trial, determine to execute him, and take him to the Roman governor to confirm the verdict.[58] When the governor, Pilate, is reluctant to condemn Jesus, the leaders and the crowd pressure him to crucify Jesus.[59] The Romans carry out the execution, but the chief priests, teachers of the law, and elders stand at the foot of the cross, mocking and ridiculing Jesus as he dies.[60] After Jesus is dead, the chief priests and Pharisees ask that a military guard be assigned to his tomb.[61] And after Jesus rises from the dead, the chief priests and elders bribe the guards to lie and say that his disciples came at night and stole the body.[62]

Matthew's emphasis is hardly anti-Semitic, as some have suggested. He is a Jew, after all, writing for a Jewish audience, telling the story of a Jew who is the focus of God's story. Matthew drives home the point that the very people Jesus came to save utterly rejected him because they failed to understand the sort of kingdom the prophesied King intended to institute.

Later, when the resurrected Jesus appeared to his disciples, he told them, "All authority in heaven and on earth has been given to me."[63] And he commissioned them to "go and make disciples of all nations."[64] The earthly kingdom may be delayed. But due to the totally unexpected twist in God's story, Jesus will rule in and through humans who are citizens of a hidden but very real Kingdom of the heart. In that new community of faith, which is focused on Jesus, aspects of the eternal community will become a reality in the here and now. Until Jesus comes again.

Discussion Questions

1. The four Gospels comprise 190 pages in my Bible. The Epistles take up only 155. What does this suggest to you?

2. Matthew's Gospel was directed to Jewish readers and speaks to specific Jewish concerns. What are those concerns, and how does Matthew deal with them?

3. Understanding the thesis of a Gospel can make us more sensitive to its portrayal of Jesus. Read any chapter of Matthew's Gospel. How does understanding that Matthew presents Jesus as the messianic King help you know Jesus better?

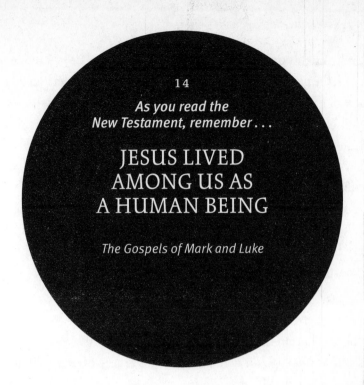

*As you read the
New Testament, remember . . .*

JESUS LIVED
AMONG US AS
A HUMAN BEING

The Gospels of Mark and Luke

The Pivotal Event

"If you are willing," the man choked out, "you can make me clean."

It was almost a question, almost an expression of faith, certainly an expression of anguish. Jesus' response was immediate.

"I am willing," he said. And then in an act that brought a flood of tears to the leper's eyes, Jesus reached out his hand and touched him.[1]

Digging Deeper into the Gospels of Mark and Luke

The people in the Roman Empire of Jesus' time would have loved social media. They would have delighted in LinkedIn. They would have friended as many other people as possible on Facebook and eagerly sent and collected "likes." This notion of a powerful role for social media among ancient Mediterranean peoples probably seems strange.

Yet it highlights one of our problems in reading the New Testament: We lack the perspective that could be gained only by immersion in the world of the first century. For instance, the reason that social media would have fit the people of the first century is that theirs was an honor/shame culture. Social media, with its power to "friend" and "like," would have powerfully reinforced social mechanisms that were actively used to define the frequently shifting status of individuals.

As we look at Mark's and Luke's Gospels through the lens of Mediterranean culture, we meet Jesus as his contemporaries experienced him. And we better understand how Mark's and Luke's distinctive portraits contribute to our understanding of God's story.

Honor in the First Century

In the Mediterranean world when Jesus lived, the first source of a person's honor—we would say *status*—was his family of origin. Respect based on one's family of origin is *ascribed honor*. In the world of the first century, ascribed honor played a central role in how a person was viewed by others. Thus, Mark's very first words tell us the focus of his Gospel: "The beginning of the good news about Jesus the Messiah, the Son of God."[2] If the primary benchmark of one's level of honor in first-century society was the status of the father—and that *was* the test—then Jesus was worthy of ultimate honor. He was no less than the Son of God himself.

This claim to the highest possible ascribed status for Jesus is immediately supported. John the Baptist, himself a subject of Old Testament prophecy, came to "prepare the way for the Lord."[3] When Jesus is baptized by John, God himself acknowledges Jesus as "my Son, whom I love."[4] Then, in the desert, Jesus overcomes the tempter and is attended by angels.[5] Each of these events supports the claim that Jesus is special, acknowledged to be the Son of God. Any madman might show up claiming to be the Messiah. But the testimony about Jesus' identity provided by John, by God himself, and by angels marks Jesus as unique, even as it supports Mark's thesis.

In the first century, a person began life with an honor rating ascribed to him on the basis of his father's or his family's honor. This honor could be raised or lowered, based on how the individual behaved. If the community considered an individual's actions appropriate to his status, his honor—the respect others felt he deserved—increased. If the community judged one's behavior inappropriate, his honor decreased.

One of the major ways in which a person's actions were judged in those days was by his generosity—that is, by how willing he was to use his resources, including his influence, to gain favor for others. Mark presents Jesus as the Son of God, an identity that implies unique influence with God himself. Mark then takes pains to show that Jesus generously distributed God's gifts to others and that the community recognized his generosity. Again and again, Mark describes miraculous healings, including the resurrection of a dead girl. After healing a man with leprosy, Jesus sends him away with a "strong warning" not to "tell this to anyone."[6] The warning underlines the fact that Jesus' generous gift of healing was not given with any consideration of what he might gain in return. But the leper "went out and began to talk freely,"[7] the appropriate response of one who is deeply grateful for the gift he's been given. The result is that people "came to [Jesus] from everywhere."[8]

This recognition by the "crowd"—a word that's repeated in Mark no fewer than thirty-two times—clearly signals to Mark's readers that Jesus' contemporaries held him in highest regard. Jesus acted as a generous patron should. He used his influence with God to win gifts of healing and deliverance for those who appealed to him. In the many stories of healings embedded in the Gospels, we see evidence that the crowds treated Jesus as the Son of God. That is, they approached him as one who could gain them divine favor because of his unique position and his influence with the Father.

It's interesting that our text describes a visit by Jesus to his home-town of Nazareth.[9] When he began to teach in the synagogue, the people "took offense at him."[10] Mark tells us they asked, "Isn't this the carpenter? Isn't this Mary's son and the brother of James, Joseph, Judas and Simon?"[11] They could not get past Jesus' human identity. They saw him simply as a member of their humble community, a common builder, a man whose family of origin was no more special than any-one else's in Nazareth. But in refusing to honor Jesus as the Son of God, they cut themselves off from God's gifts. "He could not do any miracles there, except lay his hands on a few sick people and heal them."[12]

This is indeed one of the themes of Mark's Gospel and the others. The reader is provided with evidence about Jesus' identity. The Jews may acknowledge him as the promised Messiah and put their trust in him, or they may reject him. The non-Jewish inhabitants of the Roman Empire can look at the evidence that Jesus is the Son of God, and may put their trust in him. Or they may view him, as his neighbors in Nazareth did, as a mere human being. The choice each makes will determine whether or not God's favor flows to him or her through the one whom God acknowledges as his Son.

Honor Challenges

Challenges are another feature of the honor/shame culture of the first-century Mediterranean world. In that culture, honor, or status, was treated as a limited commodity. There was only so much honor to go around. Therefore, a person who wanted to increase his status or repu-tation in the community was forced to compete with others. In order for one to gain honor, another would have to lose honor.

As Jesus achieved increasing honor by using his influence with God to channel gifts of divine healing and deliverance, others in Jewish society lost honor. These were the religious elite. The emergence of Jesus, who "taught them as one who had authority, not as the teachers of the law,"[13] undermined the level of respect that the population had for the recognized religious authorities. The response to Jesus by the elites was predictable. In an effort to regain their lost honor, the religious leaders launched negative honor challenges: obvious and unmistakable attempts to reduce Jesus' status. Mark records at least a dozen of these.

As Mark's Gospel unfolds, we see the religious elite challenge Jesus about fasting, about picking grain on the Sabbath, and about healing on the Sabbath.[14] When they publically charge Jesus with being in league with the prince of demons, Jesus ridicules the notion.[15] Later, when they criticize Jesus for the failure of his disciples to perform a traditional hand-washing ritual before eating, Jesus confronts the leaders. He points out that they have used the "tradition of the elders" to "nullify the word of God" and states, "You do many things like that."[16]

In each confrontation, Jesus bests his accusers. But in time, he refuses to play the game on their terms. When challenged to perform a miraculous sign, he refuses. Miracles were no parlor trick to Jesus. The public miracles he performed were expressions of God's love and concern for the sick or demon possessed. They were performed for the benefit of others. It would demean Jesus and cheapen God's grace if he performed a miracle for his own benefit.

As the religious leaders continue to pose negative honor challenges, Jesus finally challenges them in return. Overturning the tables of money changers in the Temple courts, Jesus accuses the leaders of turning God's "house of prayer" into a "den of robbers."[17] Unable to meet this challenge and others, and desperate over the realization that Jesus is stripping them of the honor they think of as their right, "the chief priests and the teachers of the law . . . began looking for a way to kill him."[18] The text tells us that "they feared him, because the whole crowd was amazed at his teaching."[19]

By this time the leaders are truly desperate, as Jesus openly attacks them in his parable of the tenants who kill the owner's son because they want his inheritance for themselves.[20] Mark tells us the leaders would have arrested him then, but "they were afraid of the crowd; so they left him and went away."[21] But the die is cast. The chief priests and elders, the Pharisees and Sadducees are committed. Jesus cannot be discredited. So he must be killed.

A Last, Desperate Effort

Like Matthew, Mark makes it clear that the crowds honored Jesus as one of the greatest of the Old Testament prophets.[22] This fell short of Peter's conviction that Jesus was the Messiah.[23] But the religious leaders were not confused over who Jesus claimed to be. On the night when Jesus was seized and dragged before the Sanhedrin, the high priest asked Jesus, "Are you the Messiah, the Son of the Blessed One?"[24]

Jesus answered bluntly, "I am." And he continued, "You will see the Son of Man sitting at the right hand of the Mighty One and coming on the clouds of heaven."[25]

Despite the evidence provided by Jesus' healings and exorcisms that he was indeed the Son of God, the leaders chose to condemn him. But they faced another problem. How would the crowds, who had honored Jesus and delighted in the religious leaders' embarrassment, respond?

Honor in first-century society was an unstable commodity. It could be gained. But it could also quickly be lost. The leaders' task now was to publicly strip Jesus of his honor; to degrade him and thus deprive him of the allegiance of the crowd.

Ideally, in the honor culture of the first century, those who benefited from another's generosity would remain loyal to him even if he suffered reversals. Certainly, in Judea there were thousands of families whose members had had their sight restored or paralysis lifted. One could have expected these people to remain loyal even in Jesus' darkest hours. But like his twelve disciples, when the critical moment arrived, "everyone deserted him and fled."[26]

The effort to degrade Jesus began in the Sanhedrin. "Some began to spit at him; they blindfolded him, [and] struck him with their fists."[27] In the morning, Jesus was bound and dragged before Pilate to be accused like a common criminal. When the crowd was given a choice of releasing Jesus or a terrorist named Barabbas, the chief priests (who by demeaning Jesus had demonstrated their superiority and regained their lost honor), stirred up the crowd to choose Barabbas. As for Jesus, they shouted, "Crucify him!"[28]

Mark's account of the death of Jesus emphasizes details that were utterly degrading in the eyes of first-century people. Jesus was flogged.[29] He was ridiculed and mocked by "the whole company of soldiers."[30] When Jesus stumbled under the weight of the cross he was forced to carry, another man was made to carry it for him. He was crucified between two robbers, and "those who passed by hurled insults at him, shaking their heads and saying, 'So! You who are going to destroy the temple and build it in three days, come down from the cross and save yourself!'"[31] He was even the butt of insults by the "two rebels" who were crucified with him.[32]

In the first century, crucifixion was the most horrific death possible. No Roman citizen could be condemned to crucifixion. That penalty was reserved for the worst of criminals. It's no wonder that the apostle Paul later described Christ's cross as "a stumbling block to Jews and foolishness to Gentiles."[33] But it is here that Mark turns the significance of Jesus' death upside down. Far from being degrading, Jesus' crucifixion is the ultimate proof of God's generosity. The Cross reveals God's commitment to show grace even to a depraved and rebellious humanity.

The ideal generous patron in first-century culture was a person who dispensed his gifts freely, without thought of anything he might gain by the giving. The appropriate response to such generosity was gratitude. Any worthy individual would show gratitude by praising the giver and offering his service in return. Even when a recipient showed himself to be unworthy, a generous patron might continue to give him gifts, hoping by his goodness to awaken an appropriate response in the recipient. While Jesus was with his disciples, he spoke of his approaching death, explaining, "The Son of Man did not come to be served, but to serve, and to give his life as a ransom for many."[34] By casting the Crucifixion as a voluntary act, the Gospel writer Mark showed that Jesus' death could no longer be categorized as degrading. It became the noblest of deaths, a death suffered for the benefit of others.

In Christ, God went far beyond every expectation of generosity. Jesus gave his life to provide the gift of life for those who had proved themselves to be his enemies. This is a theme that the apostle Paul emphasizes in Romans, where he writes, "Very rarely will anyone die for a righteous person, though for a good person someone might possibly dare to die. But God demonstrates his own love for us in this: While we were still sinners, Christ died for us."[35]

But was the death of Christ truly a noble sacrifice? Is Jesus truly the Son of God, as declared in Mark's thesis statement?[36] Mark's Gospel, like the others, concludes not with the Crucifixion, but with the Resurrection. Though in his humanity, Jesus was descended from King David, the apostle Paul writes to the believers in Rome, "[He] was declared to be the Son of God in power according to the Spirit of holiness by his resurrection from the dead."[37] The Resurrection vindicated Jesus' claims, restored his honor, and confirmed his identity as the Son of God.

How Luke Defines Jesus

Luke's portrait of Jesus has much in common with Matthew's and Mark's. He tells many of the same stories. The narrative follows the same basic script. Yet there are subtle differences. How does Luke want us to see Jesus?

The answer is powerfully suggested in his genealogy of Jesus. Luke traces Jesus' line back to Adam and the Creator. The implication is clear: Through Luke's eyes, we are to look at Jesus as a human being—in fact, as the *ideal* human being. First-century philosophers and moralists expressed the notion of an ideal human with the term *arête*. This term, meaning "excellence," reflects the belief that what is excellent fulfills the purpose for which it was created. In locating Jesus in the stream of humanity, Luke implies that Jesus is everything that a human was originally meant to be. But any first-century observer would have felt uncomfortable with Luke's narrative account of Jesus' words and actions, which simply do not fit the prevailing first-century stereotype of the ideal human.

We see this almost immediately. An angel appears to the priest Zechariah at the Jerusalem Temple. The same angel greets a young girl named Mary in Galilee. Mary, barely in her teens and from a family not even worth identifying, believes the angel's promise of a virgin birth. "I am the Lord's servant," she immediately responds. "May your word to me be fulfilled."[38] Mary is identified as "blessed . . . among women."[39] Zechariah, meanwhile, has been struck dumb "because," the angel tells him, "you did not believe my words."[40] Neither Mary nor Zechariah has responded as we might expect.

Throughout his Gospel, Luke tells stories that juxtapose men of high status with women of significantly lower status—due to their gender and other circumstances. For example, a woman "who lived a sinful life"[41] slips into the home of Simon, a respected and wealthy Pharisee, who has invited Jesus for dinner. The woman washes Jesus' feet with her tears, but Simon has not shown him even the minimum level of courtesy that custom required. The woman leaves forgiven, for she "loved much."[42]

Later, on a Sabbath day, Jesus heals a woman who has "had a spirit of infirmity [for] eighteen years."[43] When the ruler of the synagogue, a spiritual leader and authority, rebukes Jesus, Jesus angrily condemns him as a hypocrite. The ruler thinks nothing of untying an ox on the Sabbath so it can get a drink, but cares nothing for the suffering of this "daughter of Abraham."[44]

In another incident, the disciples are in the Temple courts, where wealthy men are ostentatiously depositing large sums of money into the Temple treasury. Jesus points out a poor widow who has deposited all that she had—"two very small copper coins"—and he says, "This poor widow has put in more than all the others."[45] In each of these pairings, the woman is praised and the man put to shame.

For first-century observers, their discomfort would increase when they came to the now-familiar story of Mary and Martha.[46] In that ancient Hebrew society, men were expected to operate in the public sphere, while women were expected to live and function in the private confines of the home. Typically, the only men a respectable Jewish woman would speak with were her male relatives, and even this was within the home rather than in public. A woman's opinion carried so little weight that she was not allowed to testify in a rabbinic court. So when Mary chose to sit with the men, listening to Jesus teach while Martha busily prepared a meal for everyone, we would expect Martha to be commended and Mary rebuked. But Jesus reversed this cultural norm. He gently rebuked Martha and said, "Mary has chosen what is better, and it will not be taken away from her."[47]

First-century observers might have felt a similar shock when they read Luke's account of the Resurrection. To whom did the angels appear at the site of the empty tomb? To *women*.[48] And who were the first to carry the message of Jesus' resurrection? Mary Magdalene, Joanna, Mary the mother of James, and others.[49]

In presenting Jesus as the ideal human being, Luke makes it clear that Jesus was not simply a man of his times. In fact, Jesus challenged the stereotypes that shaped first-century culture.

As we read through Luke, we gain many fascinating insights into the changes that Jesus modeled. In the first century, table fellowship—sharing a meal—was a significant social activity. When Levi chose to follow Jesus, he held a banquet for his friends: "tax collectors and others."[50] Jesus also attended, scandalizing the Pharisees and teachers of the law, who asked the disciples why Jesus would eat and drink with "tax collectors and sinners."[51] Jesus answered for himself, saying, "It is not the healthy who need a doctor, but the sick. I have not come to call the righteous, but sinners to repentance."[52] With this statement, he signaled his intention to fashion a new, inclusive community that would embrace everyone who responded to his call.

We see something similar when Jesus traveled to his hometown of Nazareth and taught in the synagogue.[53] Luke gives us more details than Matthew or Mark about this event. Jesus' friends and neighbors were "amazed at the gracious words that came from his lips,"[54] but they became enraged when Jesus reminded them of times in their history when God chose to show favor to pagans rather than to Jews.[55] The new community that Jesus intended to form was modeled on his own perfect manhood and would include many more than just the "chosen" people.[56] Members of the "out" group were to become part of the "in" group. Jesus made this same point in his parable of the great banquet: When those who were invited refuse to come, the doors are thrown open so that the outcasts may come in.[57] We see this theme also in the story of the good Samaritan, which teaches us to extend our concept of neighborliness to include our enemies.

This, of course, would have been most disquieting to a first-century reader of Luke's Gospel, who lived in a world in which social strata and behavioral norms were clearly defined. Yes, a person was stereotyped by family, gender, ethnicity (such as the despised Samaritans), and occupation (such as the hated tax collectors). But these stereotypes also gave each person a clear sense of identity and of how he or she fit into the social order. Everyone knew how to treat others and how others would treat them.

Then Jesus appeared. By his treatment of women, Samaritans, tax collectors, and sinners; by his compassion for the poor, the powerless, and the sick; and by his implied inclusion of foreigners, he shattered the familiar categories. For people whose identity was rooted in social status, this was a frightening prospect indeed.

We hear the uncertainty in Peter's voice when he says, "We have left all we had to follow you!"[58] Truly, the disciples had left everything. They had left their families, their occupations, their hometowns—everything by which they had identified themselves and by which others knew them. But Jesus had an answer.

"Truly, I say to you, there is no one who has left house or wife or brothers or parents or children, for the sake of the kingdom of God, who will not receive many times more in this time, and in the age to come eternal life."[59]

Jesus told them the truth. They and all the millions of others who would trust in Jesus would form a new community. They would be adopted into God's family and be identified as the children of God. In that family, in the community that formed around Jesus, they would learn how to live as Jesus lived. They would find a new and satisfying way of life.

Discussion Questions

1. Scan Mark's Gospel and locate at least three honor challenges. What were Jesus' opponents trying to do? How did his response increase his own honor and decrease that of his opponents? Have you ever experienced anything similar to an honor challenge? Explain.

2. Both Mark and Luke tell about Jesus' rejection in Nazareth (Mark 6; Luke 4). How do the differences in the accounts relate to the theme of each Gospel?

3. Read through the Gospel of Luke. Note each passage where the writer, or Jesus, seems to challenge stereotypes or provide an example to be followed in the new community that will form around Jesus.

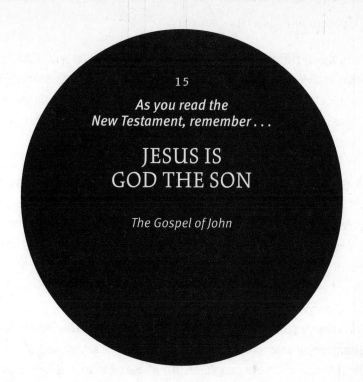

15

*As you read the
New Testament, remember . . .*

JESUS IS
GOD THE SON

The Gospel of John

The Pivotal Event

Nicodemus wrapped his cloak more tightly around himself, pulling it up to cover his mouth and chin. He slipped into the entry of the place he'd been told he would find Jesus.

He didn't particularly want to meet with Jesus. But he couldn't figure the man out. Like other powerful men who sat with him on the Sanhedrin, he acknowledged that God must be with this unusual man who had burst onto the scene teaching and performing miracles. "We know," Nicodemus said when he met with Jesus, "that you are a teacher who has come from God. For no one could perform the signs you are doing if God were not with him."[1]

Digging Deeper into the Gospel of John

The very first words of John's Gospel shout it: We're going back to the beginning!

In the beginning was the Word, and the Word was with God, and the Word was God. He was with God in the beginning. Through him all things were made; without him nothing was made that has been made. In him was life, and that life was the light of all mankind.[2]

Though John's Jesus is the same Jesus we've seen in Matthew, Mark, and Luke, he's also a Jesus we haven't fully seen in the other Gospels.

John's first words alert us to the fact that there are major differences between the Old Testament story and the New Testament story about to unfold. John is truly taking us back—back to a new beginning.

The Original Beginning

God's story as told in the Old Testament begins with the Creator fashioning a universe. He makes beings in his own image and likeness. His intent is to create people he can love and who will love him in return. God gives these human beings free will so that they might freely choose to love him. For an unspecified time, the first humans, Adam and Eve, live within the circle of God's love. Then the antagonist appears, planting seeds of doubt, and the first couple exchange their intimate relationship with the Creator for independence, never imagining the full consequences of that decision.

We're familiar with this account, and we've seen the major themes of God's story emerge through the experience of Abraham's descendants. But now, as John alerts us to a new beginning, it's important to understand an important difference between the two ways God tells us his story.

There is no real parallel between the way God's story is told in the Old Testament and the way God's story is told in the New Testament. True, it is all one story. The Old and the New Testaments belong together as one book. But even so, the one harmonious, unified story is told in different ways in the two testaments.

The New Testament was completed by the end of the first century of the modern era. Nothing that happened after that is revelatory. Church history, with its focus on councils, popes, schisms, and reformations, is *not* the framework in which God's story is worked out. Although the Old Testament and New Testament include historical events that enable us to understand and enter into God's story, we are *not* to look to events during the most recent two thousand years to understand God's story.

The New Beginning

I began this chapter on John's Gospel by noting that it opens in a radically different way than Matthew, Mark, or Luke. Though each Gospel is about Jesus, each writer's portrait of Jesus has a different theme. What about John's Jesus? The very first words, the very first chapter, tell us that Jesus is God himself—the Creator and Source of life. Jesus was present at the beginning, both with God and as God. As John's Gospel unfolds, the writer makes it clear that the one God exists in three persons: Father, Son, and Spirit.

John also makes it clear that God the Son, who is coequal and coeternal with the Father, entered—as a true human being—the universe he created.[3] In Jesus, God came to those who were his own, but they rejected him. "Yet," John tells us, "to all who did receive him, to those who believed in his name, he gave the right to become children of God—children born not of natural descent, nor of human decision or a husband's will, but born of God."[4]

In these words, John further defines the new beginning that his Gospel is about to introduce. God's story in the Old Testament was told through the history of the nation of Israel. Now, in the New Testament, God's story will be told through *individuals*—individuals who receive Jesus, who believe in his name, and who, by faith, become children of God.

This is why we need to read John as a new Genesis. Genesis and John both introduce us to God. Each is about relationship. Genesis depicts the fall of humanity, by way of Adam's choice of independence. John depicts God's restoration of humanity, by way of faith in Jesus.

The word *faith*, or *belief*, occurs no fewer than ninety-eight times in the Greek text of John's Gospel. It's important not to confuse *faith* (belief that leads to a *response* of trust and commitment) with *agreement* (belief that begins and ends with *knowledge*). James notes that "even the demons *believe*" (agree) that God exists.[5] They are absolutely certain that he's real, having rebelled against him in the dark, distant past. But that sort of belief isn't what John calls *faith*. And that sort of "belief in God" brings no benefit to the believer. No, what John means by "believing in," or "having faith in," is a *faith response*—of trust and commitment—to the person of Jesus. To believe in Jesus is to place such confidence in him that we commit ourselves completely to him. We rely totally on him for forgiveness of our sins and for our ultimate salvation.

The faith response also means we commit ourselves to Jesus daily, trusting him so completely that we live our lives *his* way. In a very real sense, placing our faith in Jesus means that we turn away from the independence that Adam chose—with its reliance on emotion, understanding, perception, and desires—to choose to live according to God's will. Jesus states it succinctly: "I seek not to please myself but him who sent me."[6] This is the door that biblical faith throws wide open for us. As God's redeemed and restored children, we can choose not to please ourselves but to please God. And that choice leads to real life and true community, here and now as well as eternally.

A Journey through John's Gospel

The Gospels of Mathew, Mark, and Luke are organized chronologically. John's is not. Instead, he focuses on a number of miracles performed by Jesus. These accounts are usually followed by extended teachings. Through each miracle, we learn more about God the Son. In the teachings, we are shown the appropriate faith response.

John passes over some of the early miracles recorded in the other Gospels, saying simply that "many people saw the signs he was performing and believed in his name."[7] The miracles had an impact on the religious leaders, too. But the leaders did not believe. One of them, Nicodemus, came to visit Jesus. He admitted, "We know that you are a teacher who has come from God. For no one could perform the signs you are doing if God were not with him."[8] Jesus stunned Nicodemus by telling him, "No one can see the kingdom of God unless they are born again."[9]

Genesis begins with God breathing life into Adam, a life Adam threw away when he cut his ties with God to go his own way. Here at the beginning of John's Gospel, we have a vision of life restored: "Everyone who believes may have eternal life in [Jesus]."[10]

The well-known John 3:16 follows: "For God so loved the world that he gave his one and only Son, that whoever believes in him shall not perish but have eternal life." The lines are clearly drawn. Each individual must choose. The choice is between a new, eternal, spiritual life or continuing death. "Whoever believes in [Jesus] is not condemned, but whoever does not believe stands condemned already because they have not believed in the name of God's one and only Son."[11]

The next miracle is a quiet one. Jesus speaks to a Samaritan woman, reveals her secrets, and announces himself as the Messiah. The woman believes and hurries to tell her neighbors about Jesus. Many of them come to see him for themselves.[12] Their response stands in sharp contrast to the response of the religious leaders when Jesus, "some time later," heals an invalid by the pool of Bethesda in Jerusalem.[13]

The leaders' initial reaction is to criticize Jesus for healing on the Sabbath. But when Jesus refers to God as "my Father," they are scandalized.[14] They view God as the Father of their nation (in the sense of *founder*), but Jesus is affirming a personal father/son relationship with the Creator. His claim arouses a murderous rage among the religious leaders: "Not only was he breaking the Sabbath, but he was even calling God his own Father, making himself equal with God."[15]

Jesus responds by reaffirming the relationship: "The Father . . . has entrusted all judgment to the Son, that all may honor the Son just as they honor the Father."[16] The truth is, Jesus says, "Whoever hears my word and believes him who sent me has eternal life and will not be judged but has crossed over from death to life."[17]

Jesus' claim is verified by the testimony of John the Baptist, by the witness of the Father through the miracles Jesus performs, and by "the very Scriptures that testify about me."[18] Again the issue is clearly drawn. To cross over from death to life, one must believe in (i.e., put one's trust in) Jesus as the Son of God.

The first five chapters of John's Gospel clearly focus on Jesus' identity and on the life-or-death response that each individual must make.

The next miracle is witnessed by a great crowd of people. Jesus feeds thousands with five barley loaves and two small fish.[19] The miracle brings to mind *manna*, the "bread from heaven" with which God fed Israel in the wilderness during the time of Moses.[20]

This miracle by Jesus excites the crowd. They imagine an endless supply of "bread from heaven to eat," and they implore Jesus to "always give us this bread."[21] Jesus responds by declaring, "I am the bread of life. Whoever comes to me will never go hungry, and whoever believes in me will never be thirsty."[22]

As Jesus develops this metaphor, many draw back, uncertain of what he means when he says, "Whoever eats my flesh and drinks my blood remains in me, and I in them," and "The one who feeds on me will live because of me."[23] Jesus is God's supernatural provision, both of eternal life and of all that is needed to sustain that life. Through faith in Jesus, the life that Adam lost can be restored. And through continuing reliance on Jesus—the metaphorical feeding on Jesus as the bread of life—our newly restored life can be sustained and nurtured.

The healing at Bethesda, which Jesus performed on a Sabbath, as well as reports of miracles he performed in Galilee were now the subject of whispered speculation among the people. *Is he a good man or a deceiver?*[24] When it comes time for the autumn Feast of Tabernacles, Jesus slips into Jerusalem anonymously. Halfway through the festival, he begins to teach openly in the Temple courts. Speculation intensifies. Could this Jesus be the Messiah? Temple guards sent to arrest Jesus return empty handed.[25]

The next time Jesus speaks to the people, he claims, "I am the light of the world."[26] The phrase "I am" (Greek, *ego eimi*) is found frequently in John's Gospel. It is Jesus' way of identifying himself as the "I Am" (in Hebrew, *Yahweh*) of the Old Testament.[27] "Whoever follows me," Jesus says, "will never walk in darkness, but will have the light of life."[28]

Light and darkness are sharply contrasted in John's Gospel and also in his three epistles. Light and darkness here are essentially moral terms that are closely linked to truth. As Jesus puts it, "If you hold to my teaching, you are really my disciples. Then you will know the truth, and the truth will set you free."[29]

In Robert Louis Stevenson's *Kidnapped*, there's a scene in which the hero, young David Balfour, goes to his uncle's home after his father's death. Arriving after dark, David is ushered into the ancient family manor by his uncle and led to a tiny kitchen, where the aged man has been eating gruel by the light of a single candle. His uncle tells him to climb a stone stairway, where he will find a place to sleep. The uncle refuses David a candle, so David stumbles upward into pitch darkness, his hands pressed against the cold stone wall. Suddenly a flash of lightning illumines the scene. David looks down in horror. The stairway opens onto empty space, with jagged rocks far below. The uncle intended for David to fall to his death. Only that sudden flash of light reveals the truth.

As the Light of the World, Jesus, too, reveals the truth. We wander about in darkness, in the grip of distorted desires, deceived by our illusions about what will benefit us and what will lead to harm. Jesus' teachings are the only safe guide to a fulfilling life. No wonder the disciples who "hold to [his] teaching" come to know—that is, to *experience*—the truth.

The religious leaders react angrily to Jesus' words. They claim that as descendants of Abraham, they have always been free in their covenant relationship with God. Jesus denies the claim and asks, "Why is my language not clear to you? Because you are unable to hear what I say. You belong to your father, the devil."[30] The argument ends with Jesus' assertion: "Very truly I tell you, . . . before Abraham was born, I am!"[31]

Jesus' next miracle drives home his message, as he restores sight to a man born blind.[32] The Pharisees investigate the healing, but even though they are unable to deny the miracle, they refuse to credit Jesus. These religious leaders, who claim to see, are the ones who are truly blind.

In the discourse that follows, Jesus claims, "I am the good shepherd" and "I am the gate for the sheep."[33] In the Old Testament, spiritual and political leaders are depicted as shepherds, and every Israelite knew there was only one opening into the pens where sheep were kept at night. As the good shepherd, Jesus will lay down his life for his sheep. His opponents, who claim to be shepherds, are actually thieves and robbers, intent only on killing and destroying for their own benefit.[34] The simple fact that these men do not recognize the good shepherd or acknowledge the miracles he performed in the name of the Father proves that they are not his sheep.

Jesus performs one more notable miracle. When Lazarus, a family friend, falls mortally ill, his sisters send for Jesus. But Jesus waits, arriving only after Lazarus has been dead for three days. Saying, "I am the resurrection and the life,"[35] Jesus goes to the site of the tomb and calls Lazarus back to life. The fact of the miracle is incontestable. But the religious leaders meet and determine that Jesus must die. "From that day on they plotted to take his life."[36]

The final week of Jesus' life begins with his triumphal entry into Jerusalem, where crowds hail him as the Messiah, the "king of Israel."[37] But John's account of Christ's final week focuses squarely on what happens at a supper that Jesus shares with his disciples just before his crucifixion. Warning his disciples that he will be with them "only a little longer," Jesus begins to prepare them for the era that lies ahead.[38]

His first words of instruction recall a key theme in the Old Testament. In the Torah, God calls his people to build a community of love. Now Jesus tells his disciples, "A new command I give you: Love one another. As I have loved you, so you must love one another. By this everyone will know that you are my disciples, if you love one another."[39] This is one of those themes that bind the Old and New Testaments together. The vision of a loving community is developed extensively in the New Testament epistles.

But the emphasis in this Last Supper teaching is on *promise*, not on command. Although Jesus will soon be absent from the flesh, he will nevertheless answer prayers offered in his name.[40] And Jesus will send the third person of the Trinity, the Holy Spirit, "to help you and be with you forever,"[41] and to provide divine guidance.[42] Jesus then describes the relationship that will exist between himself and believers in the coming era. He portrays himself as a vine and believers as branches. If we "remain in" him—that is, if we live in organic connection with him—his life will flow into us and enable us to "bear much fruit."[43] This organic connection is essential, Jesus says, because "apart from me you can do nothing."[44] This connection is maintained by loving Jesus so much that we keep his commandments.[45] Here again, Jesus repeats his new "command" to "love each other."[46]

Jesus then warns his disciples. In the future, they will live out their relationship with Jesus in a hostile world. "If the world hates you," Jesus says, "keep in mind that it hated me first."[47]

The thought of Jesus' leaving was devastating for the disciples. But Christ encouraged them. It was actually for the disciples' good that he was leaving, he said. "Unless I go away, the Advocate [the Holy Spirit] will not come to you; but if I go, I will send him to you."[48]

John's account of Jesus' Last Supper teachings concludes with a prayer that Jesus offers for the disciples and for all believers.[49]

John now moves into territory similar to that of the other three Gospels. Jesus is arrested and tried before the supreme religious council of the Jews. He is condemned to crucifixion by the reluctant Roman governor, executed, and buried. But on the third day, Jesus rises. He appears to many of his followers and spends time with his disciples, specifically taking time to reinstate Peter, who had denied three times during Jesus' trial that he even knew Jesus.

John sums up the purpose of his Gospel in John 20:31: "These are written that you may believe that Jesus is the Messiah, the Son of God, and that by believing you may have life in his name."

The Bridge

We've seen that each Gospel has a theme and purpose. John's Gospel presents Jesus as God the Son, urging all to respond to him with unwavering trust. It is John's Gospel that serves as our bridge into the New Testament epistles. The Old Testament tells God's story through the history of the Jewish people, with the threads of the story gradually woven into a narrative that spans centuries. John's Gospel, with its emphasis on the individual's faith response to Jesus as God the Son, is the perfect bridge into the New Testament era.

Though God's story as told in the New Testament is essentially the same story told in the Old Testament, it is told in a stunningly different way. There is nothing in the epistles that matches the interaction of the nation and people of Israel with other ancient nations and peoples. God's New Testament people are not identified with any nation at all. In fact, believers are to live their lives in essentially pagan societies, in a world that John says "is under the control of the evil one."[50] Christians will have to struggle all their lives against the corrupting beliefs and values of the societies in which they live. They will need every resource that God provides—the resources that Jesus promised in his Last Supper teaching. They will need the love and support of one another, gathering in little colonies planted on hostile shores. They will need prayer and the promise that Jesus will respond to pleas uttered in his name. They will need an organic relationship with Jesus that is maintained by love-motivated obedience to his words. And they will need to rely on the Holy Spirit, who will guide and empower them.

Perhaps most of all, they will need to understand that God's story is no longer being told in the history of a nation. *God's story is being told in and through the experience of each individual believer.*

Today, *we* are the tellers of God's story. The narrative of our lives is the medium through which God speaks—to us and to others. Along with the Gospels, the New Testament epistles instruct us on the story our lives are to tell.

Just how this affects our reading of the New Testament is something we will soon discover.

Discussion Questions

1. In this chapter, we emphasize and reemphasize the idea that God's story is told in different ways in the Old and New Testaments. Explain in your own words what this means.

2. What differences can you identify between the first three Gospels (Matthew, Mark, and Luke), which are all written from a similar vantage point, and John's Gospel? Why does the author view John as "Genesis revisited" and as a bridge into the New Testament epistles?

3. Quickly read through John 14–17. What themes do you see in this teaching of Jesus that reappear in the New Testament epistles?

16

*As you read the
New Testament, remember...*

WE ARE TO FOCUS ON THE NEW COVENANT, NOT THE OLD

Acts and the Epistles

The Pivotal Event

No one would have recognized Peter now. Once he'd been a blustering coward who lashed out when a serving maid accused him of being a follower of Jesus. Now he stood boldly in front of the rulers who had engineered the Savior's death, confidently proclaiming, "Salvation is found in no one else, for there is no other name under heaven given to mankind by which we must be saved."[1]

Digging Deeper into Acts and the Epistles

Historians have traditionally been fascinated by great men and great wars. I understand their concentration on leaders such as Peter the Great, who set a new course for Russia, or Adolf Hitler, whose vision of a thousand-year Reich led to the deaths of millions of people. Such men were larger than life, with an almost incalculable impact on their contemporaries and on our own times. That's the traditional approach to understanding history. Historians discover all they can about the great leaders—what they were like, what influences shaped them, what motivated their actions, and how they affected their own times and ours.

But recently some historians have shifted focus from the "great men and great conflicts" model to pay closer attention to what is called "the other side of history." This shift in focus can be credited to the fact that we have thousands upon thousands of letters, journals, and memoirs dating from America's Civil War. These writings provide fascinating insights into the thoughts and emotions of ordinary citizens as the conflict drew near, burst into flame, and died out at Appomattox. This "other side of history" has to do with the experience of ordinary men and women who lived and died in obscurity. The other side of the American Civil War is reflected in answers to long-unasked questions: What was it like to be a woman of the South in the 1860s? What was it like to be new recruit in the Union Army?

This recent fascination with the other side of history gives us a fresh perspective on the New Testament epistles. The Old Testament unfolds God's story through the experiences of a people and a nation: Israel. Acts and the Epistles challenge us to ask what it means to be an ordinary Christian, anytime and anyplace.

True, times and circumstances change. First-century Christians lived in a different world than the one twenty-first-century Christians inhabit. But despite the many differences, what it means to be a Christian in any age or culture shapes an individual's experience in similar ways. And it is in and through the lives of ordinary believers that God's story is told today.

The Acts of the Apostles

Acts begins with an excited but uncertain group of men and women huddled together in Jerusalem. Their risen Lord has promised them,

"You will receive power when the Holy Spirit comes on you."[2] And so they wait.

Then, on the Jewish festival day of Pentecost, the Holy Spirit came, filling and empowering them, bonding them to Jesus and to each other.[3] Empowered by God's Spirit, this unlikely group of men and women set out to invite the entire world to return to God through trust in Jesus. They began, as Jesus had said, "in Jerusalem" and went to "all Judea and Samaria, and to the ends of the earth."[4]

Acts pays almost no attention to governors or kings, except to mention them in connection with Peter's or Paul's activities. The focus in Acts is squarely on ordinary people who are affected by the gospel—on Peter, whose powerful preaching launched the Christian movement in Jerusalem; on Stephen, the first martyr; on Cornelius, the first non-Jewish believer in Jesus; on Paul, a persecutor of Christians who became the most fervent promoter of the faith; on Lydia, a businesswoman, who became the first convert in Europe; on a Philippian jailer; on a slave girl, whose owners were infuriated when Paul cast out an evil spirit that had enabled her to tell the future; and on converts such as Priscilla and Aquila, who joined in Paul's drive to spread the gospel throughout the Roman Empire. Each of these individuals represents the other side of history. Peter and Paul might have merited passing mention in a contemporary history, though no history of the time actually mentions them. Contemporary histories barely mention Jesus himself, though the historian Tacitus remarks that one "Christos" was reputedly the cause of some riots among the Jews of Rome. In fact, the very people whom history ignores are the focus of Acts, as God's story continues to unfold in a truly unexpected way.

This latest twist in God's story is so familiar to us that we may miss the change of direction represented in John's Gospel, Acts, and the Epistles. Yet that change truly is radical. The history of Israel was shaped by the nation's response to the Torah, a law given to a nation. That law envisioned a society in which God's people might experience rest and a foretaste of the eternal community of love that God is committed to provide for his own. But the prophet Jeremiah wrote of a future in which the Lord would make a new covenant with the people of Israel. In describing the new covenant, the Lord states, "It will not be like the covenant I made with their ancestors."[5]

There are many differences between the covenant of the law and the new covenant of grace. One difference in particular is important for us not to overlook. The covenant of the law had to do with the nation of Israel. That is, the blessings and disasters associated with the Mosaic law were linked to *national* loyalty and obedience. When we read Jeremiah's promise of a new covenant, we find God describing how he will relate to *individuals*. Notice Jeremiah's emphasis on the *people* of Israel as individuals, rather than on the nation of Israel as a people.

> "I will put my law *in their minds*
>   and write it *on their hearts*.
> I will be *their* God,
>   and they will be my people.
> No longer will they teach their neighbor,
>   or say to one another, 'Know the LORD,'
> because they will *all* know me,
>   *from the least of them to the greatest*,"
>
> declares the LORD.
>
> "For I will *forgive their wickedness*
>   and will remember their sins no more."[6]

The promised new covenant was instituted by the death of Jesus, who announced, "This cup is the new covenant in my blood, which is poured out for you."[7] The apostle Paul is particularly aware that his is a new covenant ministry.[8] His mission is to reach individuals with the gospel, to fashion them into communities, and to encourage the inner transformation promised in Jeremiah. In this, Paul is clearly focused on those whose stories lie on the other side of history—a side of history that is also the focus of both John and Acts and that provides a context for the New Testament epistles.

The mission of Peter and Paul and the other evangelists in the early church was to spread the story of Jesus and extend God's invitation to forgiveness and transformation in Christ. Paul's strategy is laid out clearly in the book of Acts. Along with a team of believers, Paul traveled to major population centers in the Roman Empire. There he began to preach and teach—first in the local synagogues; and then, as individuals responded to the gospel message, in whatever venue was available. At first, Paul taught the core of believers who gathered in each community; but after a relatively short time, he moved on to other cities. The mission of further evangelizing the cities and outlying areas was left with the young Christian communities that Paul had established. But these were truly young churches. To further instruct them, Paul wrote letters, which were quickly copied and passed from church to church, as were letters written by other leaders, such as Peter, James, and John. Paul also regularly sent individuals he was mentoring, such as Timothy and Titus, to visit the churches and to provide further instruction in Christian doctrine and lifestyle. In essence, the collection of letters assembled as our New Testament served, then and now, as a handbook of new-covenant living. What the Torah did to present the possibility of community to the people of Israel, the New Testament epistles do for us today.

It shouldn't surprise us that God's story in both Testaments is told within the same basic framework. Each assumes God's role in Creation, fashioning humans in his own image and likeness. Each assumes human freedom, with individuals able to choose to love God or to reject his love. Each assumes the Fall, with Adam declaring independence from God and passing on to his descendants the bent to go one's own way. Each assumes that choices have consequences and that God will permit each person's choices, even when those choices lead to suffering for others or eternal punishment for the individual. Each assumes that God continues to love every individual and that he will ultimately bless all who respond to his invitation to return to him. Each assumes that humans are redeemable and that God is eager to forgive. Each Testament assumes that ultimately God will establish the eternal community of love that has always been his intent.

The Old Testament describes how God's story was worked out within this framework through Israel's experience. The New Testament, with its new-covenant focus on individuals, is about how God's story is to be worked out in the lives of people living on the other side of history. The New Testament, in particular, asks,

- What does it mean for one to be a child of God?
- What does it mean to live a righteous life?
- What does it mean to live as a Christian in the world?
- What does it mean for us to be in community?

Reading the New Testament for answers to these questions anchors us securely in God's story. And as we live out the answers in our daily lives, God's story will be told and retold through our personal stories.

To hear the answers, we need to learn to read the Epistles as *story* rather than as theology. In the past, for example, when I read Paul's teaching in Romans 2 that non-Jews are held accountable to a "law" embedded in the conscience and will be judged by it, even as the Jews are responsible to the law of Moses, I used to ask, "How does this passage inform my understanding of God's relationship with the lost, and especially with those who have never heard of Jesus?" This is reading for *theology*. As I've read the text, I have identified a concept that I can relate to other concepts in my theological system. But in effect, I've relegated Paul's comments to the world of ideas—to an abstract, essentially impersonal world. I have failed to ask how this text affects people like me who are struggling to live within God's story.

Today I read this same passage from a different, distinctively *story-oriented* perspective. I see that Paul is referring to a terrible conflict that goes on in the heart of every human being. The Jew has a law, given by God through Moses, that clearly states God's expectations. In acknowledging that the law is God-given, the Jew agrees that what the law expects from him or her is right. But the Jew, in attempting to live according to God's law, constantly falls short. And this, Paul argues, isn't the experience of Jews alone. Non-Jews find themselves in the same situation. They may not have the law of Moses, but they do have a *conscience*. And conscience demonstrates that God created human beings with an innate realization that right and wrong exist, and with a belief that we are expected to do what is right. Though the specific actions that are judged "right" or "wrong" may differ by culture and society, every individual struggles with right/wrong issues in life. Everyone feels a responsibility to make right choices, yet too often we do the very things that we ourselves judge to be *wrong*—even as we acknowledge that we might have made another choice that would have been *right*. To experience this inner conflict is part of what it means to be human, and it's a testimony to the harmony of the Bible's story with reality.

To limit a New Testament passage to the realm of theology and treat it primarily as a source of abstract ideas is to *intellectualize* the New Testament. And if we simply intellectualize the teachings in the New Testament letters, we will surely miss how God intends his story to be worked out in our lives.

Let me be clear here. I'm not suggesting it is wrong to study theology. Nor is it wrong to explore the theological implications of what we read in the Bible. In a sense, theology serves as a framework within which we can better understand God's story, even as God's story provides the raw material out of which we are to construct our theology.

Without a theological framework, we're sure to misunderstand God's story. But it is clearly wrong to isolate theology from story. Yet it is the story, as told in Scripture, that is authoritative, and it must always be allowed to stand in judgment of our theology.

I suspect that our tendency to intellectualize what we read in the Bible is one reason why so few Christians experience the Bible as the living, vital, transforming book it is meant to be. We read it as theologians, attempting to fit this concept with that until we suppose we know "the truth." But in Scripture, truth is a revelation of reality, and we are called to *live* the truth rather than simply know it.

When we come to the New Testament with a sensitivity to its story, we come in full awareness of our humanity. We come to Scripture as weak and vulnerable beings, living with uncertainty and struggling to survive in a world beyond our control. We approach Scripture as flawed creatures, yet we are loved by God and love him in return, inviting Scripture to speak to us in our humanness. We open ourselves up to God and to others, eager to let God's story inform our lives and enable our own individual stories to make sense.

This approach to reading the New Testament is possible only because of what Paul expresses in 1 Corinthians 10:13. There the apostle makes it clear that "no temptation has overtaken you except what is common to mankind." *Peirasmos,* the Greek word translated "temptation," identifies a test, trial, or temptation. Though *peirasmos* has been translated as "temptation" here, the words *test* or *trial* capture Paul's intent more precisely. We are constantly faced with difficult choices. We are pushed and pulled by insistent voices all around us. We are driven by thoughts and desires we hardly dare to acknowledge. Yet none of the tests or trials we experience is unique. The stress, the fears, the doubts and uncertainties we face are all "common to mankind." Though the details of my life may differ from yours, you and I both understand what it means to know joy, grief, anger, rejection, and the host of emotions that surge within the human soul. When we come to Scripture in our humanness, aware of our need to understand God's story so that our own stories can have meaning within his story, God speaks to our hearts. And God shapes both us and our stories.

In Our Humanness

We humans are a broken people, living in a broken world. We don't need to know God's story to understand that. All we need to do is listen to the stories of those around us, stories that most people hide out of shame while pretending everything is right with them and the world. Each of us has stories we dare not tell, even though such stories are all around us. We seldom hear the story of the little girl who was ignored by her parents and now feels worthless and unworthy of love. We seldom hear the story of the child whose mother regretted she hadn't had an abortion, a child who now feels unheard and is driven to be the center of attention. We seldom hear the story of the boy whose father demanded perfection, who though today a successful and wealthy man, is still tormented by the conviction that no matter how successful he becomes he'll never be good enough to win his father's approval. We seldom hear the stories of girls who were sexually molested and who carry unmerited burdens of guilt and shame, or the stories of those who find themselves in the grip of depression. We usually don't know which of our neighbors are struggling to meet their house payments, are threatened with the loss of their jobs, or are worried about choices their children are making. Chances are that those we see at church every Sunday aren't aware of moments when we wonder anxiously what the latest tests the doctor ordered will reveal, or aware of the pain of arthritis that makes walking an agony. We may not tell even our best friends about the hurt and conflict in our marriages, or about our fears concerning the future. And we almost never hear the stories of those struggling with addiction. They're silent about the shame they feel as they surrender again and again to their craving for alcohol, drugs, gambling, or pornography.

Because we seldom tell our own stories about such things or hear others tell their stories, we tend to assume that our fears and failures are unique, something that we alone experience. And then God speaks to us in the words of Paul and tells us that no trial has overtaken us that is not common to mankind. The very things that challenge us most, the things that in our minds isolate us from others, are the common experiences of all humanity. Experiencing such trials is a part of what it means to be human, fallen creatures in a fallen world. But then Paul continues, "God is faithful; he will not allow you be tested beyond what you can bear. But *when you are under the pressure of painful trials*, he will also provide a way out so that you can stand up under it."[9]

Note that the text does not say God will change our circumstances or remove the pressure. In fact, the way out is to stand up under the trial. God's new-covenant story is a story of *redemption* and *transformation*. For now, however, it's enough to remember that we are to come to Scripture, and especially to the New Testament, with a growing awareness of our brokenness as fallen human beings. It is in our brokenness, in our weakness, that God's story becomes our story and that his story is told through ours.

In the next four chapters, we'll see how the New Testament speaks to those of us who live on the other side of history. And we'll discover how to read the New Testament as individuals who are being redeemed as we live in community in a hostile world.

Discussion Questions

1. What does it mean to say that the New Testament is all about people "on the other side of history"?

2. Read any two consecutive chapters in Acts. How do they either support or challenge the "other side of history" approach?

What significance do you find in the replacement of the Mosaic covenant at the institution of the new covenant?

3. Explain the contrast between reading the New Testament for its theology and approaching it from the perspective of brokenness. What differences can you see in the two approaches? What has been your approach when you read the Bible, and especially the New Testament?

17

*As you read the
New Testament, remember...*

WE ARE GIVEN
A NEW IDENTITY
IN CHRIST

The Epistles

The Pivotal Event

Paul had hated to leave. Still, he hadn't abandoned the young church he'd established in Ephesus. Paul sat down to write a letter that would serve as a handbook on spiritual warfare for the church. The very first thing that Paul dealt with as he wrote was the identity of these new believers.[1]

Digging Deeper into the Epistles

They had looked forward to the empty nest. Time to travel. Time to renew their relationship. Time to be by themselves. But then their daughter met an eleven-year-old boy who needed a family. And she kept insisting, "You've got to meet him!"

A few days ago, he celebrated his twelfth birthday in their home.

It was an unexpected adoption. The boy is of a different race. He's active, full of energy—so talkative, so much a child. Needing so much of their time, giving so much joy. Yet there's no doubt that our friends' unexpected adoption means a totally new life and a totally different future for their new son.

The apostle Paul reminds us that life is like this for you and me in our relationship with God. Writing to the believers in Ephesus, Paul tells us that God chose us "for adoption to sonship through Jesus Christ, in accordance with his pleasure and will."[2] In the Roman Empire, adoption as a son was special. The new son's ties to his old family were severed completely. Allegiance was owed only to the father of the adoptive family. And all the resources of the new family were available to the adopted child. Because God was pleased to adopt us, we can look forward to a totally new life, a totally different future.

Genesis begins with the introduction of God, the central figure in the Bible's story, and then quickly introduces humanity in the persons of Adam and Eve. We immediately discover that God has created the world as a home for these very special beings who are made in his image. We discover that God's story is a love story, with the Creator as lover and human beings as his beloved. But all too soon Adam and Eve declare independence from God. Terrible consequences flow from that choice. And it raises the question, Can sinful human beings ever be restored to their original state of harmony with the Creator?

Paul answers this question in the first chapter of his letter to the Ephesians. And the answer, perhaps surprisingly, is *no*. Human beings cannot be restored to an Edenic state of innocence. What God has chosen to do instead is to adopt people—lost and sinful individuals—into his own family. We are now loved as God's own precious sons and daughters.

This unexpected adoption is the first key to understanding God's story as it is told in the New Testament. It is still a love story. God is still the central figure, and we human beings are still his beloved. It is simply that the bond of love revealed in the New Testament is even stronger, even more powerful and unbreakable than the original.

The letter to the Ephesians begins by recounting the role of each person of the Trinity in bringing about this stunning new relationship we now enjoy. God the Father has "blessed us in the heavenly realms with every spiritual blessing."[3] Moreover, "he chose us in him before the creation of the world to be holy and blameless in his sight."[4] It was "in love" that he "predestined us for adoption to sonship through Jesus Christ," an action rooted in nothing except "his pleasure and will."[5] This stunning and unexpected adoption will ever be to the "praise of his glorious grace, which he has freely given us in the One he loves."[6]

Paul then moves on to discuss the role of Jesus, God the Son. In Jesus, "we have redemption through his blood, the forgiveness of sins, in accordance with the riches of God's grace."[7] God has revealed to us that he intends "to bring unity to all things in heaven and on earth under Christ."[8] Redemption, a theme introduced so powerfully in the Exodus story, is the dominant emphasis here as well, experienced not only by individuals who are adopted into God's family, but ultimately by "all things in heaven and on earth." Again the letter reminds us that "we were also chosen" in accord with "the plan of him who works out everything in conformity with the purpose of his will," in order that we "might be for the praise of his glory."[9]

The letter then focuses on the role of the Holy Spirit. Like all who were "included in Christ when you heard . . . the gospel of your salvation," we were "marked in him with a seal, the promised Holy Spirit, who is a deposit guaranteeing our inheritance until the redemption of those who are God's possession."[10]

Though adoption into God's family is unveiled only in the New Testament, it has been part of God's plan and purpose from the beginning. And each person of the Godhead has been totally invested in accomplishing that purpose. God the Father chose us, God the Son redeemed us, and God the Spirit serves as a seal of ownership, guaranteeing our ultimate transformation when Jesus returns. As believers in Jesus, we now face life from the secure position of one who is God's child and is totally loved by him.

Life as an Adopted Child

When I was in the navy, one thing troubled some of my fellow sailors. Knowing that I claimed that God had forgiven all my sins in Jesus, they couldn't understand why I didn't just do anything I wanted. "If God won't send you to hell," they objected, "why not just sin?"

They never could seem to grasp my response: "I *am* doing anything I want to. I just don't *want* to do the things you're talking about. Knowing that God loves me changes my *want to*." The confidence that I am a child of God, and that he loves me just as I am, creates a desire in me to please him.

This is the point the apostle John makes in his first epistle:

> See what great love the Father has lavished on us, that we should be called children of God! And that is what we are! . . . Dear friends, now we are children of God, and what we will be has not yet been made known. But we know that when Christ appears, we shall be like him, for we shall see him as he is. *All who have this hope in him purify themselves, just as he is pure.*[11]

The truth that we can now approach life as adopted sons or daughters of God—that is, *secure in God's love*—is hard for many believers to grasp. They're too aware of their own penchant for sinning and too aware of the flaws of others in the faith community. Paul deals with the tension between *identity* and *lifestyle* in his second letter to the Corinthians.

After reviewing several problems in the church at Corinth, Paul complains, "Brothers and sisters, I could not address you as people who live by the Spirit but as people who are still worldly—mere infants in Christ."[12] The believers in Corinth were "acting like mere humans," not like sons and daughters of God.[13] Yet in his second letter, Paul reassures them. He has learned to fix his eyes "not on what is seen, but on what is unseen."[14] Paul is realistic about the faults and the flaws in these young believers. Yet he also knows that "what is seen is temporary, but what is unseen is eternal."[15]

In developing this thought, Paul contrasts behavior with "what is in the heart."[16] There, deeply embedded within us, is the love for the Father that animated Jesus as he lived out his life here on earth. Thus, it is "Christ's love [that] compels us."[17] It is Christ's love that will bring about our transformation toward Christlikeness.

After all, Paul argues, Christ died for all. The purpose of his death was to effect the transformation that the new covenant promises; an inner transformation that produces a new way of life, "that those who live should no longer live for themselves but for him who died for them and was raised again."[18]

Paul argues that it is simply unthinkable that God's purpose in Christ's death should fail. That purpose was to transform human beings who have been adopted into God's family so that those who have the new life that God provides should stop living for themselves and live for God's glory instead. God's intention is not to achieve conformity to an external standard, but to bring about an inner transformation that powers a godly lifestyle. "So from now on," Paul writes, "we regard no one from a worldly point of view."[19] Instead, we realize that "if anyone is in Christ, the new creation has come: The old has gone, the new is here!"[20] We now rely on what is in our hearts, where God has planted new life in Christ.

Thus, Paul characterizes his ministry as one of *reconciliation*, of helping believers bring their lives into harmony with who they truly are as God's adopted children. And how is this done? Paul's answer is that we model our ministry on God's, namely, "that God was reconciling the world to himself in Christ, not counting people's sins against them."[21] No longer are our sins and failures the issue, for "God made him [Jesus] who had no sin to be sin for us, so that in him we might become the righteousness of God."[22]

When we approach life as God's adopted sons and daughters, we do so with full realization that we are a beloved and forgiven people. Sin, judgment, and condemnation simply are no longer issues, for Christ, in his death and resurrection, provides both forgiveness and new life. Understanding this, we can live without fear, without guilt, and without shame. We can recognize and acknowledge our failures, for we are confident that as we come to know God better and love him more, he will transform us from within. In fact, he is already at work in us.

We do not glorify God by hiding our flaws and pretending to be "good Christians." It is by living authentic lives with others, sharing honestly who we are, that Jesus is glorified. The truth is, God's Spirit is *already* at work within us, making us more and more like Jesus. As we live openly and honestly with others, they will see that change in us and will meet Jesus in us.

At the conclusion of Ephesians 1, Paul prays that we might "know the hope to which he has called [us], the riches of his glorious inheritance in his holy people, and his incomparably great power for us who believe."[23] That "great power" is the same "mighty strength he exerted when he raised Christ from the dead."[24] It is *resurrection power*. As that transforming power is exercised in human beings who have been adopted into God's family, his story is being told today.

Understanding Redemption

Paul goes to great lengths in Ephesians 1 to let us know how precious we are as God's adopted children. It's stunning, then, to read the first words of Ephesians 2: "As for you, you were dead in your transgressions and sins." Even worse, "you followed the ways of this world and of the ruler of the kingdom of the air [Satan], the spirit who is now at work in those who are disobedient."[25] And Paul goes on: "All of us also lived among them at one time, gratifying the cravings of our flesh and following its desires and thoughts. Like the rest, we were by nature deserving of wrath."[26]

Paul makes it very clear that nothing we've done, and nothing we have been, has commended us to God or merited our adoption into his family. It was only because of God's "great love for us" that he extended mercy to us by giving us life in Christ, "even when we were dead in transgressions."[27] It is only by grace that we have been saved.[28] That word, *saved*, takes us back to the roots of the doctrine of redemption in the Old Testament. There we meet the people of Israel, enslaved and helpless.

Each of the three Hebrew words translated *redeem* or *ransom* is "cast against the background of helplessness. Each finds human beings captured, held captive by the power of forces they cannot overcome. Only by the intervention of a third party can bondage be broken and the person freed."[29]

In Egypt the bondage was physical, and God acted to free his captive people by acts of judgment that turned Egyptian society upside down. In the New Testament, the bondage is spiritual—captivity to "the cravings of our flesh."[30] We are spiritually dead, and though we may struggle to live as our conscience demands, we can never break free of death's grip. Nevertheless, Paul tells us, "God, who is rich in mercy, made us alive with Christ even when we were dead in transgressions."[31]

God could not free us from spiritual bondage and provide us with renewed spiritual life through miraculous works of power, as he did when he freed the Israelites from Egypt. Though the events in Exodus, by which God reclaimed his people, serve as a model for our redemption as individuals, that redemption could only be accomplished by

God himself, in the person of Jesus, stepping into the universe he had created and reclaiming us through his death and resurrection.

> These passages [where the word *redemption* is found] make it clear that Jesus' life is the price of redemption (Matthew 20:28; Mark 10:45). The redemption price, the "precious blood of Christ, a lamb without blemish or defect," was paid to release people from "the empty way of life" received from their forefathers (1 Peter 1:18-19). Redemption is a release "from all wickedness" (Titus 2:14). The redemption that Jesus accomplished by his blood is an eternal redemption (Hebrews 9:11-12), intended to so cleanse us that "we may serve the living God" (Hebrews 9:14). Thus, redemption in the NT focuses on the condition of the believer, who had been locked in a wicked and empty way of life, and on the price of redemption, the blood of Christ. It also focuses on the result of redemption, a commitment by the believer to serve God.[32]

As Paul continues his exposition in Ephesians 2, he wants us to understand clearly that redemption is a work of God alone, "that in the coming ages he might show the incomparable riches of his grace, expressed in his kindness to us in Christ Jesus."[33] Truly, it is by grace we have been saved, and throughout the coming ages, it is God alone who will be glorified by our redemption.

The Impact of Redemption

The unruly mob of freed slaves who hurried out of Egypt were led by God's fiery-cloudy pillar, which guided them to Mount Sinai and on to a new land and a new life.

The New Testament uses similar imagery to depict our redemption in Christ.

The apostle Peter, in his first letter, draws an analogy between the experience of Noah and our experience of redemption.[34] Just as Noah was carried through the waters of judgment in the ark and deposited safely in a new world, so too believers are carried safely through the waters of divine judgment in Christ, and brought into a new world in which we "do not live the rest of [our] earthly lives for evil human desires, but rather for the will of God."[35]

We see the same imagery in the New Testament's references to Christ's Kingdom. Through Jesus, God "has rescued us from the dominion of darkness and brought us into the kingdom of the Son he loves, in whom we have redemption, the forgiveness of sins."[36] In this Kingdom, we are "all children of the light and children of the day. We do not belong to the night or to the darkness. . . . For God did not appoint us to suffer wrath but to receive salvation through our Lord Jesus Christ. He died for us so that whether we are awake or asleep, we may live together with him."[37]

As redeemed children of God, we are forgiven, and we are being transformed. But the redemption that God has in mind goes even further: "The creation itself will be liberated from its bondage to decay and brought into the freedom and glory of the children of God."[38] Paul pictures the creation as "groaning as in the pains of childbirth right up to the present time," even as we ourselves "groan inwardly as we wait eagerly for our adoption to sonship, the redemption of our bodies."[39] The world in which we live is not the world God created; it is but a fallen replica, subject to death and decay. The Fall corrupted not only *human* nature, it corrupted *all* of nature. And though Christ's sacrificial death provided redemption for the universe as well as for human beings, the full impact of all that he accomplished on the cross will not be realized until the end of history.

Of greater immediate impact is another aspect of redemption that Paul now introduces. "We know," he writes, "that in all things God works for the good of those who love him, who have been called according to his purpose."[40] This does *not* mean that everything that happens to God's adopted children is *good*. In fact, many of the "all things" we experience are terrible, devastatingly painful, and traumatic. But Paul *is* saying is that *in all things*, God is at work with the *good* (Greek, *agathos*—benefit, profit) of his children in view. Put simply, God is at work to redeem the evil that occurs in our lives and to transform it into experiences that will benefit us.

We cannot fully understand the doctrine of redemption without seeing this aspect of God's work in our lives or without understanding that our transformation into the likeness of Jesus is the primary benefit that God has in mind for us.[41]

Here's an example: A woman named Carolyn grew up in a physically and emotionally abusive home, with a mom she believed resented and hated her. Her early years were not only deeply painful but also scarring. Yet many years later, when she volunteered to work at a shelter for single abused women and their children, she discovered that her pain had been a gift. She not only understood the women who came to the shelter, she also loved them; and they loved her in return. By transforming Carolyn's pain and her scars, God redeemed the sins that her parents had committed against her, transforming them into a source of empathy and hope for the women she worked with.

The apostle Paul writes about a similar experience. In 2 Corinthians 1:4, he praises God "who comforts us in all our troubles, so that we can comfort those in any trouble with the comfort we ourselves receive from God." Paul depicts our sufferings as the sufferings of Christ overflowing into our lives, and he shows that the comfort we find in Christ overflows to others. God redeems our distress, and in the process enables us to comfort others.[42]

The apostle Peter speaks to those who desire to "love life and see good days" but are buffeted by undeserved suffering. He quotes from Psalm 34:12-16, which lays out the normal course of events: *do* good to *see* good. Because God's eyes are on the righteous, we can expect good to be rewarded.[43]

Peter then looks at the unusual situation in which a person who is eager to do what is right suffers for it. In that case, the children of God are not to be afraid; they are rather to recognize that Jesus is Lord and meet the challenge with a positive attitude, being ready to explain how they live in hope despite injustice.[44] In everything, Peter adds, it is important to keep a clear conscience, for "it is better, if it is God's will, to suffer for doing good than for doing evil."[45]

Peter then points us to the example of Jesus, who died because of the sins of others, not because of any sins of his own. In this case of ultimate injustice, the righteous one was executed, and the unrighteous, who deserved punishment, seemed to have escaped. But even this terrible injustice was redeemed. It was through Jesus' death that we were brought into relationship with God. As for Jesus, though "he was put to death in the body," he was "made alive in the Spirit."[46] History's greatest injustice was redeemed in such a way that *we* were saved and the resurrected Jesus was glorified.

The point of Peter's illustration is clear. So many of the "all things" in our lives are painful. So many traumatic experiences have scarred us in ways that others can never understand. But God is a God of redemption. He has saved us and adopted us into his family as dearly loved sons and daughters. Through the redemption that is available in Christ Jesus, God is at work today, transforming us into his likeness. And among the wonders of his grace, God is redeeming our past, even our most painful experiences.

Discussion Questions

1. Compare and contrast how the love relationship between God and humanity is developed in Genesis and in the New Testament.

2. Compare and contrast how the theme of redemption is expressed in the Exodus story, and the way this theme is developed in the New Testament.

3. How would your life and your feelings be affected if you were convinced that as God's adopted child, you are totally loved and totally forgiven?

*As you read the
New Testament, remember . . .*

WE ARE CALLED TO LIVE AS NEW-COVENANT PEOPLE

The Epistles

The Pivotal Event

For a man brought up as a Pharisee, proud of his commitment to the Torah and dedicated to strict observance, Paul's discovery that God would accept him only on the basis of his faith in Jesus was a jolting surprise. Years later, he sat down to write the book of Romans, a powerful treatise in which God promises that "the righteous requirement of the law" will be "fully met in us."[1] As Paul explains, "If the Spirit of him who raised Jesus from the dead is living in you, he who raised Christ from the dead will also give life to your mortal bodies because of his Spirit who lives in you."[2]

Digging Deeper into the Epistles

I don't remember much from my studies as a philosophy major at the University of Michigan. After all, I received my bachelor's degree in

1958, well over half a century ago. But I do remember a dictum credited to Immanuel Kant that *ought* implies *can*. As Kant puts it in *Religion within the Boundaries of Mere Reason*, "If the moral law commands that we ought to be better human beings now, it inescapably follows that we must be capable of being better human beings."[3]

Even before two world wars and the Holocaust shattered our belief that humanity is evolving morally toward an era of peace and prosperity, there was abundant evidence to the contrary. Even when we agree on what we *ought* to do, and even if we *can* live by that moral imperative, most people, at times, choose *not* to. We might be free to do our best, but all too often we choose to do our worst.

In the earliest chapters of God's story, we're introduced to two human beings who were created with a truly free will. This was both a blessing and a curse. A person with a totally free will has the option to make right and beneficial choices, but he or she also has the option to make wrong and disastrous choices. Still, in the case of Adam and Eve, free will was an absolutely necessary gift. God had no interest in creating puppets. He was committed to creating beings in his own image and likeness.

There was an even more compelling reason for Adam and Eve to be given free will: It was necessary in order for them to make the one essential choice on which the Creator's vision depended. God's ultimate intention was, and is, to fashion an eternal community of people who will not only love God and be loved by him, but will also be infused with the kind of love displayed within the Trinity. There is no way this kind of love can be coerced. It must be given freely. To make it possible for us to freely choose to love God, it must be possible for us to choose *not* to love God.

As the story unfolds, Adam and Eve chose independence rather than intimate relationship with their Creator. His love was rejected, and humans were supposedly free.

Christian theologians such as Luther and Erasmus have debated whether fallen human beings still have a will that is free to love God. But in the Bible, the developing story focuses our attention on what we humans *do* rather than on what we *might* do. The Bible tells us that one of Adam's sons chose to murder his own brother, and that as the ages passed, human society deteriorated until "every inclination of the thoughts of the human heart was only evil all the time."[4]

In Romans 1, the apostle Paul traces the path of this deterioration. Later, he argues that both Jews and Gentiles continually fall short of an appropriate response to God's "kindness, forbearance and patience."[5] Paul offers proof of his argument by quoting Psalm 14:1: "There is no one righteous, not even one."[6] *Ought* might well imply *can*, but history and our own personal experience make it all too clear that *ought* does not imply *will*.

God's Choice

As the story in Genesis continues, we see God's response to Adam's declaration of independence. God reaches out to the first pair. He offers history's first blood sacrifice and cloaks Adam and Eve in the skins of the slain animals.[7] In this, he opens a door through which Adam's offspring might approach God. Without violating humanity's free will, God may not be able to override the terrible consequences that flow from the choice that Adam made, but God will not give up on humankind. He will walk through history alongside us, honoring our freedom to choose, yet prepared with responses of his own, whatever choices we make—responses that will ultimately bring about the future he has always envisioned for those he loves.

The continuous interaction between humanity's free choices and God's responses is a major element in God's story. We see this with exceptional clarity in the establishment of the law. All the Torah's moral and ritual laws, its ways of worship and celebration, are intended to shape a community here on earth that will reflect aspects of the eternal community of love that will be established at history's end. But as Deuteronomy 28 makes clear, in order to experience a community of love, each generation of Israelites must choose to be loyal to God and live according to the Torah. With loving care, God carefully lays before his people the benefits of obedience and the disastrous consequences of disobedience. He wants each generation to fully understand how significant their choices are. As we will see, human choice is a major element in the way God's story unfolds in the New Testament, as well.

Before we continue exploring the New Testament, though, it's important to be clear on one point: The story in both Testaments derives its structure and direction from *covenants*. Several of these covenants—the Abrahamic, the Davidic, and the new covenant—can be defined as *promise covenants*. Each contains statements of what God intends to do. Each is given legal status as a binding commitment (promise) by its identification as a covenant. Each of these promise covenants is unconditional. Finally, complete fulfillment of each promise covenant will take place at history's end. All that God promises will be realized in the *eschaton*, the "divinely ordered climax of history,"[8] when God puts an end to evil, sin, and suffering, and establishes an eternal community of love.

These characteristics of the promise covenants help us better understand what's different about the law-based covenant. First, under the law, God's intentions are contingent on human choice. Thus, Deuteronomy 28:1 begins, "If you fully obey the LORD your God and carefully follow all his commands I give you today, [*then* is implied] the LORD your God will . . ."

Second, the conditions stated in the Mosaic law are predicated on the choices of the Israelites as a *people* or *nation*; that is, as a corporate entity. Redemption from Egypt established God's claim on Israel as his own cherished possession. The law defines how the people as a whole might experience rest, security, and God's blessings in their lifetimes. But God's people could experience those blessings only if they, collectively, were loyal to God and carefully followed his commands and decrees.

In our reading of the Old Testament, we've all seen the choices that generation after generation of God's people made. Kant may have been philosophically correct in arguing that *ought* implies *can*. But God's story makes it very clear that whatever might be *possible*, we humans consistently, universally make wrong choices.

Old and New Covenants

The Bible refers to the Old Testament law in a variety of ways. In the original language, *law* is *torah*, a broad term meaning "divine instruction." It is also called "the Law," "the Law of Moses," and "the Old Covenant." The term *old covenant* emerges from Jeremiah's prediction that "'the days are coming,' declares the Lord, 'when I will make a new covenant with the people of Israel and with the people of Judah. It will not be like the covenant I made with their ancestors.'"[9] The writer to the Hebrews comments, "By calling this covenant 'new,' he has made the first one obsolete; and what is obsolete and outdated will soon disappear."[10]

Paul, too, is critical of the Old Testament law. Whatever benefits the Old Covenant might have offered Israel, the law could impart neither life nor righteousness. "For if a law had been given that could impart life, then righteousness would certainly have come by the law."[11]

The law given through Moses at Sinai had several functions. First, it served to reveal the moral character of the Creator. Second, it established God's expectations for the behavior of his people. As a statement of expectations, the law served to direct the choices of God's people, with blessings promised for corporate obedience and disastrous consequences for corporate disobedience. But Paul identifies a third function of the law. With its revelation of God and its explicit statements of his expectations, the law is intended to make human beings "conscious of our sin."[12] In this, the law is like a mirror, reflecting to us the truth that we all fall short and are sinners.

But the law was never intended to be a road map for individual salvation or private blessing. Salvation has always been rooted in a faith response to God.[13] All too often, the ability of a godly individual to enjoy a comfortable life hinges on choices made by other people. Habakkuk mourns in his complaint about injustice in his day that when "the wicked hem in the righteous . . . justice is perverted."[14]

Paul argues powerfully that we are declared righteous on the basis of our faith, "apart from the works of the law."[15] This shocked his Jewish readers, who assumed that their standing with God and their salvation depended on conforming to the law's demands. It seemed that Paul's "by faith" teaching robbed the law of meaning, and that because the law was given by God, Paul's *gospel of grace* must be flawed. But Paul responds, "Do we, then, nullify the law by this faith? Not at all! Rather, we uphold the law."[16] That is, we uphold the law by reframing our understanding of its function. The sages and rabbis did not realize the limitations of the law:

- It could reveal God and his character.
- It could guide the people of Israel into a way of life that would bring corporate blessing.
- It could function as a mirror, reflecting how far we fall short of God's righteousness.
- But it could not save us from the consequences of our sinful rebellion.

With these limitations in mind, we can better understand Paul's insistence that we "are not under the law, but under grace."[17] The law, that "obsolete" system, which nevertheless reveals something of God's moral character and continues to unveil us as sinners, has no role at all in the transformation of those who have been adopted into God's family.

The Good, the Bad, and the Ugly

"The law is holy, and the commandment is holy, righteous and good," Paul writes in Romans 7:12. The law is good in that it provides a trustworthy portrait of righteous behavior. The law is also good in that through it, "sin might be recognized as sin."[18]

What's bad about the law is that it is totally incapable of producing righteousness. Even worse, Paul says, the law curses us. Quoting Deuteronomy 27:26, he writes, "As it is written: 'Cursed is everyone who does not continue to do everything written in the Book of the Law.'"[19] God does not grade on a curve. The law is an absolute standard. To be acceptable to God on the basis of what we do, we must "continue to do *everything*" the law requires. Thus, rather than speak life, the law speaks death and God's condemnation.[20]

All this is bad enough, but there is also an ugly side to the law. Paul teaches that our "sinful passions" are "aroused by the law" and bear "fruit for death."[21] Kant's moral imperative—*ought*—stimulates the rebelliousness in our nature and actually energizes our *won't*!

Many people have a problem with the idea that we are not under law. Because the law is "holy, righteous and good," they fear that abandoning the law means turning our backs on righteousness. But nothing could be further from the truth. God calls his adopted children to live righteous and holy lives. And because the law cannot produce righteousness in us, God takes an entirely new approach.

Life in the New Covenant

As we saw earlier, Jeremiah predicted that God would one day make a new covenant with his people, one that would "not be like" the law given in the time of Moses.[22]

The law defined how the corporate nation of Israel was to behave in order to experience present blessings. The new covenant, in addition to providing complete forgiveness of sins,[23] also *provides for the progressive inner transformation of the child of God here and now.* As Jeremiah prophesied, "'This is the covenant I will make with the people of Israel after that time,' declares the Lord. 'I will put my law in their minds and write it on their hearts.'"[24]

Jesus stunned the people who gathered to listen to his Sermon on the Mount. He reaffirmed the authority of the law but went on to say, "Unless your righteousness surpasses that of the Pharisees and the teachers of the law, you will certainly not enter the kingdom of heaven."[25] The teachers of the law, and especially the Pharisees, were dedicated to the most rigorous observance of the law possible. How could anyone's righteousness surpass theirs?

Jesus provided a series of illustrations, each of which identified a behavior required in the law, and then revealed the source from which violations of the law arose.

"You have heard that it was said . . . , 'You shall not murder. . . .' But I tell you that anyone who is angry with a brother or sister will be subject to judgment."[26]

"You have heard that it was said, 'You shall not commit adultery.' But I tell you that anyone who looks at a woman lustfully has already committed adultery with her in his heart."[27]

The law can regulate behavior, but there is nothing it can do to change what is in the human heart. And God is ultimately concerned about *who we are*, not just *what we do*.

Because every human being is born with a nature that is inherently sinful,[28] we simply must be transformed from within if we are to live righteous and holy lives. Paul's claim that "if anyone is in Christ, the new creation has come" is especially significant.[29] Peter goes even further, stating that through Christ, we "participate in the divine nature, having escaped the corruption in the world caused by evil desires."[30]

When we understand the implications of God's new-covenant promise to "put my laws in their hearts,"[31] we begin to understand the nature of the choices faced by Christians. The old covenant, the law, focused the attention of God's people on *behavior*. The new covenant focuses our attention on *character*, promising a progressive inner transformation that will produce righteous living. God's intent in giving us new life and a new nature is "that the righteous requirement of the law might be fully met in us, who do not live according to the flesh but according to the Spirit."[32]

How then are we, as God's adopted children, to use the freedom of choice he has given us? We must choose the path prescribed by the apostle Paul, to "put off your old self, which is being corrupted by its deceitful desires; to be made new in the attitude of your minds; and to put on the new self, created to be like God in true righteousness and holiness."[33]

There are many ways in which this basic choice is expressed in the New Testament. Jesus describes it by saying, "Whoever wants to be my disciple must deny themselves and take up their cross and follow me."[34] Here, the cross represents Jesus' choice to follow the will of the Father for himself, whereas our "cross" represents God's will for us individually. Jesus warns us that people who choose to save their life rather than lose their life for Jesus will ultimately lose who they might have become.[35]

Paul writes of our union with Christ in his death and resurrection, and urges us, "Do not let sin control the way you live; do not give in to sinful desires. . . . Use your whole body as an instrument to do what is right."[36]

In Galatians 5, Paul discusses the inner conflict between walking by the Spirit and walking according to our old, sinful nature, which "desires what is contrary to the Spirit."[37] He says, "The acts of the flesh are obvious: sexual immorality, impurity and debauchery; idolatry and witchcraft; hatred, discord, jealousy, fits of rage, selfish ambition, dissensions, factions and envy; drunkenness, orgies, and the like."[38]

The Spirit, on the other hand, produces "love, joy, peace, forbearance, kindness, goodness, faithfulness, gentleness and self-control."[39]

Note the key difference between the two lists: The sinful nature produces sinful acts, whereas the Holy Spirit transforms our character.

The choice we have to make, in any situation, is whether we will side with the Spirit and let him transform us, or side with our sinful nature and let it express itself in its old sinful ways.

As we look over the two lists from Galatians 5, we realize we don't need the law to tell us which actions are the right ones to take. If we are loving, kind, patient, and self-controlled, we simply will not behave according to our sinful nature. And what we will gain by choosing to be responsive to the Spirit is a deepening personal love relationship with Jesus.

As Jesus told his disciples, "Anyone who loves me will obey my teaching. . . . Anyone who does not love me will not obey my teaching."[40] It is our love for Jesus that motivates us to respond to the Spirit's promptings and not to act on the desires stirred up in our sinful nature. As we make continual choices to respond to the Spirit, he will continue to transform us into the likeness of Christ, from the inside out.

On Our Own?

Earlier, we saw something of the ugly side of the law. In Romans 7, Paul first explains the basis on which a believer is legally released from responsibility to God's law.[41] He then explains why it is so vital for new-covenant believers not to try to approach God through the law.[42] Any effort to live by rules is doomed to failure.

The law, by focusing our attention on what we *ought* to do, stimulates a reaction from our sin nature, making our struggle to do right even more difficult. There is no way the law can give new life to a person who is spiritually dead; nor is there any way the law can encourage the continuing transformation of one who has been given new life in Christ.

But we are now adopted children of God, and we have a new nature. That nature is energized as we rely on the Holy Spirit, "that we might bear fruit for God."[43] United with Jesus, whose death and resurrection have given us eternal life, "we have been released from the law so that we serve in the new way of the Spirit, and not in the old way of the written code."[44]

Later, Paul gives us an amazing promise: "If the Spirit of him who raised Jesus from the dead is living in you, he who raised Christ from the dead will also give life to your mortal bodies because of his Spirit who lives in you."[45] The same power that flowed through Jesus and raised him from the dead is now available to transform you and me.

Choice in the New Covenant

Under the old covenant, Israel was responsible to make a corporate choice to live in obedience to the divine instructions that governed their behavior. Under the new covenant, individuals are responsible to love God and respond to the Holy Spirit's promptings.

Under the old covenant, obedience brought each generation earthly blessings that reflected blessings to be experienced in the eternal community of love. Under the new covenant, responsiveness to the Spirit brings increasing transformation toward Christlikeness.

Under the old covenant, disobedience brought devastating punishments intended to produce repentance. Under the new covenant, choosing to follow the impulses of our sin natures blocks our personal transformation and leads to divine discipline intended to produce "a harvest of righteousness and peace for those who have been trained by it."[46]

In misunderstanding the law's essential message and design, the rabbis of Jesus' time read the Old Testament as a rule book, identifying some 613 commandments that Jews were required to obey. And the rabbis added hundreds of their own rulings that interpreted how the commandments were to be kept. Under the new covenant, with its focus on transformation, we do not read the Bible as a rule book.

We read the Bible in order to know God better. The better we know God and the more we come to love him, the more responsive we will be to the Holy Spirit's promptings and the more our choices will reflect God's own character.

In Romans 12:1, Paul urges us, "in view of God's mercy, to offer [our] bodies as a living sacrifice, holy and pleasing to God—this is [our] true and proper worship." Then Paul continues, "Do not conform to the pattern of this world," a pattern woven from the passions engraved within our sinful human nature.[47] Instead we are told, "Be transformed by the renewing of your mind."[48] As we read the Bible in order to meet, know, and love God, our minds will be transformed, and we will become more sensitive to the Holy Spirit's promptings. It is *then* that we "will be able to test and approve what God's will is—his good, pleasing and perfect will."[49]

Discussion Questions

1. What role does human choice play in God's story today? What do you think of the assertion that God walks through life with us, responding to and interacting with our choices?

2. Saint Augustine is credited with saying, "Love God, and do what you please." What in this chapter suggests that Augustine may have been correct? What suggests that Kant's "*ought* implies *can*" may be wrong?

3. As a community, the people of Israel were intended to display God's character and goodness. As individuals, God's adopted children are also called to display God's character and goodness. What do you see as essential for Christians to succeed in this calling?

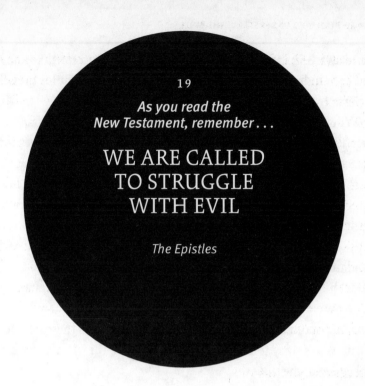

19

*As you read the
New Testament, remember . . .*

WE ARE CALLED TO STRUGGLE WITH EVIL

The Epistles

The Pivotal Event

In his later years, the apostle John, the last surviving disciple of Jesus, made a note on a torn fragment of papyrus: "The whole world is under the control of the evil one."[1] Then John went back to the letter he was writing, which is all about love. "Do not love the world or anything in the world. . . . For everything in the world—the lust of the flesh, the lust of the eyes, and the pride of life—comes not from the Father but from the world."[2]

Digging Deeper into the Epistles

Not too many decades ago, people assumed a black-and-white moral world. There was general agreement on what was considered *good* and what was considered *bad*. But times have changed. Today we live in a world awash in shades of gray. And the commonly accepted notion is that each individual should be free to decide what's right for himself or herself.

When Paul argued that we are not under law but under grace, he wasn't repudiating the moral standards expressed in the Old Covenant. In fact, Paul teaches that Christ, in his death, "condemned sin in the flesh, in order that the righteous requirement of the law might be fully met in us, who do not live according to the flesh but according to the Spirit."[3] As the adopted children of God respond to the promptings of the Spirit, the moral choices they make will be in harmony with standards embedded in the law.

In the previous chapter, I noted three functions of Old Testament law. Now we can add one more: The law serves to confirm or refute the godliness of our choices. The Holy Spirit will not lead those who live within God's story to make choices that violate the moral standards embedded in the law.

One problem with repudiating biblical standards in favor of "what seems right" is that ideas about right and wrong change. We've seen this phenomenon clearly in the United States. At one time, a lifelong marriage relationship between a man and a woman was considered normal and right by most people. Today, many people approve of simply living together. At one time, bearing a child outside of marriage was considered wrong. But in 2010 alone, more than 1.6 million children were born to unmarried women, comprising 40.8 percent of all births in the United States that year.[4] The rapid growth in the percentage of births to unmarried women reflects a significant shift in our culture's view of what is right and normal.

Still, we're not to look to Scripture merely for rules to follow. We come to Scripture to meet and get to know God, to have our minds and our character transformed by his Spirit. The choices we make are to be motivated by love for God, and are to reflect the character of the "new self" we are in Jesus. But make no mistake. Actions that violate moral principles expressed in the law or in the New Testament do not flow from a transformed character. They are expressions of the old, sinful human nature.

Reenter the Antagonist

As I've noted, no story is complete without a protagonist and an antagonist. This is certainly true of the Bible's story. God is the protagonist whose story the Bible tells, the hero whose goal is to fashion an eternal community of love. Satan, the powerful angel who led a rebellion against the Creator before the material universe existed, is the antagonist. His goal is to frustrate God's efforts and to cause as much damage and pain as possible to the beings the Creator has chosen to love.

We first met Satan in the Garden of Eden, where he deceived Eve and moved Adam to reject God's love in favor of independence. After that, Satan seems to have left the stage. Except for brief reappearances in the story of Job and the story of the temptation of Jesus, the devil seems to have no strong role in the Bible's tale. But this is a complete misunderstanding of the story. Satan is active throughout the narrative of Old Testament events. Wherever we read of pagan deities in the Old Testament, we see the hand of Satan—disguised, perhaps, but actively manipulating events to lure Israel into making choices that will lead them away from God and prevent generation after generation from experiencing blessing.

Satan's hand is seen more clearly in the Gospels. In Jesus, God invaded what Satan considers his territory, and the intensified activity of demons became more visible. Again and again, Jesus came into contact with evil spirits who were oppressing individuals—spiritually, psychologically, or physically. In each case, the demon was cast out and the oppressed individual was freed.

When we read the New Testament epistles, we too often fail to recognize references to the antagonist and his followers. Yet the epistles mention him frequently, using the vocabulary of the first-century world. In that time, spirit beings were referred to as principalities, powers, rulers, authorities, dominions, and so forth. And the New Testament makes it clear that "our struggle is not against flesh and blood, but against the rulers, against the authorities, against the powers of this dark world and against the spiritual forces of evil in the heavenly realms."[5] Today, too, the antagonist is bent on corrupting the choices of God's people in an effort to block the inner transformation to which God is committed and to keep God's adopted children from fulfilling God's purposes in their lives.

Making godly choices isn't easy. We have many resources provided by our heavenly Father. But we make our choices in the face of active opposition from the world, the flesh, and the devil.

A Word about Evil

Scan the Internet or check out a dictionary, and you will find various ways of viewing evil. Though some today debate whether or not evil actually exists, the idea of evil has always been around. In his famous play *The Clouds*, Greek playwright Aristophanes commented, "Evil events from evil causes spring." William Shakespeare observed, "The evil that men do lives after them; the good is oft interred with their bones."[6] Not to be outdone, broadcast radio episodes of *The Shadow* in the 1930s were launched with the question "Who knows what evil lurks in the hearts of men?" followed by "The Shadow knows . . ." The question for us is this: How does the concept of evil play out in God's story, and what does it mean there?

The Old Testament uses a single family of Hebrew words to express the concept of evil. The verb *ra'a'* means "to be evil or bad," or more frequently, "to do harm." The masculine noun *ra'* means "evil" or "bad," whereas the feminine noun *ra'ah* means "evil" in the sense of distress or misery. As these words are used in the telling of God's story, they focus on two complementary aspects of evil. *Evil* identifies actions that violate God's intentions for human beings. And *evil* also describes the tragedy, distress, and physical and emotional harm that results from wrong moral choices. What's important for us to remember in God's story is that choices can be good or evil, and the choices we make matter. We can choose a path in harmony with God's intentions for us, or we can choose other paths. If we reject God's path as revealed in his character and in his Word, we not only do evil, but we also open ourselves up to evil . . . that is, to disastrous, painful consequences.

In viewing *choice* within the frame set by the concept of good versus evil, we must remember that God passionately desires what is best for us. He loves us completely and is eager to bless us. As God's adopted children, we are free to choose between good (that which is God's intention and desire for us) and evil (anything that is not his intention or desire for us). No matter what standard our society adopts for what is morally acceptable, we must look to God's character and his Word to know the path we should take.

In the 1960s, there was a shift in our society's view of sexual morality. Women, who desired equality with men and were convinced that men enjoyed sexual privileges that were denied to women, chose the freedom to engage in premarital sex as a way to symbolize their equality with men. The result, according to British psychiatrist Theodore Dalrymple, was a situation in which sexual relations were freed "of all social, contractual, or moral obligations and meaning whatsoever, so that henceforth only raw sexual desire itself would count in our decision making."[7] In his fifteen years of caring for the poor in London, Dalrymple saw the results of this shift in what he describes as "the chaos of the[ir] personal lives" in this most vulnerable social class.

> Here are . . . children who have children, in numbers
> unknown before the advent of chemical contraception and
> sex education; women abandoned by the father of their child

a month before or a month after delivery; insensate jealousy
. . . that results in the most hideous oppression and violence;
. . . sexual and physical abuse of children on a mass scale;
and every kind of loosening of the distinction between the
sexually permissible and the impermissible.[8]

We do not have to be evil to unwittingly choose evil. Equality for
women is a worthy standard to be pursued. But the way in which the
feminism of the 1960s sought parity—by claiming the right to be as pro-
miscuous as men—has produced untold pain and social disruption. One
outcome is that living together without marriage has become socially
acceptable, as has the fact that more than 40 percent of all infants in the
United States are now born to single mothers. And this despite the well-
known but seldom-stated fact that most single mothers and their children will likely lead lives at or below the poverty line.

Good and evil in God's story are not abstract ideas. Good and evil
are rooted in God's intentions for human beings, whether expressed
in the Old Testament law or in the character-driven terms of the New
Testament's story. God's motive in establishing what is good is not that
of a tyrant who insists on having his way, but that of a loving Creator
who desires the best for us, who seeks to guide us away from what is
harmful toward that which will bless.

The World, the Flesh, and the Devil

Earlier in this chapter, I suggested it should be easy for us to make
good choices, given all that God has provided for us. But of course it's
not that easy. One reason that it's not easy is that Satan, the antagonist in God's story, has resources of his own. And he is rabidly committed to using every device he has to corrupt our choices, even as he
successfully corrupted the choices of so many generations of God's
Old Testament people. In God's unfolding story, as told in the New

Testament, these corrupting influences are identified as the world, the flesh, and Satan himself.

The crucial term translated "world" in the New Testament is the Greek *kosmos*. As a theological term, *kosmos* makes a significant statement about the organization of human culture.

> *Kosmos* portrays human society as a system warped by sin, tormented by beliefs and desires and emotions that surge blindly and uncontrollably. The world system is a dark system (Ephesians 6:12), operating on basic principles that are not of God (Colossians 2:20; 1 John 2:16). The entire system lies under the power of Satan (1 John 5:19).[9]

In God's story, all of human society is revealed to be under the control of the evil one.[10] So we would be wise not to uncritically accept the moral beliefs and attitudes prevalent in our culture. As 1 John 2:16 says, "Everything in the world—the lust of the flesh, the lust of the eyes, and the pride of life—comes not from the Father but from the world."

Those of us who live within God's story, seeking to make his story our personal stories, must be aware that what may seem right to others may very well not be right. Satan subtly appeals to our human nature and manipulates the world we live in, which is constantly attempting to "squeeze [us] into its own mould."[11] We are to be constantly on guard, constantly seeking to know God better and to make his perspectives, values, and attitudes our own.

It's not an easy thing to live in a culture where most people uncritically adopt the values and attitudes of society. But we are called to discern, to choose the will of God, and in so doing, to discover that his will truly is "good, pleasing and perfect."[12]

While Satan weaves a web of deceit in human society, he has an ally within every human soul. In God's story, that ally is called *the flesh*. Again, it's important to understand how this term is used in

Scripture. In God's story, use of the word "flesh" in no way implies that pleasure is somehow sinful. In the Old Testament, "flesh" (*basar*) refers to humans as creatures who live in and are part of the material universe. The material universe God created as our home is filled with sights and sounds and sensations we were designed to enjoy. At the same time, the term draws attention to our frailty: "God Most High . . . remembered that they were but flesh, a passing breeze that does not return."[13]

In the New Testament, "flesh" (*sarx*) and "fleshly" (*sarkinos* or *sarkikos*) draw attention to a more significant aspect of human frailty. In its theological sense, *sarx* describes humans as not simply frail but also flawed, morally twisted, and inadequate. Our understanding is distorted, and even our best efforts are hostile to the ways of God. In the New Testament's version of the story, "flesh" portrays human beings as isolated and cut off from God's life. In fact, in Galatians 5:16-26, *sarx* is appropriately translated "sinful nature,"[14] and is cast as the source of the drives that lead us to "sexual immorality, impurity and debauchery; idolatry and witchcraft; hatred, discord, jealousy, fits of rage, selfish ambition, dissensions, factions and envy; drunkenness, orgies, and the like."[15]

Here again, these actions are contrasted with the transformed character produced by the Holy Spirit—a character marked by "love, joy, peace, forbearance, kindness, goodness, faithfulness, gentleness and self-control."[16] No law can produce these qualities. And no law can suppress the sinful passions that surge within what is variously called the "old self," the "sinful nature," or "the flesh."

The evil one fully understands the potential for sin that is inherent in human nature. He understands the desires that tug at our hearts. And he craftily shapes the world system to appeal to the motives that drive the old self, even fashioning the options presented to us by the world to appear *good*. Satan is wholly evil. But Satan is good at being what he is: the opponent and the opposite of his Creator.

The Evil One

A certain TV commercial features two gazelles wearing night-vision goggles. They are making fun of a lion deep in the bush who is intent on sneaking up on them. The gazelles chuckle, ridiculing the far more powerful beast. Exposed, he is no longer a threat. The commercial reminds me of imagery in Peter's first letter: "Your enemy the devil prowls around like a roaring lion looking for someone to devour."[17] Then Peter gives us the antidote to the evil one: "Resist him, standing firm in the faith."[18]

Many Christians today tend to ignore the reality of Satan and demons. They may agree that such beings exist (after all, Satan is mentioned in the Bible), but invisible powers that can't be seen with the naked eye hardly seem real to us. What impact can they have on the "real world"? Other Christians, however, overemphasize the spirit world and see Satan and demons in every experience. Either extreme is likely to distort our understanding of God's story.

The writers of the New Testament take Satan and the demonic realm seriously. Certainly the apostle Paul joins Peter in his concerns about the devil's activities. Paul writes, "Our struggle is not against flesh and blood, but against the rulers, against the authorities, against the powers of this dark world and against the spiritual forces of evil in the heavenly realms."[19]

Now and then we catch a glimpse in the Bible of what Paul calls "the devil's schemes."[20] That phrase is important because it reminds us that Satan and his demons are far from all-powerful. Satan may prowl about looking for unwary saints, but he is not able to confront us openly and simply overpower us. No wonder he prowls about and schemes.

Paul identifies one of Satan's schemes as the fostering of unforgiveness,[21] and he warns us against holding on to anger, which will "give the devil a foothold."[22] He also says that those who resist the truth have fallen into "the trap of the devil, who has taken them captive to do his will,"[23] and that "the god of this age has blinded the minds of unbelievers, so that they cannot see the light of the gospel."[24] Even believers are vulnerable to Satan's evil influence, as reflected in Peter's question to Ananias in Acts 5:3: "How is it that Satan has so filled your heart that you have lied to the Holy Spirit?"

We know from the Gospels, as well as from the apostle Paul's experience with his personal disability,[25] that evil spirits can influence our physical health. This should hardly surprise us. Medical science is increasingly aware of how such things as depression and stress impact health. If psychological factors can affect our physical health, we shouldn't doubt that spiritual influences can have as great an impact, or even greater.

Ephesians is probably the most important book in the Bible for exposing Satan's strategies and for helping us understand the resources that enable us to stand against the devil's schemes. There Paul urges us to be strong in the Lord's mighty power[26] and reminds us that whatever powers evil wields, Christ is far greater. Christ has made a "public spectacle" of the powers and authorities of darkness, "triumphing over them by the cross."[27] In his resurrection, Jesus was raised "far above all rule and authority, power and dominion," and God has placed "all things under his feet."[28]

Though Satan and demons are not to be feared, they are to be taken seriously. We must be aware that Satan is active in our world and that we may be attacked by demons. Satan cannot take away the eternal life that God has given us, but he will do everything he can—working through the world, the flesh, and a variety of subtle schemes—to keep us off the path that God has marked out for us.

Shades of Gray?

We live in a world where the difference between right and wrong is often difficult to distinguish. Our society is awash with competing views, and the media is filled with subtle messages designed to shape our beliefs and attitudes and desires. It is important to remember Scripture's warning that "the whole world [*kosmos*] is under the control of the evil one."[29]

Despite our position as adopted children of God, despite the gift of a new nature, and despite the presence of the Holy Spirit in our lives, it is not easy for us to "no longer live the rest of [our] earthly lives for evil human desires, but rather for the will of God."[30] The world, the flesh, and the devil continually assault us, seeking to lure us away from God's path and God's will. Yet our choices are far more significant than we may realize.

The Gospel of Mark records the first time that Jesus spoke to his disciples about his coming death and resurrection.[31] Then Jesus spoke about the future that awaited his disciples. "Whoever wants to be my disciple," he told the gathered crowd, "must deny themselves and take up their cross and follow me."[32] Here the Cross represents God's will for Jesus, while our cross represents God's will for each of us as individuals. Then Jesus adds, "For whoever wants to save their life will lose it, but whoever loses their life for me and for the gospel will save it. What good is it for someone to gain the whole world, yet forfeit their soul? Or what can anyone give in exchange for their soul?"[33]

The challenge is far clearer in the original Greek, where both *life* and *soul* are translations of the same Greek word, *psuche*, which is used here as a reflexive pronoun. We might paraphrase it like this: "Whoever wants to save themselves will lose themselves, but whoever loses themselves for my sake and the gospel will save themselves. What good is it to gain the whole world, and in the process forfeit the selves God intends us to be?"

God is committed to our transformation. Our old selves are destined to be put off; and at the Resurrection, we will be fully our new selves in Christ. As God's adopted children, we are called to experience inner transformation now, gradually becoming more and more like

Jesus. But the progress of that transformation requires that we choose daily to live by the will of God.

Our choices count far more than we might expect. The antagonist knows this full well, and he marshals all the resources of the world, the flesh, and his demonic forces against us.

Living within God's story demands commitment and alertness. We need to live in constant, conscious touch with Jesus, seeking always to choose his will. We need to live in the book that tells God's story, reading it not as a rule book but as a love letter—one that invites us to trust our Savior, put our hand in his, and step confidently into the future he has designed for us.

As we do, we can be sure that no shade of gray will prevent us from clearly seeing God's way.

Discussion Questions

1. How closely do you examine the choices you make each day? What would you discover if you thoroughly examined just the choices you make by habit?

2. How closely have you examined your beliefs and attitudes about issues that are important to you? Which beliefs are most likely to have been uncritically adopted from the social group you most closely identify with?

3. To further explore how Satan and his demons can influence you directly, check out the spiritual warfare section at your favorite bookstore.[34]

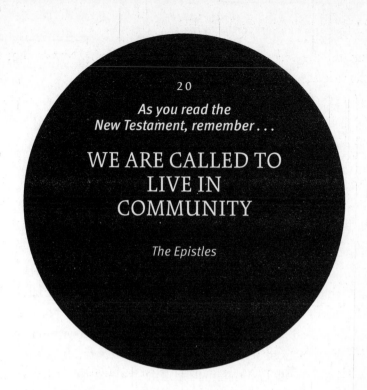

*As you read the
New Testament, remember...*

WE ARE CALLED TO LIVE IN COMMUNITY

The Epistles

The Pivotal Event

John sat back on his stool and peered at the letter he had been writing.
Bending close, for his aging eyes were dimmer now, he read what he had
written: "Dear friends, let us love one another, for love comes from God.
... Dear friends, since God so loved us, we also ought to love one another."[1]

Digging Deeper into the Epistles

As the apostle Peter looked around at the culture of the first century,
where Christianity had blossomed, he observed the attitude of those
who didn't know Christ. "They are surprised," he wrote, "that you do
not join them in their reckless, wild living, and they heap abuse on you."[2]
Many, if not most, Christians had abandoned the way of life their critics
maintained. "You have spent enough time in the past doing what pagans
choose to do—living in debauchery," Peter wrote.[3]

But living for the will of God in a world that is under the control of

Satan seems almost impossible. The entire *kosmos*, the world system, is rife with attitudes and values and beliefs that the evil one has tuned to human cravings that are deeply rooted in our sinful nature, our old selves. The values of this world, the "craving for physical pleasure . . . [and] for everything we see, and pride in our achievements and possessions"[4] comes naturally to us. Especially with the pressure we feel to be just like the people around us.

The ancient Israelites had a similar problem. Canaan was inhabited by pagan people who worshiped nature gods on whom the fertility of the land was believed to depend. Sex was a major element in these religions, as human orgies were believed to stimulate the gods to copulate, which was supposed to enhance the productivity of the land. The religions of Canaan also featured many occult practices, practices forbidden to God's people because they involved contact with evil spirits.

Two courses of action were taken to protect the Israelites from moral and spiritual contamination. The first was expressed in God's command to drive out or exterminate the inhabitants of Canaan.[5] Like the Genesis flood, this was a divine judgment on sins that had reached their full measure. The command to drive out the Canaanites was also intended to insulate Israel from the pernicious influence of the lifestyle practiced by these pagan nations.

The second course of action taken to protect the Israelites was to provide them with the law. The law, as I've argued, is not to be understood as an arbitrary set of rules that God's Old Testament people were to follow. Rather, the law of Moses was a carefully designed framework intended to create a community that would reflect elements of the eternal community of love that God will establish at the end of history. Within such a community, where each individual was valued and his or her rights were protected, individuals would find a safe place. They would be nurtured in a community in which everyone shared a common faith, and they would grow in their knowledge of and love for God, who loved them first.

There's a beautiful picture in the Old Testament of what this might have looked like if only Israel had remained loyal rather than turning aside to worship pagan deities and adopt pagan practices. In Deuteronomy 6:4-9, Moses calls on God's people to love the Lord with heart, soul, and strength, and to have his commands engraved on their hearts. Then Moses describes a pattern of nurture. God's people are to repeat God's commands "again and again" to their children, "when you are at home and when you are on the road, when you are going to bed and when you are getting up."[6] The words and ways of God were to be woven into the shared lives of families and communities, and the way people lived out their faith in every situation was to be explained by reference to the words of God.

But Israel ignored the way of life set out in the Torah and instead adopted the ways, values, attitudes, and beliefs of the pagan peoples around them. The community of love that might have been remained an unrealized dream.

Community Now

Adoption into God's family for both Jews and Gentiles constituted an unexpected twist in God's eternal plan. God has always loved and valued human beings. But now we are loved not simply because we are created in his image, or because we are members of a chosen people, but because we are adopted sons and daughters, precious to a God whose nature is that of a Father.

The resurrection of Jesus and the events of Pentecost marked an additional radical change. No longer were God's people to have a national identity. Instead, his sons and daughters would be scattered throughout all the nations and peoples of the earth. There, in cultures welcoming or hostile, individuals would be called to live out God's story, experiencing transformation toward the likeness of Jesus.

For transformation to take place in the face of challenges from the world, the flesh, and the devil, God's new covenant people would also need to experience community. They must, as in the Old Testament ideal, be anchored in a community in which each person is loved and valued, where they share a common faith, where God and his ways are talked about and woven into shared lives.

God designed a community in which his Old Testament people could be nurtured. God has also designed another community, within which our transformation is to take place today. That community is called the church. No, not the place where we assemble to sit on pews for an hour on Sunday mornings. The church the New Testament envisions is made up of smaller groups of believers: close friends deeply invested in one another's lives, who come together to offer love and support, and to encourage one another to follow Jesus more closely.

Picture after picture of the church functioning as community is found in the New Testament. We see the church functioning this way in Paul's exhortation to the Romans:

> Love must be sincere. Hate what is evil; cling to what is good. Be devoted to one another in love. Honor one another above yourselves. Never be lacking in zeal, but keep your spiritual fervor, serving the Lord. Be joyful in hope, patient in affliction, faithful in prayer. Share with the Lord's people who are in need. Practice hospitality. . . .
>
> Do not be proud, but be willing to associate with people of low position. Do not be conceited.[7]

We see it in the selfless attitude that undergirds these little communities of Christians, as described in Philippians 2:

> Make my joy complete by being like-minded, having the same love, being one in spirit and of one mind. Do nothing out of selfish ambition or vain conceit. Rather, in humility value others above yourselves, not looking to your own interests, but each of you to the interests of the others.[8]

And in Ephesians, Paul writes:

> I pray that you, being rooted and established in love, may
> have power, together with all the Lord's holy people, to grasp
> how wide and long and high and deep is the love of Christ,
> and to know this love that surpasses knowledge—that you
> may be filled to the measure of all the fullness of God.[9]

This is the heart of Paul's prayer: that the Christians in Ephesus would be "rooted and established in love." The love Paul has in mind is love for the other members of God's family with whom they share their lives. It is in living and loving together that we experience the width and depth, the length and height, of Christ's love, as Jesus loves us through our brothers and sisters. This is a reality that we are meant to experience in communities formed around our devotion to Jesus. As we experience this family love, our core is strengthened and we are "filled to the measure of all the fullness of God."

God's story took an unexpected twist following the death and resurrection of Jesus. The focus shifted from the people of Israel to individuals from every tribe and tongue and nation who, through faith in Jesus, are adopted into God's family. The Old Covenant expired.[10] In its place, the promised New Covenant was inaugurated. Sins were forgiven, and those who were adopted were given a new life, a new self. And a process of inner transformation was initiated within God's adopted children.[11]

Today, God's children are scattered across a world that is firmly in the grip of the evil one. That world is populated by people who simply do not understand the relationship they are intended to have with God. And they don't understand how that relationship guides the actions and shapes the attitudes of believers. Surely if the people of Israel needed a community, a safe place, we followers of Jesus also require community. We need a supportive network of relationships within which we are known, welcomed, loved, and valued, and where commitment to following Jesus is encouraged and affirmed. And this is exactly what the church—as described in Scripture—is designed to be.

Three Images

The New Testament has three primary images of what the church is and how it is to function. The first image is that of a family. God is our Father, and all believers are brothers and sisters. The focus is on nurturing close, loving relationships. In this loving community, transformation is encouraged and experienced.

The second image is that of a living body. Christ is portrayed as the head of this body and believers as body parts, each with his or her own contribution to make to the health and well-being of the other parts of the body. This image is developed in Romans 12, 1 Corinthians 12, and Ephesians 4. Appropriately, each passage also deals with spiritual gifts—that is, ways in which the Holy Spirit works through individuals to nurture spiritual and psychological transformation in other believers. These passages also emphasize that spiritual gifts operate in the context of loving community relationships.

The third image, found in 1 Peter 2, is that of a holy temple. Peter pictures believers as living stones "being built into a spiritual house to be a holy priesthood."[12] Here the context emphasizes the wonder of our belonging to God—"Once you were not a people, but now you are the people of God"[13]—and also the importance of living "as foreigners and exiles" in the world.[14] We who live within God's story are to "abstain from sinful desires, which wage war against your soul."[15]

Each of these three images emphasizes the connection that must prevail between believers. The family image emphasizes the close and intimate relationships that exist within an extended family—or *should*. The body image emphasizes an organic union in which each member is a part of a living whole. The temple image emphasizes the way in which individual living stones are laid so that together they form an edifice that brings glory to God.

In some ways, it was easier in the first century for the church to actually serve as the church. Within Mediterranean societies, there already existed structures called *collegia*, a Latin term meaning "joined in law." Collegia were simply small groups of people that might function as a guild or a social club. Some collegia were formed as burial societies, to ease the financial burden on families when a member died. The collegium model could easily be adapted for church gatherings. Thus, up until the third century, Christians met primarily in homes as small groups of believers whose purpose was to worship Jesus and encourage mutual commitment to follow the Lord. In these smaller home meetings, it was easier to become family, easier to function as a body and a holy temple. In these smaller home meetings, believers could and did develop the community God intends for his people. When persecution came, as it did, or when people in the world heaped abuse on the believers, the community was available to provide support and to remind individuals that others shared their burdens, beliefs, and convictions.

Today, too many kids are growing up outside of community, isolated and vulnerable to the distorted values and beliefs of the surrounding youth culture. Too many adults struggle with depression or loneliness, or are overwhelmed by circumstances, all without the loving support of a Christian community.

Still, there have been moments in church history when community was viewed as an indispensable element of the Christian life. Celtic Christianity was marked by an appreciation of the need for community. The class meetings of the early Wesleyan movement also provided this kind of experience. Today, initiatives such as the church multiplication movement in Southern California seek to rebuild community as a solid basis for evangelism. But for too many of us, "church" still means attending large, impersonal gatherings focused on the transmission of biblical information rather than on enabling believers to experience—and to be—the true church, the community of love that is at once family, body, and temple.

The large-gathering model should not discourage us. Many congregations have already sensed a need to encourage community and have formed smaller home groups. And even if a particular church focuses more on programs than on people, there's no reason not to invite a few Christian friends to meet regularly with a view toward building community. As always, God responds to the choices we make. Whatever the future holds for us, it will be a future that we ourselves help to construct.

The Story in Review

God's story is one story, its elements in the two Testaments similar and yet different. The themes we've seen in the Old Testament are repeated, with variations, in the New Testament. God is the same Person in Old and New Testaments. He is the Creator of both the seen and unseen universe. He is the source and giver of life. And God is the lover of humankind, which he created in his own image and likeness.

In both Testaments, human beings, the objects of God's love, are alienated from him. With Adam's choice to live independently of God, humans experienced spiritual death (Genesis 2:17). The grip of spiritual death is demonstrated in the Old Testament, while the reality is explained more fully in the New Testament. Love and death provide the essential tension in God's story. Will the Creator, who deeply loves human beings, be able to give life to the dead? Will God be able to fashion an eternal community of love in which a restored humanity loves him and one another as deeply as he loves them?

In both Testaments the story involves an antagonist. The antagonist is Satan, who with a vast number of angels rebelled against the Creator before the material universe was fashioned. In the story, Satan embodies all that is evil, while God embodies all that is good. It is Satan who teases and tempts Adam and Eve, moving Adam to declare independence from God. And it is Satan who, lurking behind the scenes sketched in both Testaments, is constantly looking for ways to thwart God's plan to fashion the eternal community of love and to encourage the continuing isolation of humans from their Creator.

COMPARISONS AND CONTRASTS

	The Story in the Old Testament	The Story in the New Testament
God's Identity	Creator, lover of humankind	Creator, Redeemer, Father of adopted children
Our Identity	Created in God's image	Adopted into God's family
Our Nature	Fallen, fiercely guarding independence	Dual nature: fallen (old self), new creation (new self)
Story Line	God's struggle to maintain a relationship with Israel	Christ's suffering to win a new relationship with all humankind
Story Focus	Israel as God's chosen people and nation	Individuals as adopted children of God
Key Event	Redemption from slavery in Egypt (physical)	Redemption by Jesus from sin's grip (spiritual)
Framework	Law covenant	New covenant
Community	Defined by and laid out in the Torah	Defined as family, body, and holy temple
Challenge	Obedience to the Torah	Responsiveness to the Spirit
Settings	A nation in the midst of pagan peoples/nations	Individuals living in essentially pagan societies
Calling	To display God's person and character in national and community life	To display God's person and character in personal and community life
Obstacles	Satan the antagonist, the world, our fallen sinful nature (the flesh)	Satan the antagonist, the world, our fallen sinful nature (the flesh)

As the story unfolds, we realize that God has chosen to respect rather than override the choices that humans freely make. Rather than treating humans as puppets and forcing them to do what is right, God interacts with human choices. Their choices will have consequences, but whatever choices humans make, God will be prepared with a response that will ensure his final victory over the antagonist and the ultimate establishment of an eternal community of love.

In what the New Testament calls "the fullness of time,"[16] the king who was promised in the Davidic covenant appeared. As prophesied, this descendant of King David, Jesus, was more than human. He was a man who was, at the same time, God himself. According to his story as told in the Gospels, despite clear evidence of his identity, he was rejected by his own people, condemned to death, and crucified. On the third day, he rose again—transformed—and entered the presence of God the Father, where he is now the supreme power in the universe and is poised to return to take up the throne promised him in the Davidic covenant.

It is at this point that the story takes its radical turn. The Old Testament's focus was on Israel as a nation and a people. After Jesus' death and resurrection, the focus shifts to individuals. Individuals who trust in Jesus as he is presented in the gospel are adopted into God's family. Their sins are forgiven, they are given spiritual life, and a process of transformation is initiated. Although God's adopted children must struggle against the world, the flesh, and the devil, they have resources. In the new life they have been given, they become *new selves*. They have the Holy Spirit indwelling them, and he energizes their new selves as they choose to live by God's will. And they have a new community, the church, within which their transformation is encouraged.

Just as the people of Israel had a choice—to love God and others and to abide by the Torah—so the adopted children of God have a choice. We are to love God and others and to respond to the promptings of the Holy Spirit. We are to put off the old self, which is driven by sinful impulses, and put on the new self, which is spiritually alive and motivated by love for God. And as we live for God, our choices will be guided by a growing knowledge of who God is, which we gain by reading Scripture as a story rather than as a rule book.

God's story—of sin and loss, of helplessness and redemption, of choice and consequence, of hope and transformation—is being written in the lives of his adopted children today.

And it is being read by everyone around us.

DISCUSSION QUESTIONS

1. What kinds of persecution or abuse do Christians in your community experience because of their faith? What do you think is the reason for such abuse—or the reason for the lack of abuse?

2. In this chapter, we argue that Christians are called to experience transformation in the context of community. How does the church you attend encourage or discourage the building of community? What has been your experience with Christian community?

3. What does it mean to say that God is telling his story today in and through the lives of his adopted children?

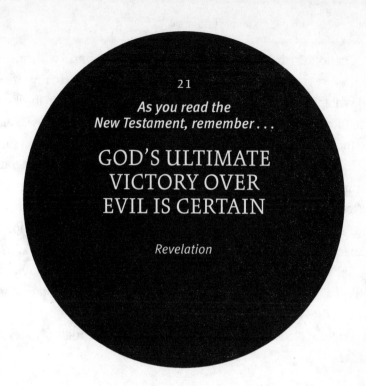

21

*As you read the
New Testament, remember...*

GOD'S ULTIMATE VICTORY OVER EVIL IS CERTAIN

Revelation

The Pivotal Event

Emperor Domitian was dead. Soon John, the last of the apostles of Jesus, would be free to return to Asia Minor and the churches he'd taken under his care. But as his final Lord's Day in exile waned, John saw a vision. What he saw was the ultimate triumph of God.

Digging Deeper into Revelation

My mother's favorite magazine was called *Revelation*. Later, the name was changed to *Eternity*. The magazine was the work of Donald Grey Barnhouse, pastor of Philadelphia's Tenth Presbyterian Church and an influential Bible teacher in the 1940s and '50s. When the state of Israel was founded in 1948, Barnhouse was certain the stage was set for the return of Jesus. That was my mother's conviction too.

Charlotte Richards was a small, slightly plump woman with brown hair, a very sweet face, and a deep devotion to Scripture. In my office, as I write, I have the Bible she studied so intently. Right up until she died fifty years ago, my mother was certain that Jesus' return was just around the corner. But she hasn't missed it. The apostle Paul reminds us that "the Lord himself will come down from heaven, with a loud command, with the voice of the archangel and with the trumpet call of God, and the dead in Christ will rise first. After that, we who are still alive and are left will be caught up together with them in the clouds to meet the Lord in the air. And so we will be with the Lord forever."[1]

But there's much more at stake than the rapture of individual believers. There are cosmic issues waiting to be settled. There is evil to vanquish, judgment to execute, and an eternal community of love to establish. No wonder Revelation both fascinates and frustrates its readers.

The Revelation Conundrum

That word *conundrum* isn't one we use often, but it's appropriate here. A conundrum is a puzzle, mystery, poser, problem, riddle, or enigma. Pick any of those words, and it has been applied to the last book in God's story, Revelation.

Some have assumed that Revelation was written as a subversive document in response to the persecution of Christians by Emperor Domitian (AD 81–96). It was a lot safer to rail against Rome when no one knew that was what you were doing.

During the Reformation, some attempted to match images in Revelation with events in church history. Revelation was thought to capture some eighteen centuries of Christian history, and it supposedly came down on the side of the Protestants by depicting the Roman Catholic Church as the Great Whore and as apostate Babylon.

Later, others insisted that Revelation should be divided into seven repetitive segments, each containing a description of history between the First and Second Comings of Christ.

Yet another approach to this puzzling book sees the whole narrative as symbolic. Revelation simply provides a general portrait of the conflict between good and evil (with good eventually winning, of course).

A final approach uses Revelation 4:1 as an interpretive key. There, Jesus tells the apostle John, "Come up here, and I will show you what must take place after this." What follows is John's description, from the vantage point of heaven, of a series of divine judgments that batter the earth. These culminate in the ultimate defeat of Satan and the creation of a new heaven and a new earth.

Why So Difficult?

There are a number of reasons why the events described in Revelation are so difficult for us to understand. One reason is that so much is symbolic. Some of the symbols are explained in the text. For instance, bowls of incense represent the prayers of God's people.[2] The great dragon is Satan,[3] and the waters represent peoples and nations.[4] Some symbols can be understood from their earlier use in the Old Testament. For instance, the four horsemen are found in Zechariah and Ezekiel, where they represent the execution of God's purposes.[5] Other images are not as clear. Nearly all of the symbols, even those that are explained in the text, are unfamiliar to modern readers, making the book seem even more mysterious. There is, however, yet another hurdle we face in interpreting Revelation.

Imagine yourself as a farmer in Massachusetts in 1764. You're walking behind a plow, holding the horse's reins, when suddenly you are transported to twenty-first-century Los Angeles. There you are shown a network of concrete paths along which strange, horseless vehicles hurtle at unbelievable speeds. You reach a city crowded with towering structures, windows aglow with light. But there are no fires in the structures. And you watch in amazement as strange, metal-winged cylinders filled with people leap, roaring, into the sky and disappear into the distance. Then, just as suddenly, you are back in 1764, standing in your field. You simply have to tell your neighbors what you've just witnessed!

You hurry to the farm over the hill, eager to share. But when you find your neighbor, you realize you don't have words to describe what you've seen. How could a person living in 1764 talk about a modern superhighway? How could he or she describe an SUV? How could he or she explain jets taking off from a busy airport? In 1764 there simply weren't words capable of describing these things that seem commonplace to you and me.

It was much like this for John as he penned Revelation. What John saw in his vision was real. But living near the end of the first century, he simply didn't have words to describe what he saw. So he did the best he could. For instance, when John says he saw "the stars in the sky" falling to earth "as figs drop from a fig tree when shaken by a strong wind,"[6] he was using images available in his time to describe something that people in our day might well describe in very different terms.

How Shall We Read Revelation?

From a story perspective, we must read Revelation as a description of future events. God's story has shown its protagonist and antagonist battling over creatures that the Creator loves. The tension in the story is created when these creatures, human beings, reject the Creator's love and declare independence, making themselves vulnerable to the antagonist, Satan. But every good story has a dénouement. And God's story must reach a point at which loose ends are drawn together and good triumphs over evil. Certainly God's story in the Bible is incomplete without such an ending.

The picture drawn in Revelation reflects themes introduced by the Old Testament prophets. As the end approaches, the scattered people of Israel are assembled again in the Promised Land.[7] But rather than launching a time of blessing, the final act opens with suffering and tribulation, as foreign hordes gather to invade a "peaceful and unsuspecting people."[8] Then God acts, to "send fire" on the invaders.[9] Through his intervention, God says, "The nations will know that I the LORD am the Holy One in Israel."[10] Similar glimpses are found in the New Testament. We hear Jesus warn of a dreadful time of "great distress, unequaled from the beginning of the world."[11] This time is associated with Jesus' return and linked to Daniel's prophecy of an "abomination that causes desolation."[12]

We read Paul's description of a coming antichrist, "the man doomed to destruction," who will be overthrown by the splendor of Christ's return.[13] And we are reassured that God is just and ready to "pay back trouble to those who trouble you. . . . This will happen when the Lord Jesus is revealed from heaven in blazing fire with his powerful angels."[14]

As we read, we realize that God clearly intends for his story to have a decisive ending—an ending in which good triumphs and evil is put away forever. With almost 70 percent of the verses in the book of Revelation containing allusions to the Old Testament, we can hardly understand the last book of the Bible without referring to the Old Testament's promises of a definitive conclusion to God's story. Though we can't be dogmatic about the interpretation of events described in Revelation, neither can we read through the book without being convinced that it does indeed herald God's ultimate triumph.

A Look into the Future

It's AD 96, just after the death of Emperor Domitian. John, the elderly apostle, has been exiled to the island of Patmos in the Aegean Sea. He is visited there by the glorified Jesus and is given a revelation "to show his [Jesus'] servants what must soon take place."[15] The sight of Jesus stuns John, who falls at his feet. John is then commissioned to write "what you have seen, what is now and what will take place later."[16]

Chapters 2 and 3, the "what is now" portion of Revelation, contain letters dictated by Christ to churches in seven cities in Asia Minor. Then John is brought into heaven to be shown "what must take place after this."[17] As John watches, a "mighty angel" presents a scroll sealed with seven seals, and in a thundering voice asks, "Who is worthy to break the seals and open the scroll?"[18] In response, Jesus steps forward as the Lamb of God, while heaven and earth ring with praise.[19]

As John watches from his vantage point, the Lamb breaks the seals. As each seal is broken, war, famine, and devastating plagues batter the earth.[20] As additional seals are broken, thousands who have been murdered because of their loyalty to Jesus cry out for justice.[21] When the sixth seal is opened, the universe shudders.[22] At that, the inhabitants of the earth call out to the mountains, "Fall on us and hide us from the face of him who sits on the throne and from the wrath of the Lamb!"[23]

But God remains gracious. During a period of calm before the next season of judgment is unleashed, 144,000 servants of God, drawn equally from Israel's twelve tribes, are sealed and set apart as witnesses.[24] Their mission is successful, for the next thing John sees is a "great multitude" who "have come out of the great tribulation; they have washed their robes and made them white in the blood of the Lamb," and now are shepherded by Christ himself.[25]

But more judgments are coming. The opening of the seventh seal reveals seven angels who are given seven trumpets.[26] As each angel sounds his trumpet, the earth is further savaged, and demonic beings are released to torment earth's population.[27] Yet John adds in wonder, "The rest of mankind who were not killed by these plagues still did not repent of the work of their hands; they did not stop worshiping demons, and idols of gold. . . . Nor did they repent of their murders, their magic arts, their sexual immorality or their thefts."[28]

This first catalog of coming judgments is stunning, and it certainly fits with Jesus' warning of a time of "great distress, unequaled from the beginning of the world."[29] Then another angel appears and announces, "There will be no more delay!"[30] The end announced by the prophets "will be accomplished."[31]

John now describes two "witnesses" who will preach and perform miracles in Jerusalem for three and a half years (1,260 days). They will be killed, but three and a half days later, they will be resurrected and taken into heaven.[32]

At this point, John clearly resorts to symbolic images. As history draws to a close, Satan will not be alone in his struggle against God.

Chapter 13 pictures an unholy trinity, with Satan joined by two individuals identified as "beasts." The conflict intensifies, and more angels announce that "the hour of [God's] judgment has come."[33] Angels deliver seven plagues and pour out seven "bowls of God's wrath."[34] But still the remaining humans, rather than repenting, "cursed God" on account of the plagues.[35]

John now describes the rise and fall of "Babylon the Great," which has joined Satan in persecuting believers. The city of Babylon, representing human culture, is destroyed by her allies and collapses in ruins.[36] As the judgments that devastate the earth come to a close, all in heaven shout, "Hallelujah! For our Lord God Almighty reigns. Let us rejoice and be glad and give him glory!"[37]

A Clear Vision

Although chapters 5–18 of Revelation are filled with uncertain images, John's subsequent description of future events seems crystal clear. Nothing that follows is difficult to understand. Some may not like what they read. They may wish to interpret it away. But John no longer must struggle to find words to describe what he sees. Familiar words, the kind his readers will understand, will suffice.

What John sees first is Jesus, preparing to return to earth at the head of heaven's armies.[38] On earth, the two beasts assemble a vast human army "to wage war against" the returning Christ. But their resistance is in vain. The two beasts are "thrown alive into the fiery lake of burning sulfur," and the members of their human army are killed.[39]

Then an angel seizes Satan, chains him, and confines him in the abyss, a word describing a "bottomless" or "unfathomable" place. Satan is sealed away "to keep him from deceiving the nations anymore until the thousand years were ended."[40] Those who were killed during the Great Tribulation are restored to life to reign with Christ during the ensuing thousand-year period.[41] Many believe it is during this period of Christ's rule on earth that some Old Testament prophecies—such as Isaiah's prediction of an era of peace when "the wolf and the lamb will feed together"[42]—will be fulfilled.

But the era of peace will end when Satan is "released from his prison" and goes out "to deceive the nations."[43] For a thousand years, humans will have not been subject to pressure from a corrupt world system or from Satan.[44] But humanity's sinful nature will retain its grip, and when Satan is freed, he will succeed in gathering millions of followers—"in number they are like the sand on the seashore"—eager to march "across the breadth of the earth and [surround] the camp of God's people, the city he loves."[45] This final rebellion will be put down decisively. Fire from heaven will destroy the rebel army, and Satan will be "thrown into the lake of burning sulfur."[46]

With the prophecies of the Old and New Testaments fulfilled during the Tribulation and millennial-kingdom periods, history will come to an end. The material universe will be dismissed and the dead recalled to face final judgment. Those whose names are "not found written in the book of life" will be "thrown into the lake of fire."[47]

The stories of these millions end in tragedy. But we need to remember that Jesus once said that "eternal fire [is] prepared for the devil and his angels."[48] In the story as God tells it, there is no question that innumerable human beings will share that fate. We need to remember that throughout God's story, he has respected our freedom as human beings to choose. And at all points in the story, God has encouraged us to choose wisely. He has revealed his existence in the Creation; he has spoken clearly through the human conscience and in Scripture; and he has proclaimed his love in the sacrifice of his Son. Whether or not a person responds to any of these messages, his or her choice will be permitted by God. He does not *send* anyone to eternal punishment. We choose our own destiny.

In Revelation 21, the scene shifts once again. The dead have been judged. The lost, now lost forever, have been dismissed into the lake of fire. At last, God is ready to welcome the redeemed into his eternal Kingdom of love. The first creation has been dismissed, and John sees "a new heaven and a new earth."[49] In this new creation, God is ever present with his people. The eternal community of love becomes a reality:

> I heard a loud voice from the throne saying, "Look! God's dwelling place is now among the people, and he will dwell with them. They will be his people, and God himself will be with them and be their God. 'He will wipe every tear from their eyes. There will be no more death' or mourning or crying or pain, for the old order of things has passed away."
>
> He who was seated on the throne said, "I am making everything new!"[50]

Then John describes the new Jerusalem, the capital of the new world that God will fashion. Though John provides some details about the city,[51] it's clear that what is most important is humankind's restored relationship with God, which John also describes.

No longer will there be any curse. The throne of God and of
the Lamb will be in the city, and his servants will serve him.
They will see his face, and his name will be on their foreheads.
There will be no more night. They will not need the light of a
lamp or the light of the sun, for the Lord God will give them
light. And they will reign forever and ever.[52]

As John's vision comes to a close, Jesus speaks and assures him, "Look,
I am coming soon!"[53] This promise is repeated, and the final words we
read from Jesus are, "Yes, I am coming soon."[54]

To this promise John can only respond, "Amen. Come, Lord Jesus."[55]

His Story Becomes Ours

God's story is our story. Some of us have entered into the story joyfully,
affirming its truth, and have quickly found our place. In a very real
sense, we have discovered who we are by relating ourselves to God's
story. Others choose to believe other stories and let those stories shape
their identity. The tragedy is that those other stories are illusions cast
by God's antagonist, webs woven to ensnare us and blind us to the
true story.

As to whether we can know for certain that God's story is true,
definitive proof will be presented only when Jesus comes again, as the
story promises. So we each must, by faith, choose a grand narrative
that we believe describes ultimate reality. In the past, people advanced
a number of arguments to convince doubters that it was more reasonable to believe the Bible than to believe the arguments for competing narratives, such as evolutionary theory. If we're uncomfortable
with the old arguments, I suggest we evaluate the options based on
story. Which of the available narratives—the Bible's story, the evolution story, the new stories that are coming into our culture through
Eastern religions and neo-pagan faiths—best fits life as we know it?

Which story best explains the almost universal awareness that something beyond the material world exists? Which story best fits our idealism and our hunger for what is good? Which story accounts for the flaws and failures of human societies? Which story best fits our pangs of conscience, our awareness that it is we who choose and are responsible for our choices? Which story best fits our sense that somehow we are significant, and that this life simply can't be all there is?

All these questions underscore why it's important for us to approach and read the Bible as story. Not as a compilation of rules to follow. Not as a collection of things we're supposed to believe. When we approach the Bible as story, we come to it to meet the God who tells us his story. We sense how much like him, and how far from him, we are. As we journey with him across the centuries—and now millennia—as he reaches out in love, we see how rebellious and unresponsive we truly are. Yet we discover in Jesus the ultimate gift of sacrificial love, and we learn of additional gifts that God is eager to give us—namely, adoption into his family, new and transformed selves, and his very presence to lead us and guide us.

And now we glimpse the end of the story. We see good triumphant and evil vanquished. We see all who respond to God's invitation restored. And we see a new world established as the setting for an eternal community of love.

The choice is clear. Will we reject God's story and be left outside forever? Or will we believe and embrace his story, and as a result find our place in it for eternity?

Discussion Questions

1. "From the point of view of story, we must read Revelation as a description of future events." How does reading Revelation as a prophetic depiction of the future fit the Bible's overall story?

2. Read through Revelation in one sitting, without stopping to puzzle over details, and then respond to the following statement:

"Though we can't be dogmatic about the interpretation of events described in Revelation, neither can we read through the book without being convinced that it does indeed herald God's ultimate triumph." Do you agree or disagree? Why?

3. When we read the Bible as story, our choice is clear. Explain why you agree or disagree. What choice have you made?

Notes

CHAPTER 1: IT'S ALL ABOUT LOVE

1. Romans 1:20
2. Romans 1:19
3. Isaiah 40:26
4. John 10:27, 29
5. Romans 1:21
6. Romans 10:17
7. 1 Corinthians 2:2
8. 1 Corinthians 2:6
9. Genesis 1:10, 12, 18, 21, 25
10. Genesis 1:3-5
11. Genesis 1:27
12. Genesis 1:28
13. Genesis 2:9
14. Genesis 2:15
15. Genesis 2:16
16. Genesis 2:17
17. Genesis 1:26, italics added
18. 1 John 4:8
19. Genesis 2:18
20. Genesis 2:20
21. Genesis 2:23

CHAPTER 2: ADAM CHOSE INDEPENDENCE

1. Lysander in William Shakespeare, *A Midsummer Night's Dream*, act 1, scene 1, line 134.
2. Genesis 2:16-17
3. John 14:23-24
4. Genesis 3:1
5. Genesis 3:2-3
6. Genesis 3:4-5
7. Genesis 3:6
8. 1 Timothy 2:14
9. Genesis 2:18
10. Genesis 3:9-10
11. Genesis 3:12
12. Genesis 2:17
13. Lawrence O. Richards, *New International Encyclopedia of Bible Words* (Grand Rapids: Zondervan, 1999), 408.
14. Ephesians 2:1-3
15. 1 Kings 11:4
16. Ecclesiastes 1:13
17. Ecclesiastes 1:2
18. Genesis 3:23-24
19. Genesis 3:22
20. Genesis 3:21
21. Leviticus 17:11

CHAPTER 3: SATAN PLAYS A MAJOR ROLE IN THE BIBLE'S STORY

1. Genesis 3:24
2. Leviticus 17:7, NKJV
3. Deuteronomy 32:17, NKJV
4. Psalm 106:37, NKJV

5. See, for example, Matthew 7:22 and 9:33.
6. Matthew 25:41
7. Revelation 12:7
8. Revelation 12:7-9
9. Job 38:4, 7
10. Genesis 1:2
11. Ibid.
12. Ibid.
13. Genesis 1:28
14. Genesis 3:15
15. Ezekiel 28:15
16. 2 Corinthians 4:4
17. John 12:31
18. Ephesians 2:2
19. Matthew 12:24
20. Job 1:8
21. Job 1:11

CHAPTER 4: GOD IS OBLIGATED TO JUDGE

1. Genesis 6:13-14
2. Henry Wadsworth Longfellow, "There Was a Little Girl," *The World's Best Poetry*, vol. 1 (Philadelphia: J. D. Morris, 1904), 169.
3. Genesis 4:3
4. Genesis 4:7
5. Romans 2:14-15
6. Romans 3:10, referencing Psalm 14:3
7. C. S. Lewis, *Mere Christianity* (1952), in *The Complete C. S. Lewis Signature Classics* (San Francisco: Harper, 2002), 81.
8. Genesis 4:9
9. Habakkuk 1:3-4
10. Habakkuk 1:3
11. Habakkuk 1:7
12. Habakkuk 2:4-5
13. Habakkuk 2:6-8
14. Habakkuk 2:9
15. Habakkuk 2:12-14
16. Habakkuk 2:15-17
17. Lewis, *Mere Christianity*, 55.
18. Genesis 4:12
19. Genesis 6:6-7
20. Deuteronomy 7:2, 5
21. Genesis 15:13-14, 16
22. Deuteronomy 18:9-13
23. 2 Thessalonians 1:6-7
24. Genesis 9:6
25. Genesis 8:21-22
26. Romans 13:4
27. Genesis 4:7

CHAPTER 5: GOD'S COVENANT PROMISES ARE UNCONDITIONAL

1. Genesis 12:1
2. Genesis 12:4
3. Genesis 12:1
4. Genesis 3:15
5. Genesis 12:2
6. Ibid.
7. Ibid.
8. Genesis 17:5
9. Genesis 12:3
10. Ibid.
11. Genesis 12:7; see also Genesis 15:18.
12. Genesis 16:1, 3
13. Genesis 15:3
14. Genesis 15:5
15. Genesis 15:18
16. Hebrews 6:16-18
17. Romans 4:18-25
18. Numbers 23:23, NKJV
19. Numbers 25:3, NLT
20. See, for example, Amos 9:1-10.
21. See 2 Kings 14:25.
22. Jonah 1:2; 3:4
23. Jonah 1:4, 17; 2:10
24. Jonah 3:5, 10
25. Joel 2:13-14
26. 2 Samuel 7:16
27. Jeremiah 31:32-34
28. Genesis 12:3
29. See 2 Corinthians 3:18.

CHAPTER 6: REDEMPTION MUST COME FIRST

1. Exodus 3:7-8
2. Ben E. King, Jerry Leiber, Mike Stoller, "Stand By Me" (1961).
3. Exodus 2:23
4. Acts 7:23-25
5. Psalm 78:42-43
6. Lawrence O. Richards, *New International Encyclopedia of Bible Words* (Grand Rapids: Zondervan, 1998), 576.
7. Exodus 6:6
8. Richards, *New International Encyclopedia of Bible Words*, 512.
9. Author's paraphrase of Romans 1:18-32, with quotes taken from Romans 1:21, 29 (NIV).
10. Ephesians 2:1, 3
11. 1 Peter 1:18-19
12. Titus 2:14
13. Hebrews 9:14
14. Richards, *New International Encyclopedia of Bible Words*, 518.
15. Exodus 7:9
16. Exodus 7:11
17. Exodus 7:13
18. Exodus 10:2
19. See, for example, Exodus 6:7; 7:17; 8:10, 22; 31:13.
20. Exodus 14:4, 18
21. Ephesians 2:2
22. 2 Corinthians 4:4
23. 2 Timothy 2:26
24. Revelation 12:9
25. 1 John 5:19
26. Ephesians 6:12
27. Ephesians 6:11
28. Rick Warren, *The Purpose Driven Life*, Expanded Edition (Grand Rapids: Zondervan, 2012), 28.
29. Exodus 3:15

CHAPTER 7: GOD'S LAW IS AN EXPRESSION OF LOVE

1. "Teen Trends: Killer Numbers," *Dr. Phil*, aired September 3, 2012.
2. Deuteronomy 4:6
3. Matthew 22:37-40
4. Leviticus 19:15; cf. Exodus 23:3, 6
5. Leviticus 19:10; 23:22
6. Exodus 23:10-11
7. Leviticus 25:36-37; Deuteronomy 15:1-3, 7-11
8. Deuteronomy 15:13-15; see also Leviticus 25:39-54.
9. Deuteronomy 14:28-29
10. Ibid.
11. Genesis 3:16
12. Deuteronomy 23:17
13. Proverbs 5:18
14. Proverbs 6:26
15. Leviticus 18:6. See also Leviticus 18:12.
16. See Deuteronomy 22:13-30.
17. Exodus 20:12
18. Lawrence O. Richards, *New International Encyclopedia of Bible Words* (Grand Rapids: Zondervan, 1998), 370.
19. Deuteronomy 7:6.
20. Deuteronomy 7:12-14
21. Galatians 3:25, NLT

CHAPTER 8: GOD INTERACTS WITH OUR CHOICES

1. Deuteronomy 30:19-20
2. Isaiah 28:12
3. Ibid.
4. Isaiah 28:13
5. Deuteronomy 28:1
6. Deuteronomy 28:3-10
7. Deuteronomy 28:11, 13
8. Deuteronomy 28:15
9. Deuteronomy 28:16-29
10. Deuteronomy 28:37

11. Deuteronomy 28:64-66

12. Amos 5:12

13. Amos 4:6, 10

14. Genesis 15:6

15. Deuteronomy 30:19, italics added

16. 1 Samuel 13:13

17. 1 Samuel 15:11

18. Jonah 3:1-10

19. 2 Kings 20:1-6

20. Joel 2:12-14

21. Jeremiah 26:2-3

22. Ibid.

23. Deuteronomy 32:16

24. Deuteronomy 32:17, NKJV, ESV, NLT

25. Exodus 7:8–11:10

26. Numbers 22:1–25:3

27. Jeremiah 2:11

28. Amos 5:12

29. Ruth 1:1

30. Ruth 1:16-17

31. See Romans 8:28.

CHAPTER 9: GOD'S FOCUS IS ON OUR LIFE HERE ON EARTH

1. 1 Thessalonians 4:16-17

2. Matthew 22:32, italics added

3. Ibid.

4. Genesis 6:5, ESV

5. George G. Hunter III, *The Celtic Way of Evangelism: How Christianity Can Reach the West . . . Again* (Nashville: Abingdon, 2010), 19–20.

6. Genesis 4:7, NASB

7. See Genesis 4:1-17.

8. See Genesis 27:1-46.

9. See Genesis 29:31-35.

10. See Genesis 34:1-31.

11. See Genesis 37:1–50:21.

12. See Exodus 1:1–2:10.

13. See Exodus 20:1-13.

14. See Joshua 2:1-24.

15. See Joshua 7:1-26.

16. See Judges 16:23-30.

17. See Ruth 1:1-22.

18. See 2 Samuel 15:1-12.

19. Psalm 3:1-6

20. Psalm 73:2-3

21. Psalm 73:13-14

22. Psalm 73:23-26

23. See Romans 12:6-8, 9-10, 13, 14-16.

24. Romans 12:21

25. See Romans 13:1-7.

26. See Romans 14:1–15:6.

CHAPTER 10: THE MEN AND WOMEN OF THE BIBLE ARE OUR MENTORS

1. See 1 Samuel 21:1-9.

2. Thomas Carlyle, quoted in E. D. Hirsch, *The New Dictionary of Cultural Literacy: What Every American Needs to Know* (New York: Houghton Mifflin, 2002), 434.

3. Herbert Spencer, *The Study of Sociology* (New York: D. Appleton, 1874), 30–37. See also Robert L. Carneiro, "Herbert Spencer as an Anthropologist," in John Offer, ed., *Herbert Spencer: Critical Assessments of Leading Sociologists* (London/New York: Routledge, 2000), 582–585.

4. See 1 Samuel 17.

5. See 2 Kings 20:1-11.

6. Lawrence O. Richards, *New International Encyclopedia of Bible Words* (Grand Rapids: Zondervan, 1998), 593.

7. 1 Samuel 21:1-9

8. 1 Samuel 22:22

9. 1 Samuel 25:2-3

10. 1 Samuel 25:3

11. 1 Samuel 25:8

12. 1 Samuel 25:31

13. 1 Samuel 25:33

14. 2 Timothy 3:16

CHAPTER 11: GOD SPEAKS TO EACH OF US TODAY

1. 2 Samuel 12:1-15; see also 2 Samuel 1:1-16.
2. Romans 2:17-18
3. Romans 2:14-15
4. See Romans 3:9-12, 22-23.
5. Joseph Fletcher, *Situation Ethics: The New Morality* (Louisville: Westminster John Knox, 1966).
6. 2 Samuel 5:17
7. Romans 3:2
8. 2 Samuel 5:22-25; also, compare 2 Samuel 5:19-25 with 1 Chronicles 14:8-16.
9. Exodus 3:15
10. Exodus 28:15
11. See 1 Samuel 23 and 30.
12. Deuteronomy 18:18
13. Deuteronomy 18:22
14. Jeremiah 27:1-22
15. Jeremiah 28:1-9
16. Jeremiah 28:12-14
17. Jeremiah 28:15-16
18. Deuteronomy 13:1-5
19. 2 Kings 14:25
20. Jonah 3:4
21. Jonah 3:10
22. Ibid.
23. Jonah 4:2
24. 1 Peter 4:11
25. Hebrews 3:15
26. Hebrews 4:1
27. Psalm 95:7-8
28. Hebrews 4:10
29. Hebrews 4:11
30. Hebrews 4:12
31. Hebrews 4:13

CHAPTER 12: GOD REVEALS HIS HEART

1. Malachi 3:10
2. Malachi 3:14
3. Haggai 2:19
4. Amos 2:6-7
5. Amos 3:2
6. Ezekiel 33:11
7. See Ezekiel 33:1-9.
8. Joel 1:1-12; 2:1-11
9. Joel 1: 13-20; 2:12-17
10. Joel 2:26–3:21
11. Joel 2:13-14
12. 1 Thessalonians 4:13-17
13. Isaiah 14:1-3; 27:12-13; 43:1-8; 66:20-22; Jeremiah 16:14-16; 23:3-8; 30:10-11; 31:8, 31-37; Ezekiel 11:17-21; 20:33-38; 34:11-16; 39:25-29; Hosea 1:10-11; Joel 3:17-21; Amos 9:11-15; Micah 4:4-7; Zephaniah 3:14-20; Zechariah 8:4-8
14. Joel 2:2
15. Joel 2:11
16. See Isaiah 2:12, 19; 3:6, 9; 4:3-4; 24:1, 3, 6, 19-21; 26:20-21; 65:13; Jeremiah 15:11; 30:7; Ezekiel 13:5; 14:22; 30:3; Daniel 9:27; 12:1; Joel 1:15; 3:14; Hosea 3:5; Amos 5:18-20; Zephaniah 1:14-15, 18; Zechariah 13:8; 14:1; Malachi 3:1-5; 4:1.
17. Isaiah 9:7
18. See Isaiah 2:1-4; 4:2-6; 11:1-13; 32:1-5; 33:17-24; 35:1-10; 52:7-10; 60:1–61:6; 66:15-23; Jeremiah 31:1-27; 33:14-26; Daniel 2:31-45; 7:1-28; 9:20-27; Ezekiel 20:33-42; 34:20-31; Hosea 3:4-5; Joel 2:28–3:2; 3:9-21; Amos 9:9-15; Obadiah 1:15-21; Micah 4:1-5; Zechariah 2:1-13; 14:1-21.
19. Malachi 3:15
20. Malachi 3:16-17
21. Amos 5:24
22. Isaiah 45:22
23. Isaiah 5:24-25
24. Isaiah 49:8
25. Online sales copy for David J. Neville, *A Peaceable Hope* (Grand Rapids: Baker, 2013), http://bakerpublishing group.com/books/a-peaceable-hope /320560.

26. Ibid.
27. Hosea 2:2
28. Hosea 2:3
29. Hosea 2:13
30. Hosea 4:1-2
31. Hosea 6:11–7:1

32. Hosea 7:13
33. Hosea 8:5, 7
34. Hosea 11:6
35. Hosea 11:1
36. Hosea 11:8-9
37. Hosea 14:4

CHAPTER 13: JESUS IS THE KING PROMISED IN THE OLD TESTAMENT

1. Luke 1:32-33
2. Daniel 7–8
3. Matthew 1:1, ESV
4. Matthew 2:6, referencing Micah 5:2, 4
5. Matthew 3:3, from Isaiah 40:3
6. Matthew 3:17
7. Matthew 4:2
8. Matthew 4:11
9. Matthew 5:1-11
10. Matthew 5:20
11. Matthew 5:17-48
12. Matthew 5:48
13. Matthew 6:1-34
14. Matthew 7:7-12
15. Matthew 7:15-20
16. Matthew 7:28-29
17. Matthew 10:1
18. Matthew 9:33
19. Matthew 9:34
20. Matthew 10:34-35
21. Matthew 11:20-24
22. Matthew 11:28-29
23. Matthew 12:8
24. Matthew 12:14
25. Matthew 12:23
26. Matthew 12:24
27. Matthew 12:38-40
28. See Matthew 13.
29. Matthew 13:24, 31, 33, 44-45, 47
30. Isaiah 2:2-4; Micah 4:1-9;
    Matthew 13:3-13
31. Isaiah 60:10-12; Matthew 13:24-30, 37-43
32. Isaiah 49:3; 61:3; Matthew 13:31-32

33. Isaiah 1:26; 26:2; Matthew 13:33
34. Isaiah 26:2; Matthew 13:44
35. Isaiah 66:12-14; Joel 3:18;
    Amo 9:13-15; Matthew 13:45-46
36. Malachi 3:18–4:3; Matthew 13:47-50
37. See Matthew 13:11; Luke 8:10.
38. Matthew 14:1-12
39. Matthew 14:13-34; 15:21-39
40. Matthew 15:1-20
41. Matthew 15:21-28
42. Matthew 15:29-39
43. Matthew 16:1-4
44. Matthew 16:13-28
45. Matthew 16:16
46. Matthew 20:25-28
47. Matthew 21:1-17
48. Matthew 21:23
49. Matthew 21:24–22:46
50. Matthew 23:1-39
51. Matthew 24:1-41
52. Matthew 24:15
53. Ibid.
54. Matthew 24:30
55. Matthew 24:36
56. Matthew 25:31-46
57. Matthew 26:1-5, 14-16, 47-56
58. Matthew 26:57-68; 27:1-2
59. Matthew 27:11-26
60. Matthew 27:41-44
61. Matthew 27:62-66
62. Matthew 28:11-15
63. Matthew 28:18
64. Matthew 28:19

CHAPTER 14: JESUS LIVED AMONG US AS A HUMAN BEING

1. See Mark 1:40-42.
2. Mark 1:1

3. Mark 1:3; see also Isaiah 40:3.
4. Mark 1:11

5. Mark 1:13
6. Mark 1:43-44
7. Mark 1:45
8. Ibid.
9. Mark 6:1-6
10. Mark 6:3
11. Ibid.
12. Mark 6:5
13. Mark 1:22
14. See Mark 2:18–3:6.
15. See Mark 3:22-30.
16. Mark 7:3, 13
17. Mark 11:15-17
18. Mark 11:18
19. Ibid.
20. Mark 12:1-11
21. Mark 12:12
22. Mark 8:27-29
23. Mark 8:29; see also
    Matthew 16:16.
24. Mark 14:61
25. Mark 14:62
26. Mark 14:50
27. Mark 14:65
28. Mark 15:13
29. Mark 15:15
30. Mark 15:16
31. Mark 15:29-30
32. Mark 15:27, 32
33. 1 Corinthians 1:23
34. Mark 10:45
35. Romans 5:7-8
36. Mark 1:1
37. Romans 1:4, ESV
38. Luke 1:38
39. Luke 1:42
40. Luke 1:20
41. Luke 7:37
42. Luke 7:36-50, ESV
43. Luke 13:11, NKJV
44. Luke 13:15-16
45. Luke 21:1-3
46. Luke 10:38-42
47. Luke 10:42
48. Luke 24:1-8
49. Luke 24:9-10
50. Luke 5:29
51. Luke 5:30
52. Luke 5:31-32
53. Luke 4:14-30
54. Luke 4:22
55. Luke 4:25-29
56. Deuteronomy 7:6; 14:2
57. Luke 14:16-24
58. Luke 18:28
59. Luke 18:29-30, ESV

CHAPTER 15: JESUS IS GOD THE SON

1. John 3:2
2. John 1:1-4
3. John 1:14
4. John 1:12-13
5. James 2:19, italics added
6. John 5:30
7. John 2:23
8. John 3:2
9. John 3:3
10. John 3:15
11. John 3:18
12. John 4:1-30
13. John 5:1-9
14. John 5:17
15. John 5:18
16. John 5:22-23
17. John 5:24
18. John 5:31-40
19. John 6:1-15
20. Exodus 16
21. John 6:31, 34
22. John 6:35
23. John 6:56-57
24. John 7:12
25. John 7:45-46
26. John 8:12
27. Exodus 4:13; 6:2-8
28. John 8:12
29. John 8:31-32
30. John 8:43-44

31. John 8:58
32. John 9:1-12
33. John 10:7, 9, 11, 14
34. John 10:1, 8-10
35. John 11:25
36. John 11:53
37. John 12:13
38. John 13:33
39. John 13:34-35
40. John 14:14

41. John 14:16
42. John 14:26
43. John 15:5, 8
44. John 15:5
45. John 15:9-12
46. John 15:17
47. John 15:18
48. John 16:7
49. John 17:1-26
50. 1 John 5:19

CHAPTER 16: WE ARE TO FOCUS ON THE NEW COVENANT, NOT THE OLD

1. Acts 4:12
2. Acts 1:8
3. See 1 Corinthians 12:13
4. Acts 1:8
5. Jeremiah 31:32

6. Jeremiah 31:33-34, italics added
7. Luke 22:20; see also Hebrews 8–10.
8. 2 Corinthians 3:6-18
9. 1 Corinthians 10:13, author's paraphrase

CHAPTER 17: WE ARE GIVEN A NEW IDENTITY IN CHRIST

1. See Ephesians 1:5; 6:10-17.
2. Ephesians 1:5
3. Ephesians 1:3
4. Ephesians 1:4
5. Ephesians 1:4-5
6. Ephesians 1:6
7. Ephesians 1:7
8. Ephesians 1:10
9. Ephesians 1:11-12
10. Ephesians 1:13-14
11. 1 John 3:1-3; italics added
12. 1 Corinthians 3:1
13. 1 Corinthians 3:3
14. 2 Corinthians 4:18
15. Ibid.
16. 2 Corinthians 5:12
17. 2 Corinthians 5:14
18. 2 Corinthians 5:15
19. 2 Corinthians 5:16
20. 2 Corinthians 5:17
21. 2 Corinthians 5:19
22. 2 Corinthians 5:21
23. Ephesians 1:18-19
24. Ephesians 1:19-20
25. Ephesians 2:1-2

26. Ephesians 2:3
27. Ephesians 2:4-5
28. Ibid.
29. Lawrence O. Richards, *New International Encyclopedia of Bible Words* (Grand Rapids: Zondervan, 1998), 515–516.
30. Ephesians 2:3
31. Ephesians 2:4-5
32. Richards, *New International Encyclopedia of Bible Words*, 517.
33. Ephesians 2:7
34. 1 Peter 3:18–4:2
35. 1 Peter 4:2
36. Colossians 1:13-14
37. 1 Thessalonians 5:5, 9-10
38. Romans 8:21
39. Romans 8:22-23
40. Romans 8:28
41. Romans 8:29
42. 2 Corinthians 1:5-7
43. 1 Peter 3:10-13
44. 1 Peter 3:14-15
45. 1 Peter 3:17
46. 1 Peter 3:18

CHAPTER 18: WE ARE CALLED TO LIVE AS NEW-COVENANT PEOPLE

1. Romans 8:4
2. Romans 8:11
3. Immanuel Kant, *Religion within the Boundaries of Mere Reason and Other Writings*, trans. and ed. by Allen Wood and George di Giovanni (Cambridge, UK: Cambridge University Press, 1998), 70, italics in the original.
4. Genesis 6:5
5. Romans 2:4
6. Romans 3:10
7. Genesis 3:21
8. The English word *eschaton* was coined in 1935 by Protestant theologian Charles Harold Dodd, who defined it as the "divinely ordered climax of history"; see www.etymonline.com/index.php?term=eschaton.
9. Jeremiah 31:31-32, as quoted in Hebrews 8:8-9.
10. Hebrews 8:13
11. Galatians 3:21
12. Romans 3:20
13. Compare Genesis 15:6 and Romans 4:1-3.
14. Habakkuk 1:4
15. Romans 3:28
16. Romans 3:31
17. Romans 6:14
18. Romans 7:13
19. Galatians 3:10
20. Romans 7:9-11
21. Romans 7:5
22. Jeremiah 31:32
23. Jeremiah 31:34; Hebrews 8:12
24. Jeremiah 31:33; see also Hebrews 8:10.
25. Matthew 5:20
26. Matthew 5:21-22
27. Matthew 5:27-28
28. Compare Romans 7:5-25; Galatians 5:13-24; Colossians 2:11, 13.
29. 2 Corinthians 5:17
30. 2 Peter 1:4
31. Hebrews 10:16
32. Romans 8:4
33. Ephesians 4:22-24
34. Mark 8:34
35. Mark 8:35-36
36. Romans 6:12-13, NLT
37. Galatians 5:16-17
38. Galatians 5:19-21
39. Galatians 5:22-23
40. John 14:23-24
41. Romans 7:1-4
42. Romans 7:4-6
43. Romans 7:4
44. Romans 7:6
45. Romans 8:11
46. Hebrews 12:11
47. Romans 12:2
48. Ibid.
49. Ibid.

CHAPTER 19: WE ARE CALLED TO STRUGGLE WITH EVIL

1. 1 John 5:19
2. 1 John 2:15-16
3. Romans 8:3-4
4. Joyce A. Martin et al., "Births: Final Data for 2010," US Centers for Disease Control and Prevention, *National Vital Statistics Reports* 61, no. 1 (August 28, 2012), www.cdc.gov/nchs/data/nvsr/nvsr61/nvsr61_01.pdf.
5. Ephesians 6:12
6. Marc Antony, in William Shakespeare, *Julius Caesar*, act III, scene 2, lines 74–75.
7. Theodore Dalrymple, *Life at the Bottom: The Worldview that Makes the Underclass* (Chicago: Ivan R. Dee, 2001), xi.
8. Ibid.
9. Lawrence O. Richards, *New International Encyclopedia of Bible Words* (Grand Rapids: Zondervan, 1998), 639.

10. 1 John 5:19
11. Romans 12:2, PHILLIPS
12. Romans 12:2
13. Psalm 78:35, 39
14. Galatians 5:17, 19, 24, NLT
15. Galatians 5:19-21
16. Galatians 5:22-23
17. 1 Peter 5:8
18. 1 Peter 5:9
19. Ephesians 6:12
20. Ephesians 6:11
21. 2 Corinthians 2:10-11
22. Ephesians 4:26-27
23. 2 Timothy 2:26
24. 2 Corinthians 4:4
25. 2 Corinthians 12:7-10
26. Ephesians 6:10
27. Colossians 2:15
28. Ephesians 1:21-22
29. 1 John 5:19
30. 1 Peter 4:2
31. Mark 8:31-32
32. Mark 8:34
33. Mark 8:35-37
34. For a good introduction, may I suggest my own book, *The Full Armor of God: Defending Your Life from Satan's Schemes* (Chosen, 2013).

CHAPTER 20: WE ARE CALLED TO LIVE IN COMMUNITY

1. 1 John 4:7, 11
2. 1 Peter 4:4
3. 1 Peter 4:3
4. 1 John 2:16, NLT
5. See Numbers 33:51-52, 55.
6. Deuteronomy 6:7, NLT
7. Romans 12:9-13, 16
8. Philippians 2:2-4
9. Ephesians 3:17-19
10. Galatians 3:23-25
11. 2 Corinthians 3:18
12. 1 Peter 2:5
13. 1 Peter 2:10
14. 1 Peter 2:11
15. Ibid.
16. Galatians 4:4, ESV

CHAPTER 21: GOD'S ULTIMATE VICTORY OVER EVIL IS CERTAIN

1. 1 Thessalonians 4:16-17
2. Revelation 5:8
3. Revelation 12:9
4. Revelation 17:15
5. Compare Revelation 6:1-8 with Zechariah 1:8-12; Ezekiel 5:15; and Ezekiel 14:21.
6. Revelation 6:13
7. Isaiah 11:1-16
8. Ezekiel 38:11
9. Ezekiel 39:6
10. Ezekiel 39:7
11. Matthew 24:21
12. Matthew 24:15
13. 2 Thessalonians 2:3, 8
14. 2 Thessalonians 1:6-7
15. Revelation 1:1
16. Revelation 1:19
17. Revelation 4:1ff
18. Revelation 5:2
19. Revelation 5:6-14
20. Revelation 6:1-8
21. Revelation 6:9-10
22. Revelation 6:12-14
23. Revelation 6:16
24. Revelation 7:1-8; 14:3
25. Revelation 7:9-17
26. Revelation 8:1-2
27. Revelation 8:1–9:19
28. Revelation 9:20-21
29. Matthew 24:21
30. Revelation 10:6
31. Revelation 10:7
32. Revelation 11:3-12
33. Revelation 14:7
34. Revelation 15:1–16:21
35. Revelation 16:21

36. Revelation 17:1-18; 18:9-24
37. Revelation 19:6-7
38. Revelation 19:11-16
39. Revelation 19:17-21
40. Revelation 20:3
41. Revelation 20:4
42. Isaiah 65:25
43. Revelation 20:7-8
44. Revelation 20:1-3
45. Revelation 20:8-9
46. Revelation 20:10
47. Revelation 20:11-15
48. Matthew 25:41
49. Revelation 21:1
50. Revelation 21:3-5
51. Revelation 22:1-2
52. Revelation 22:3-5
53. Revelation 22:12
54. Revelation 22:20
55. Ibid.

About the Author

LARRY RICHARDS has had a varied career. After discharge from the US Navy in 1955, he earned a BA in philosophy at the University of Michigan, where he was elected to Phi Beta Kappa. He received a ThM degree from Dallas Theological Seminary in 1962, and a PhD in 1972 from a joint program between Garrett Biblical Seminary and Northwestern University.

Upon graduation from seminary, Richards served as an editor at Scripture Press and then taught in the graduate school at Wheaton College. He began his writing career there, with books for teens and a series of textbooks on Christian education. The Christian Educators Project of Talbot Theological Seminary identified Richards as "the most prolific and influential evangelical Christian educator during the last half of the twentieth century." In 1972, Richards left full-time teaching for a full-time writing and speaking ministry.

Today Richards continues writing and teaching. He and his wife, Sue, who is also a writer, live in Raleigh, North Carolina.

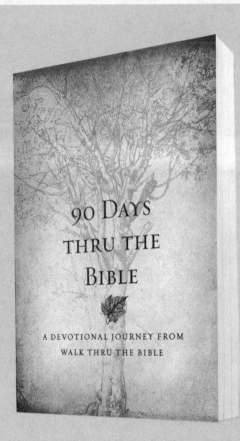